This I Believe: 2

THE PERSONAL PHILOSOPHIES
OF ONE HUNDRED THOUGHTFUL
MEN AND WOMEN IN ALL WALKS
OF LIFE—TWENTY OF WHOM ARE
IMMORTALS IN THE HISTORY
OF IDEAS, EIGHTY OF WHOM
ARE OUR CONTEMPORARIES OF
TODAY—WRITTEN FOR

EDWARD R. MURROW

Edited by RAYMOND SWING

SIMON AND SCHUSTER
NEW YORK · 1954

FIRST PRINTING
LIBRARY OF CONGRESS CATALOG CARD NUMBER: 53-14364
DEWEY DECIMAL CLASSIFICATION NUMBER: 920
MANUFACTURED IN THE UNITED STATES OF AMERICA
BY KINGSPORT PRESS, INC., KINGSPORT, TENN.

Foreword

THIS IS THE second volume of "This I Believe." It contains the personal beliefs of eighty contemporaries on this troubled and shrinking planet. It also contains twenty beliefs of what we have chosen to call "immortals," men and women of the past whose statements have been drafted by the authorities best qualified to reconstruct their philosophies. These personal declarations were written for radio and are couched in the language of speech. Many of the contributors, especially the professional writers, have told us that it has represented their most difficult writing assignment. The condensation of a personal philosophy into a few hundred words is not easy.

We live in a time when belief does not always produce action or assertion, when dissent is often confused with subversion, when a man's belief may be subject to investigation as well as his actions— the tide runs toward the shore of conformity.

In the conduct of the radio program "This I Believe," we have been aware of the easy criticisms that can be leveled against it. One is that we ask our guests as much as possible to concentrate on their spiritual beliefs rather than their political or social convictions. We know this limits the program. No doubt we lose much that would be barbed with the stimulus of controversy, and so be stirring. But we feel that we must accept this limitation if we are to arrive at our main objective, which is to point to the common meeting ground of faiths, which is the essence of brotherhood and which in a sense provides the floor of our civilization. Not that we anticipate or desire that the faiths that are expressed should be in essence the same. Indeed we feel it something of a drawback if they repeat each other too closely, even though the common source of Christian inspiration makes this inevitable in many instances. But if each person draws his faith from his own experience as well as from the teachings which he has received, his statement should be marked strongly by his individualism, and so differ from the individualism of others.

We also can be criticized for keeping out deliberately sectarian statements and particularly making this a program exclusively for laymen. This, too, represents a limitation. But we believe it a desirable one, for it prevents a development of the program into an affirmation of doctrines, and a kind of juxtaposition of doctrines, even a competition between them. However interesting and important this might be, it would not bring us to our objective of voicing the personal beliefs of a great many interesting individuals from many walks of life.

We are aware that this program already has gathered together material for an enormously interesting social study. If anyone cares to analyze this generation, so as to arrive at an appraisal of it in relation to the civilization for which it is responsible, he will find in these beliefs some valid and indeed unique data bearing on this theme. I do not know of anything before like these earnest pronouncements of hundreds of individuals about their highest and dearest aspirations. One can perhaps anticipate the appreciation of future scholars by realizing how illuminating we should find such pronouncements from the contemporaries of Queen Elizabeth or of Lorenzo the Magnificent or King Cheops.

Some onlookers may be tempted to suspect us because of the remarkable success of the program. That is, they may attribute it to the employment of smart techniques, and it may offend them that subject matter so intimate and indeed private should be given such wide circulation. We can assure such that our success has not been made; it has happened. And it has surprised us as much as it has encouraged us. It has demonstrated that we live in a time when men and women—not all of them, of course, but a great many— are sufficiently preoccupied with their own spiritual problems and opportunities as to care to seek for strength and light and comradeship from the experience of others. And the response this program has received from abroad as well as this country has led us to realize that we have an instrument that expresses not only this generation of Americans, but, to some extent, this generation of mankind.

We can point out that this is not a volume of advocacy, but it is a document reflecting some of the beliefs of those who continue to inhabit this planet. And those who read it may find it worthwhile to measure their own beliefs against those here formulated. They may find it difficult to achieve the brevity of these statements, or they may not value the brevity. But we like the thought that "brevity is good both when we are and are not understood."

EDWARD R. MURROW

Often the convictions of one generation are the rejects of the next. That does not deny the possibility that, as time goes on, we shall accumulate some body of valid conclusions. But it does mean that we can achieve only by accumulation, that wisdom is to be gained only as we stand upon the shoulders of those who have gone before. Just as in science, we cannot advance except as we take over what we inherit, and in statecraft no generation can safely start at scratch, so personal, basic beliefs must be slowly built from our experience, but also from a study of the experience and conclusions of others. That is the reason and the value of "This I Believe."

JUDGE LEARNED HAND

Contents

CONTENTS

SECTION II—IMMORTALS

CONTENTS

The Only Area of Common Understanding

BY WARD WHEELOCK

I RECENTLY made a trip around the world on which I talked to hundreds of people in sixteen countries, people of all religions, creeds, nationalities; people with varying economic backgrounds, with wide differences in living conditions, customs, clothing, food, language, entirely different in thoughts and lives. Discussions on a hundred subjects brought out divergent viewpoints, and these were interesting because of the divergences and the reasons behind them. But I found there was one subject, and only one, common to every person. That was the subject of his beliefs, of the rules he lives by, of his scale of the relative value of things.

Since two years ago, when "This I Believe" was first published as a book, we have learned a great truth. It is a truth that, if accepted, can have an important bearing on one's attitude toward life and toward others. It is this: the beliefs such as we seek, the statement of the rules a man lives by, the scale of relative values, are the area of common understanding among all people. And I know of no other. The expression of the beliefs will never be the same, the truths as seen will never be identical. But the search for the truths, the acknowledgment of the supremacy of truth, the awareness of the law of cause and effect on the moral plane, the problem of personal application to daily living—these are present in all men.

I talked with Mohammedans, Buddhists, Hindus, Shintoists, Jews and Christians and with people of many other religions. All that was said in these talks emphasized that the basic, underlying moral and spiritual teachings of all religions are virtually the same. Even the language is often surprisingly similar. Because of this, we find men and women of all faiths equally interested in the 600-word basic beliefs of other intelligent, decent people, because each such belief is potentially applicable.

There is a great range of beliefs, for each is the most personal, the most important, and the hardest thing that any one can write. Beliefs vary as much as men vary. Hence we find that the difference in conclusions is not drawn by religion, or geography, or conditions of life, but by the difference in individuals. We often find wider divergence between the beliefs of two Kansas City people living in the same block than between a Kansas City guest and a Bombay guest, where differences of belief might be expected to be enormous. Yet even where there is a big difference in beliefs, there is a common understanding, a common interest.

To us, the tremendous interest in and growth of "This I Believe" in three years was at first inexplicable. But now we understand it. For we have learned much about people in these three years. We found that vast numbers of people of all types and all ages were searching, quietly and alone, for practical help in meeting life and its problems. They wanted to know what they could believe, how they could apply their beliefs to their lives, what their relationship to others was. They recognized that out of all their experience, and all their knowledge, and the experience and conclusions of others, they must make personal decisions concerning what they stand for, how they act, what is relatively important to them.

Many books have been written on this subject. Some are excellent. But people realized that they couldn't take ready-made beliefs and rules. They had to develop their own beliefs from their own experience—and work out the application.

"This I Believe," for the first time, made available the earnest searching and honest reporting of hundreds of decent people of varied experience and conclusions. Here was the most practical aid to the most important personal problem.

How exciting it has been to see in three short years millions of people in all parts of the United States, and in all corners of the world, discover and then eagerly listen to and read and ponder "This I Believe," using it to form their own beliefs and writing us of its great helpfulness and value to them personally.

How thrilling to hear that, when "This I Believe" was printed in Arabic with 50 per cent Arabic guests, 30,000 copies were sold in three days, a record for Cairo . . . that in Korea "This I Believe" is the most listened-to and discussed radio program . . . that the

British book is now being read throughout the Empire . . . that the German magazine series has aroused great interest . . . that the Iranian and Pakistani book will be out in '55 . . . that leading men and women of the world are writing their beliefs for the International edition to be published in a dozen languages in '55 . . . that the '52 State Department feature of "This I Believe" for foreign newspapers in 97 countries was their most successful undertaking—and repeated in '54 . . . that "This I Believe" is broadcast 2,700 times a week, covering all the U.S., and 1,600 times a week overseas . . . that "This I Believe" is featured weekly in newspapers with over 8,500,000 circulation . . . that the Library of Congress published "This I Believe" in a Braille edition for libraries and schools for the blind . . . that more and more high schools are finding it the most interesting and practical way to teach moral and spiritual values . . . that the Voice of America, which has been broadcasting "This I Believe" in six languages weekly, is expanding "This I Believe" importantly in '55 . . . that the Columbia Record Album was such a success . . . and in each instance this has happened because of deep and wide public interest causing a request to us. For there is no "promotion" or "selling" of this program.

Surely one reason, "This I Believe" has succeeded is because it has made available to people a help to which they could turn out of self-interest. It has not been an exhortation. Our guests have not preached, they have done no more than examine themselves and affirm what they have learned. And this, while it is far from persuasion, is as persuasive as a form of communication can be. Beliefs often are a taboo subject. A man may not utter anything about them even in the bosom of his family. He may lock them up beyond the challenge of possible criticism. But along comes this program, and offers him the intimate beliefs of others. It leads him to take out his own beliefs. Often he finds he is a companion of the speaker; they have come to the same conclusions, seen the same light. And that strengthens him. Often, he finds the other fellow put it better than he could have put it himself. That clarifies his thinking. Sometimes he finds the speaker has said precisely what he had been looking for, the thought which solves an ethical problem that has been agitating and disturbing him. And that inspires and invigorates him.

"This I Believe" is but an extension of a conversation at an informal luncheon of four businessmen in 1949. After business was concluded, the talk turned to the gain in material values in many people's minds and the weakening of moral and spiritual values.

It developed that there was, among the four, a great difference of opinion about religion—and a feeling that this subject was too intimate and personal a one for general discussion. But when each of the four applied his experience and knowledge to express his conclusions on the rules by which he ran his life and what was relatively important to him—this was of vital interest to all the others, and extremely helpful to them.

It was recognized that most people never discussed such things—even with their families or intimates. But we felt that while personal and intimate ("like getting undressed in public," said General Lucius D. Clay), this was a subject that could and should be freely discussed. In other words—

Why could not the conclusions reached at our luncheon be extended?

"This I Believe" is that extension.

And now I would like to express a few personal beliefs.

I believe that it is the privilege and responsibility of each person to use his mind, to study, to reason, to listen, and accept differences in opinion—but to decide for himself where he stands on all subjects affecting his life and actions.

I believe that things which will not stand up under reasonable thought must be suspect. But it also is obvious that there are many things beyond human comprehension.

I believe that the most important thing on which a man can use his brain is himself—what to do with that which he has been given, how best to develop it. What objective does he have? What does he believe? What are his rules of life?

What a man believes and what he does about it—is that man. I believe that each person should retire at times unto himself to study his experiences and his thoughts, the experiences and conclusions of others, and to formulate his own personal basic beliefs—how to live with others, how to live with himself.

I believe personally that no man can live a complete and happy life without a deep belief in a Supreme Being—and a personal relationship with Him. This takes understanding of what one has received from Him, what one owes to Him, and what one can call on from Him.

I do not believe in predestination, for I think we are given minds for development—and the greatest gift ever given is that of freedom to decide and act. But there comes a time in every person's life—and generally many times—when things become greater than he and when he must turn to Some One bigger. If one does not have Some One to turn to, one is lost and unhappy.

I am glad that I have an unshakable faith in a Supreme Being, an appreciation for what I have been given, and a realization of my obligation to develop it and to render service that will justify my existence.

I do not hope to comprehend more than a small part of what exists. It would be presumptuous to assume that I can understand the creation of the universe, what will happen to it, whether there is planned for us a future life. Man can now measure millions of light years and get seemingly impossible facts from the galaxy of stars—but the things beyond human comprehension are many. On those things, I see no value in speculation.

My sincerest hope is that "This I Believe"—in addition to helping develop moral and spiritual rules of life and values for individuals—will help to build faith in a Supreme Being as a basis for daily living.

But each person must decide that for himself. All "This I Believe" can says is: "Search deeply—and here is some help."

WARD WHEELOCK

Section I

CONTEMPORARIES

Nietzsche Stands Condemned

BY FLORENCE E. ALLEN

I BELIEVE that having faith is our most pressing need today. Faith, the substance of things hoped for, the evidence of things not seen, is the mainspring not only of individual, ethical living, but of law and civilization based on law. Love is greater than faith, said Paul, but love without faith becomes futile and barren.

It seems to me that faith in the basic ethical standards, in the ultimate victory of right, and trust in the destiny of mankind are the basis of all human advance. Therefore I believe that the doctrine of Nietzsche—that the will to power is the vitalizing force and that the Superman in pursuit of power may adapt all ethical standards to his own desires—is a definite factor in the moral disintegration that besets us. This deterioration of the human spirit is, in my opinion, the danger of our time. Our minds and souls have been deprived of their heritage of integrity and faith.

To me the lives lost in the world wars and their cruel aftermaths are not the only appalling loss. I find the lessening of our beliefs, of our established principles, of faith in the individual and of trust between nations, is equally tragic.

I believe in the ethical purpose of law. After all, law is an outgrowth of faith. At first law was the effort of the race to hold brutality in leash. It began as a series of "Don'ts"—"Thou shalt not kill," "Thou shalt not bear false witness." But in its broader development, law expresses the desire of mankind to erect and maintain positive standards of right: "Thou shalt regard the rights of others," "Thou shalt love thy neighbor as thyself." Where has mankind attempted anything finer than the attainment of justice through evidence based on fact, illuminated by moral principle? This is part of my fundamental faith. "What doth the Lord require of thee," said the prophet, "but to do justly, to love mercy, and to walk humbly with thy God?"

Our country was built upon faith. Because they had faith, our fathers established the fullest freedom in the world today.

Faith that obstacles could be surmounted made men and women venture upon the seas, dare the wilderness, cross the rivers, the plains, the Rockies and the High Sierras to open up America.

Realizing the delicate problem involved in building world organization and at the same time preserving essential national freedom, I believe that we can establish world peace. The task seems super-human; but if prehistoric man could invent the wheel and the alphabet and apply ethical standards in the group through law, I see no reason why with faith and intelligence we cannot go forward to substitute law for war. But I do not believe that it can be done without faith to set free our "disinherited minds."

For it is still and always true that they who wait upon the Lord shall renew their strength; they shall mount up with wings as eagles; they shall run and not be weary; they shall walk and not faint.

FLORENCE E. ALLEN is one of the world's leading women jurists, being Circuit Judge of the United States Court of Appeals for the Sixth Circuit (which is outranked only by the U.S. Supreme Court). Born in Salt Lake City, she took an A.B. and A.M. from Western Reserve, and her LL.B. from New York University— one of the few law schools which in her time admitted women.

Judge Allen served for a time as music critic of the Cleveland *Plain Dealer*, and was diverted from a career as concert pianist only by an accident to her arm. She still plays for her own and her friends' pleasure—at her farm in Lake County, Ohio, where, she says, she rises at 5 A.M. to tend the blackberry patch. An authority on international law, she is one of three or four women to have addressed the International Bar Association. Modest, gentle, sympathetic, she is just and can be stern. She is the author of *This Constitution of Ours*.

A Live Wire

BY VICTOR ANDRADE

WHEN MY SON Mario was at the age when youngsters are a fountain of questions, he began one of his inquisitorial series, this time on the nature of electricity. He asked, and I did my best to explain, why one notices no change in wires when they are connected to the outlet, where the electricity comes from, and then what is the source of energy. My answers in technical matters would never be distinguished by profundity, but I told him of dynamos, transforming the energy of fuels or waterfalls into electricity, and of the unharnessed energy of our sun and the millions of suns in the universe. He finally asked, "And where have these millions of stars obtained their energy?"

"My son, for those of us who believe in God, it is He who is the fount of all life and all energy. That is precisely what distinguishes us from the materialists who believe that the manifestations of life are limited by the phenomena which can be understood by the senses.

"I believe in the existence of the soul—part of a universal spirit—which transitorily animates the body, just as electricity in the wires you noticed. And just as the disconnecting of the wires from the fount of electricity did not indicate the termination of energy itself, so death is not the end of the life of the spirit but the restitution to the very fount of life. In other words, I believe in the Being Who surpasses the limitations of its physical envelopment.

"Because of this, I believe in the existence of a moral order which comes from something more eternal than social conventions, customs, ambitions and conveniences. That is the reason also for my belief in love, honesty, honor, goodness and in human solidarity. I believe in these things and in justice because I believe in a Supreme Being.

"I believe that happiness is rooted in the soul and in the subjective appreciation of the state of mind; therefore it is false to seek that happiness in the satisfaction of appetite, ambitions and sensual pleasures. I believe also that it is wrong to judge the conduct and historic process of nations through a materialistic analysis, just as I judge it to be false to measure human values by the influence which power and force give. I believe that the control over instincts and the absence of fear are much more indicative of human superiority than is the possession of physical power.

"I believe that the bonds between men, who associate in order to live in a community, go beyond the common economic interests which move them to defend their homes and possessions. I believe in the existence of ties based on religion, culture and tradition. I believe that nations who have this faith are capable of enduring the sacrifices necessary in order to attain their ideals.

"I believe in the equality of men, in this life and beyond. Because of this I am opposed to imperialism and to dictators. I do not believe that nations are chosen by God to redeem humanity nor direct it in this or that way. I believe that the search for individual and collective perfection is a common task which no single individual nor any one nation can attain with prefabricated ideals or molds of conduct."

❧⟨§⟩❧

❧§ VICTOR ANDRADE has twice been appointed Bolivia's Ambassador to the United States. He is a descendant of Bartolome Andrade, an early hero of Bolivian independence. He took his law degree in La Paz in 1930, and became successively a teacher, an under-secretary of Public Education, and an officer in the Bolivian Army during the Chaco War. He was elected to the Parliament in 1940, was Minister of Foreign Affairs in 1944, and a member of the delegation to the San Francisco U.N. Conference in 1945. The following year his government was deposed by revolution.

While in exile, he taught at the New School for Social Research in New York. In the spring of 1951, his party was returned to power by election and Mr. Andrade became Ambassador, in which post he has settled with the United States Government, Bolivia's nationalization of the tin industry. The amiable diplomat is a pianist and author of a textbook of mathematics, and a book on the Chaco War.

5

Mozart Could Laugh

FIRST OF ALL, I believe in God. I believe in God, mostly, because I have come around to believing in Him all by myself. Nobody helped me; I am one of those who would resist help, especially in things concerning the spiritual.

I came to believe in God because, over the many years, He time and time again made Himself manifest to me. To embrace the career of composer is tantamount to embracing a life of high adventure. One is constantly on the firing line, estimated, appreciated, often criticized harshly by one and all. There may be no atheists in foxholes, but there are none in the Green Room either, especially before the première of a difficult, intricate and, I hope always, courageous musical work. Also, one cannot long work in the composition of music without coming to realize that one doesn't do it all by oneself. Something else is in operation, some great life-force, something beyond description except in as strong and subtle music as one can find and write. I do not know what it is; but as God has often been kinder to me than I deserved, I like to think that all this has something to do with Him.

Secondly, I believe in music. When I am true to it, music is my friend. It consoles me in my hours of consternation, and gives me added flight in my hours of luck. Music is, mostly, faith; but, after that, it is something that makes life, always beautiful, doubly worth living. I love music. And sometimes I even feel that it loves me back—a little.

But amongst those things I believe in most is laughter. This is a sad world. In my own short lifetime, almost everything one can imagine has happened to me personally, sad things, tragic things, things which I have more times than not faced like a coward. Once, indeed, I almost lost my dear music. But even in my darkest moments, abandoned seemingly by all, I found that I was always

6

saved if I could laugh. Laughter breaks evil spells, changes luck. Laughter is on the side of God.

Mozart, tonight, sleeps in an unmarked pauper's grave. Hard was his life, and a veritable financial catastrophe. Yet this divinely perfect of all musicians knew how to laugh. Read his letters. His music laughed too. Though it is always deeply moving, passionate, elevated, it also does what many of his contemporaries—now fallen by the wayside—could not do. It laughs. Listen to it.

I was once asked what I would most deeply wish for my young son, could I bestow but one quality upon him. Without hesitation, I wrote back, "a sense of humor." I could have said, "passion," for a passionate man is a living man. But passion, too, has its dangerous extremes; too often it brings great sorrow instead of happiness. I could have said, "happiness," but how could he know that he was happy if he was never to know sorrow? So I asked for the one quality which, added to any other which he may then develop, would make it possible to live with, to expand, to enjoy. God has been kind to me. Peter is now seventeen, has a marvelous sense of humor; and the house rings with laughter when he is home from high school.

GEORGE ANTHEIL was born in Trenton, New Jersey, and can remember no time in his life when he did not wish, first and foremost, to become a musician. He studied with various masters, including Constantine Sternberg and Ernst Bloch. For a time he was a concert pianist, but in 1926 he gave up all performances and became exclusively a composer of serious music. He has written four operas, and is working on his seventh symphony. In addition, he has written many other works. His "Ballet Mécanique" caused riots in Paris and New York during the mid-twenties; but when performed again in New York on February 20, 1954, it was acclaimed by the audience and critics as a great contemporary classic. Because of his nonconformity with the musical styles of his time, he has been called "The Bad Boy of Music." He says the title scarcely fits any more— he is not bad, and, being 53, is not a boy.

You Are Greater Than You Know

BY LOUIS L. AUSTIN

I BELIEVE LIFE is a natural turning toward happiness—as children naturally turn to play.

I believe we are meant to live a full, rich life, in vigorous health, at peace with ourselves and our fellow man.

I believe there exists within every human being an unlimited capacity for joy, achievement, love and peace of mind. I believe this capacity is born of the Creative Spirit that created man, created the universe, and sustains both. I believe that you, like myself, are part and parcel of that Creative Spirit.

I had not always believed thus. In my first forty years, I believed I stood alone. In the pursuit of "success," I had gotten myself in a hopeless business tangle, which threatened me with ruin and disgrace. When, ten years later, I emerged as owner of the property involved, I paused to analyze the factors that had delivered me from disaster and presented me with so wonderful a promise.

What I saw, in my mind's eye, was a jig-saw puzzle, all put together, every piece necessary to give me this opportunity. And I had not laid a single piece! For the first time in my life, I recognized that a Power greater than my own was dominant in my affairs.

It came to me then that every man is a Partnership, made up of (1) his visible self, and (2) an invisible Spirit—the Spirit of his Maker. Everything in the workaday world since, has made my conviction unshakable that the Creator made man for the purpose of living in Partnership with Him.

Man has an important place in that Partnership—our Partner needs us as we need Him—but our place is not in the Number One spot. We are His hands and feet, following His guidance.

I believe all our difficulties—physical and mental—stem from disregarding, knowingly or unknowingly, the Creator's part in sustaining the life He has given us.

Through our Partner's guidance and inspiration, we are able to do more work and do it better than when we delude ourselves we are doing the work alone. I believe everyone, who has ever accomplished anything worthwhile, knows that the deed was achieved not by him but *through* him.

Did not Christ himself say: "The things I do, I do not of myself. It is the Father within me that doeth the works"?

Was He not also saying to us: "You are greater than you know. You are a living, working partner of the Creative Power that sustains the universe"?

Our Maker gave us two hands. One to hold to Him, the other to our fellow man. If our hands are full of—or struggling for—possessions, we can hold to neither God nor humanity. If, however, we hold fast to Him who gave us life, who is our ever-present Partner, His loving Spirit will flow through us and out to our neighbor. That is the way to joy, love, achievement and inner peace.

Surely, if we love our children, we will teach them the simple truth of their own Partnership with God. Therein lies their only real chance for a happy, fruitful life.

⊷§⦚⦚∾

§ Louis L. Austin was born in poverty and raised in an orphan asylum. For forty years, he fought for success, money and position and failed to get any of them. In 1932—when he was broke and most of the country was too—he took over an old abandoned summer resort, buried away in the mountains of West Virginia. The place had been closed for almost a quarter of a century; it was without utilities; the roads to it were virtually impassable for miles. "Lou" Austin worked hard. He rebuilt the resort. But first he changed his way of life and his philosophy. He set out to give, rather than to get. Today, he and his family—seventeen of them, including grandchildren—run a unique inn. Summer reservations are booked a year ahead. And there is no advertising. When asked how this came about, Mr. Austin replies, "I have a partner. He saw to it that our business was built for us by kind words from kind friends."

Thought for Tomorrow

BY BERNARD BARUCH

WHEN I WAS a younger man, I believed that progress was inevitable—that the world would be better tomorrow and better still the day after. The thunder of war, the stench of concentration camps, the mushroom cloud of the atomic bomb are, however, not conducive to optimism. All our tomorrows for years to come will be clouded by the threat of a terrible holocaust.

Yet my faith in the future, though somewhat shaken, is not destroyed. I still believe in it. If I sometimes doubt that man *will* achieve his mortal potentialities, I never doubt that he *can*.

I believe that these potentialities promise all men a measure beyond reckoning of the joys and comforts, material and spiritual, that life offers. Not Utopia, to be sure. I do not believe in Utopias. Men may achieve all but perfection.

Paradise is not for this world. All men cannot be masters, but none needs to be a slave. We cannot cast out pain from the world, but needless suffering we can. Tragedy will be with us in some degree as long as there is life, but misery we can banish. Injustice will raise its head in the best of all possible worlds, but tyranny we can conquer. Evil will invade some men's hearts, intolerance will twist some men's minds, but decency is a far more common human attribute and it can be made to prevail in our daily lives.

I believe all this, because I believe above all else in reason—in the power of the human mind to cope with the problems of life. Any calamity visited upon man, either by his own hand or by a more omnipotent nature, could have been avoided or at least mitigated by a measure of thought. To nothing so much as the abandonment of reason does humanity owe its sorrows. Whatever failures I have known, whatever errors I have committed, whatever follies I have witnessed in private and public life have been the consequence of action without thought.

Because I place my trust in reason, I place it in the individual. There is a madness in crowds from which even the wisest, caught up in their ranks, are not immune. Stupidity and cruelty are the attributes of the mob, not wisdom and compassion.

I have known, as who has not, personal disappointments and despair. But always the thought of tomorrow has buoyed me up. I have looked to the future all my life. I still do. I still believe that with courage and intelligence we can make the future bright with fulfillment.

⛬

BERNARD BARUCH, financier and elder statesman, has served as unofficial adviser to seven Presidents of the United States. Spanning, thus, many administrations—including both major political parties—his influence upon world affairs has been long-continuing and potent. Few men in our time have had a more constant access to the White House.

His close friendships among the great include Sir Winston Churchill, who, when in New York, is invariably Mr. Baruch's guest.

President Roosevelt, during his long tenure, made frequent use of Mr. Baruch's services. He acted as adviser to James F. Byrnes, War Mobilization Director, during the Second World War, while also heading a vital governmental fact-finding committee. A member of the New York Stock Exchange for many years, he has written extensively on economic subjects. As one of the country's most revered statesmen, he is in constant demand as speaker before important business and educational groups.

Goethe's Promise

BY BERNARD BERENSON

ALTHOUGH I AM now in old age and perhaps at its last moments, I accept life as it is, for worse as for better—accept it, love it, rejoice in it. I feel no anticipated regret, let alone present rebellion at leaving it. Is it because I feel deep down that I am not destined to leave it, that nothing of me will remain that has not already been joyously offered to everybody and everything that survives me?

Subjectively one never dies. It is only objectively that we expect to depart this life.

Believers in immortality are therefore justified in practice. They will never know that they have died, for during the very last flickers of consciousness they were alive.

My faith consists in the certainty that life is worth living, life on its own terms. I know it is limited, a tiny speck as even is the earth in the infinite. But there is the infinitely little, and reality pervades it as completely, and it is a reality I can live by. What is that but faith? Confidence in life as worthwhile, confidence in humanity despite all its devilish propensities, zest for suitable exercise of function, enjoyment of the individual human being as a work of art.

I regard myself as a Christianity graduate in the sense in which I am a college graduate. We Americans return to our alma mater on class days and pretend that we are boys again, not yet graduated but about to do so. We do not think of returning to undergraduate life despite all its sweet alluring memories. I feel toward the Church as I do toward the University, the same gratitude, the same affection, the same admiration. But the Church, even as an institution, is measurelessly more wonderful than any university, more than all universities put together. Taken as an historical entity, man-made though I hold it to be, indeed because man-made and subject to the frailties, greed, and lusts of the individuals who through the ages have composed it, there is no other creation of mankind to compare with it. It is humanity's grandest, completest, and most beautiful achievement.

But my having graduated from Christian creeds and dogmas does not mean that I retain no beliefs to guide and comfort me. I am still the religious person I always have been. I should be glad of heart to join in any worship, to partake of any sacrament whether Christian, Jewish, or Muslim, Buddhist, Taoist or Shintoist, if I did not fear that thereby I was supposed to accept literally everything each religion accepted. By graduating from myths no matter how sublime, and dogmas architectured no matter how marvelously —as marvelously as the most majestically and subtly thought out of Gothic cathedrals—I seem to myself to have concentrated and intensified my faith. Faith in what? Faith in It, and faith in Humanity.

So after a fashion I have attained Goethe's promise that what one ardently desires when young, one will realize in old age. I am not far from my *nirvana*, I am in sight of It.

And It is a feeling of oneness with the landscape, with the house, and all that therein is, with the folk that pass, with the people one frequents, with one's occupation whether mental or manual, a oneness so complete that it knows nothing outside itself. In other words, It is a mystic union.

◄§ BERNARD BERENSON was born nearly ninety years ago, the son of a Lithuanian immigrant. He graduated from Harvard and, over the years, became America's leading scholar and critic of fine arts. His study and interpretation of the Italian Renaissance, as well as his initiative and advice, are responsible for the presence of most paintings of this period in American museums. He was the first English-speaking critic to write on Cézanne, almost sixty years ago, and he is the author of twenty-eight works of art criticism. His most recent are a critical biography, *Caravaggio: His Incongruity and His Fame,* and *Seeing and Knowing,* an analysis of the nature of modern art. "B.B." is a small, delicate, aristocratic man who now lives in a beautiful house on the hills of Settignano near Florence, surrounded by his prized library and art collection. He has been described as one of the last specimens of profound humanistic training and spirit.

The Mountain Disappears

BY LEONARD BERNSTEIN

I BELIEVE in people. I feel, love, need and respect people above all else, including the arts, natural scenery, organized piety, or nationalistic superstructures. One human figure on the slope of a mountain can make the whole mountain disappear for me. One person fighting for the truth can disqualify for me the platitudes of centuries. And one human being who meets with injustice can render invalid the entire system which has dispensed it.

I believe that man's noblest endowment is his capacity to change. Armed with reason, he can see two sides and choose: he can be divinely wrong. I believe in man's right to be wrong. Out of this right he has built, laboriously and lovingly, something we reverently call democracy. He has done it the hard way and continues to do it the hard way—by reason, by choosing, by error and rectification, by the difficult, slow method in which the dignity of A is acknowledged by B, without impairing the dignity of C. Man cannot have dignity without loving the dignity of his fellow.

I believe in the potential of people. I cannot rest passively with those who give up in the name of "human nature." Human nature is only animal nature if it is obliged to remain static. Without growth, without metamorphosis, there is no godhead. If we believe that man can never achieve a society without wars, then we are condemned to wars forever. This is the easy way. But the laborious, loving way, the way of dignity and divinity, presupposes a belief in people and in their capacity to change, grow, communicate, and love.

I believe in man's unconscious mind, the deep spring from which comes his power to communicate and to love. For me, all art is a combination of these powers; for if love is the way we have of communicating personally in the deepest way, then what art can do is to extend this communication, magnify it, and carry it to vastly greater numbers of people. Therefore art is valid for the warmth and love it carries within it, even if it be the lightest entertainment, or the bitterest satire, or the most shattering tragedy.

I believe that my country is the place where all these things I have been speaking of are happening in the most manifest way. America is at the beginning of her greatest period in history—a period of leadership in science, art and human progress toward the democratic ideal. I believe that she is at the critical point in this moment, and that she needs us to believe more strongly than ever before, in her and in one another, in our ability to grow and change, in our mutual dignity, in our democratic method. We must encourage thought, free and creative. We must respect privacy. We must observe taste by not exploiting our sorrows, successes, or passions. We must learn to know ourselves better through art. We must rely more on the unconscious, inspirational side of man. We must not enslave ourselves to dogma. We must believe in the attainability of good. We must believe, without fear, in people.

❧✃✿✄☙

◄§ LEONARD BERNSTEIN, composer, conductor, pianist, is one of the important younger men of music in present-day America. Graduating from Harvard, he attended the Curtis Institute of Music. Thereafter he studied conducting with the late Serge Koussevitsky and with Fritz Reiner, becoming assistant to the former at the Berkshire Music Center in 1942. Then followed engagements as assistant conductor of the Philharmonic Symphony of New York, music director of the New York City Symphony and musical director of the Israel Philharmonic Orchestra, and guest conductor of leading orchestras here and abroad.

As composer, Mr. Bernstein operates, as it were, on two levels—the classical and the popular. In the former field he has composed a clarinet sonata, song cycles, many piano pieces, and two symphonies. Popularly, he wrote the score for the successful Broadway musical, *On the Town*, and the ballets, "Fancy Free" and "Facsimile."

15

Traitors or Heroes?

BY ANEURIN BEVAN

THERE ARE SOME subjects that simply ask to be bogged down in meaningless generalities. This is one of them. You can say, for instance: "I believe in the good, the beautiful and the true." And when you have said it, what precisely have you said? Life never shapes the problem for us in those terms. The problem is always more immediate and particular. What in a given situation is beautiful, good, or true? Or, you can say again: "I believe in doing my duty." But life would indeed be easy if it were always clear what our duty is. Usually there is a conflict of duties as there is of loyalties. In order to serve one you often have to abandon the others. I remember a man saying to me during the last war that he had no use for rebels. Then I asked him how he would describe a German living in Germany and working for the defeat of the Nazis? Judged by conventional standards, the man was a rebel and a traitor. But judged in the wider context of humanity he was a hero. All you can really say here is that a man ought not to betray his first loyalty. The fact is that few people do. The problem is one of deciding which is the first loyalty from among a number of competing ones. And the higher the intelligence, the wider the knowledge, the keener the imagination, then the more loyalties there will be competing for our allegiance, and of course, the deeper the spiritual struggle involved in sorting them out.

This is the foremost problem of our time. Many old traditions and strongly rooted beliefs are now being eroded by swiftly moving social changes. Those struggles in society are reproduced in the hearts of all who are aware of them. In a democratic community the burden of choice is cast on the individual citizen. Quite often he finds this burden insupportable. He is then ready to have it taken from him by some authority to which he can give unques-

16

tioning obedience. Here is the point where dictatorship offers relief. It also explains the infinite nostalgia expressed in the hymn:

"Change and decay in all around I see,
Oh, Thou, who changest not, abide with me."

If I am right in saying that what we have to do is decide from among a number of almost equal claims, then the mood in which we approach our fellow human beings should be one of tolerance, for the slightest shift in the balance might have resulted in a different decision. If, furthermore, I am right in saying that the search for the truth will result in a number of different answers to the extent that the circumstances are different, then to tolerance we must add imagination so that we can understand why the other truth differs from ours. We should "learn to sit where they sit."

I am now ready to answer the question. I believe imaginative tolerance to be among the foremost virtues of a civilized mind.

THE RT. HON. ANEURIN BEVAN, P.C., M.P., the son of a Welsh coal miner, went to work in the pits at the age of thirteen. Despite a pronounced impediment, he soon became noted as an orator-agitator, and at nineteen was chairman of the Tredegar Lodge of the Miners' Federation.

His parliamentary career began in 1929 when he was elected to represent the mining district of Ebbw Vale in Monmouthshire. Another new member of this Parliament was Miss Jenny Lee, the daughter of a miner, whom Mr. Bevan married several years later. Dedicated to the principle of making the Socialist Party more radical, he took a prominent part in the Socialist League and founded *Tribune*, a weekly publication.

After the General Election of 1945, he became Minister of Health and was responsible for the establishment of the National Health Service. In 1951, he served as Minister of Labour and National Service. He has recently published a book about his political beliefs, *In Place of Fear*.

Competition Is a Sin

BY HECTOR BOLITHO

BEFORE WE CAN know what we believe, we must be coldly aware of the difference between prejudices—inherited or imposed on us from outside—and conviction, bred within ourselves, through experience.

I am in my mid-fifties—a good season for adding up. I know that I have quelled the gregariousness that muddled me so much when I was a boy. I no longer need people with the nervous anxiety that hurries us towards every lighted candle when we are young. I believe that one should learn the difference between being *lonely* and being *alone*. To me, now, the perfect day is the one when I am alone, and also idle.

I hope also that I have conquered the competitive spirit. I believe that it is wrong to wish to be one up on the Joneses, and that it is a sin to plant this notion in the minds of the young.

Children are taught that they must "do" something; the heroes in their school books are men of action, not thinkers. Children are haunted by too many examinations—that prove nothing of their capacity to think. They thus develop a false sense of the value of *action*, as opposed to the value of *thought* and *motives*. There is too much adulation for the man who swims the Channel and not enough for the man who sits on the beach and contemplates the waters before him.

Modern education is riddled with this folly, and history should be rewritten for children, so that they may comprehend the motives behind action. They should be taught that actions do *not* speak louder than words, if the words are audible expressions of thought.

You have asked me this question, "What do I believe?" at a critical time in my life. Up to a month ago, I lived mostly in London, where I had to work very hard, with my rather sketchy talent.

Then I decided to change all my pattern, to live more placidly, work less, earn less, and to spend the latter part of my life trying to learn to think. So I came to live in The Close, at Salisbury. And I am writing this at a window, with the low autumn sun lighting my pen and my paper. Beyond the mown grass is the spire of the Cathedral. The slow, wise bell is calling the people to Evensong. Instead of working today, I walked a little and I read a little. I planted some geranium cuttings in sand, for next year. True, I put off a task I should have done until tomorrow. But I feel calmer within myself for this idleness, and I believe that I am right in trying to weave a new pattern, in which contemplation is the chief colour, and action is only a thread running through.

I believe also that man's greatest enemy is fear—not fear in battle, but in the moral and ethical issues of day-to-day life. Yes, fear—and selfishness with which it is curiously intertwined. They are the ultimate foe. And I do not believe that they are conquered by *action*. They are vanquished by meekness—withdrawing into a state of sublime anonymity—and an increasing fire of moral courage within one's own heart. I touch only the fringe of this knowledge yet, but I believe that I am right.

❧§❦

HECTOR BOLITHO, the British author, has more than a score of books to his credit, chiefly English biography and history. He has, however, written novels, and, with Terrence Rattigan, a play, *Greyfarm*, which was produced on Broadway. Born in Auckland, New Zealand, he traveled through that land in 1920 in the company of Edward, Prince of Wales. Since 1922 he has lived and worked in England, where his abiding interest is in Victorian history.

For many years, Mr. Bolitho lived in the Cloisters of Windsor Castle where he studied and wrote his books on Queen Victoria, on Victoria and Albert, on George VI and other Royal subjects. His latest publication is *Jinnah, Creator of Pakistan*. Though he has traveled extensively and lectured widely in the United States, he recently decided to give up his home and interests in London and retire to The Close at Salisbury where, he says, "I can write less and learn to think—a task I have merely played at during my life."

19

My Revolt Was Violent

BY FRANCES P. BOLTON

I BELIEVE WITH Seneca that "The End of Being Is to Find Out God."

When I was but twelve, death entered my life. The dear old rector of a nearby mission chapel took me on his knee and told me very gently that I must not be unhappy, for God had put my mother to sleep until the Resurrection Day. My revolt was immediate and violent. I slid off his knee and ran out the door to the sea beach where I had taken all my child agonies, for there God always seemed closer and more real than in any church. A flame of indignation consumed me as I shook my fists at the sky, calling out with all the passion within me, "That isn't true, God! And I must know what is. Do anything you want to me, but let me find truth."

My search has led me to the place from which I can say with entire simplicity that I believe that you and I are part and parcel of the stream of Universal Life—as water drops are part of the Great Sea. I believe that what we call a life span is but one of an endless number of lifetimes during which, bit by bit, we shall experience all things. I believe that we are responsible for our thoughts and actions from the moment the soul asks, "What am I?" and that once that point of development is reached there can be no turning back. I have learned that such a belief exacts the development of a courage which demands great fortitude and ever-increasing endurance to acquire. I am not too dismayed by the darkness into which mankind has betrayed itself, for I know as only women can that all new life comes out of darkness through the gateway of agony and anguish into the Light. I am convinced that could men now know how truly each one builds his own long future and so the future of Mankind, they would not continue on the path of Destruction but would turn their faces away from Darkness toward the Light.

I believe with the Ancient Aryans that, and I quote:
"Never the Spirit was born, the Spirit shall Cease to be never;
Never was time it was not; End and Beginning are dreams!
Birthless and Deathless and Changeless remaineth the Spirit
forever."

I believe that before time was, into the seeming stillness of an incalculable speed of vibration there came the moment when the Infinite drew a deep breath and form began. There was no Time nor Space but there was Motion for within the Infinite Being the concept of Universes had been born. Without Him was not anything made that was made. And there was Light and there was absence of Light. There was beauty and the absence of beauty. There was good and the negation of good. But all were within the Being and of the Essence of the Infinite God.

Made of the stardust of infinity, man has evolved even as the stars and suns, as worlds and moons, out of the essence of God. Once started on his pilgrimage begun in unconscious perfection, he will continue through Light and Darkness, through Goodness and the Negation of Goodness until in his own time he reaches Perfected Consciousness and is re-absorbed into the Infinite Being of the Godhead.

This I do humbly believe.

FRANCES P. BOLTON, at a special election in 1940, was elected to the Seventy-Sixth Congress as Representative from Ohio to fill the unexpired term of her husband, Chester C. Bolton. Thus began a brilliant legislative career. She has been re-elected to each succeeding Congress.

Long distinguished for her worldwide interest in women's and children's activities, it has been said that no member of Congress has ever accomplished more in the field of progressive legislation in both medicine and nursing than Mrs. Bolton. Among many other such measures, she sponsored the Bolton Act which resulted in the establishment of the United States Cadet Nurse Corps.

The first woman member of Congress to head an official congressional mission abroad, Mrs. Bolton is a member of the Committee on Foreign Affairs. Under her supervision, a congressional sub-committee compiled *Strategy and Tactics of World Communism*, a monograph acknowledged to be definitive. Her son, Oliver P. Bolton, was elected to Congress in 1952.

Response to the New Bombs

BY CHESTER BOWLES

THERE ARE thoughtful men who believe that weapons of mass destruction seal the doom of the civilization which we have so painfully evolved through the centuries. They believe that in the face of new laboratory-created forces, man now stands lonely and inconsequential, hypnotized by the march of events and powerless to affect them.

This may be so. But I do not believe it.

Indeed it seems to me possible that the very vastness of the challenge will create in us a response which will cut through the confusion and frustrations of our time and guide us toward a freer, richer future. Such a future will not come easily for all of our wishing. It will not come at all unless there are enough men and women, rich and poor, black, yellow and white, Christian, Jew, Moslem, Hindu and Buddhist, who are prepared to dedicate their lives to its creation.

I believe that our proper response to the new bombs is to do what we should do without them. These awful weapons only sharpen the old moral problems which have tested man since Cain and Abel.

If we are true to the best within us, we will not rush to save ourselves at the price of surrender to totalitarianism abroad or conformity at home. Instead, in this valley of deepening shadow, each of us will seek so to live that he will deserve to be saved.

The Commandments instruct us to do unto others as we would be done by—to love our neighbors as ourselves. Is it so hard to know what this means for our time?

A rich young man asked Jesus, "What must I do?" But when he heard the answer, he "went away sorrowfully, for he had great possessions." Is America not like the rich young man?

As long as two-thirds of the world is ill-clad, ill-housed and ill-fed, we have no right to relax in comfort while Communism enlists the energies of the hopeless and disinherited of the earth. As long as people live in fear, I must work with my fellow Americans to create a climate where faith can combat it. As long as cynical men tell me that freedom can be saved by borrowing the immoral methods of those who would destroy freedom, I must oppose them and persuade others to do so.

I believe that the survival of freedom depends, not on blind fate, diplomatic trickery or brute military strength, but upon the convictions by which we live. The most fundamental of these is the certainty that each individual life is a sacred, vital part of the universal whole, and that there is no force superior to the human spirit. I have seen ample evidence of this in our own day, when the millions of India under the leadership of Mahatma Gandhi achieved their freedom without violence or bitterness.

The growth of our own America has come, not from the professional realists who never weary of telling us of the things that cannot be done, but from men and women who know the power of great ideals supported by dedicated individual effort.

I believe that the democratic truths which our Declaration of Independence once held to be self-evident remain just as evident today. Consistent with our heritage, I believe each of us in his daily life has a responsibility to reinforce these truths and to help extend them to all people everywhere.

CHESTER BOWLES was born in Springfield, Massachusetts, went to Choate School and graduated from Yale. Setting himself a carefully organized schedule of study, in 1925 he entered advertising, and four years later, with William Benton, formed the firm of Benton and Bowles, Inc. In the week after Pearl Harbor, Bowles left advertising for good, and accepted the job of tire rationing in Connecticut. He became chief of the O.P.A. and resigned as Economic Stabilizer in 1946, protesting against the lifting of controls. In 1948, he was elected Governor of Connecticut but was defeated for re-election and, in 1951, President Truman appointed him Ambassador to India. A newcomer to diplomacy, Bowles upset protocol and, by his vigor, understanding and warmth, scored a high Ambassadorial success. His *Ambassador's Report* was acclaimed by critics as a major contribution to current history.

No Better Than a Criminal

BY HARRY T. BRUNDIDGE

AT ONE time in my life I wrote a great deal about crime and criminals. I don't know how many criminals I came to know personally while I was a newspaper man, and how many of them I could truthfully call my friends. But the number is large. It has not been always easy to draw the line of behavior where it belonged, between friendship and the rights of society. But I did my duty on both sides of the line. I had my friends, and I helped the law.

What has not been hard has been to know that there is no line between people. They are all basically alike, all have good in them, all have the potentiality of failure.

I have known some criminals very well indeed. I have known, too, that I was no better than they were, I was only more fortunate. I have been able to say sincerely, there, but for the grace of God, go I. And because of this contact with criminals I have been privileged to have more friends than persons usually have. And the friends I have had, some of them, have been better friends because they weren't able to make friendships with those on my side of the line. They knew I believed they had good in them. They knew I trusted them. So they trusted me. I am rich because they did.

My religion has rewarded me. Anyone whose religion is people is sure to be rewarded.

Probably a lot of people don't have any realization that criminals also are people, that there is good in them, and the good will express itself if given a chance. I am not pretending that criminals can be reformed simply by kindness or trust. I am speaking only of the attitude toward them. The men I know who are bad—and I've known some of the worst—have become bad by the play of circumstances, by obscure weaknesses in their natures, by the influence of bad associates, by drink, by one or another cause that decided their destinies.

I guess that not many formal Christians get to know criminals as individuals. So they don't apply their Christianity to them personally. Sometimes it makes me bitter to see the problems of unfortunate men pushed aside. They should have help and encouragement from the persons from whom Christianity is expected. But I am happy to say that I have known some fine churchmen who always have been ready to help someone just out of prison for whom I wanted a job. I think in particular of an archbishop who never turned me down, and of certain men in the Salvation Army who always lent a hand. Thanks to such friends I never failed to find a job for a man who wanted to go straight. Not all of them kept the jobs, or went straight. But some did. I still hear from some of them. I still hear from some of the others, too.

I have often called on friends of mine in prison. Well, I knew them. I may have been the one for whom the scriptural comment was made: "I was in prison and you visited me." I am not chiding those who have no friends in prison. I only say that if they did they would be richer not poorer. I am rich. I am richer than most because I have friends who value me for reasons that have nothing to do with my standards or their standards. We are friends because we like each other as people. That is my religion. And I thank God I have been given a life that enabled me to practice it.

⋖§ HARRY T. BRUNDIDGE is a newspaper reporter who has had an action-packed career as crusader and reformer. Working on the St. Louis *Star*, later the *Star-Times*, he exposed the so-called national medical diploma mill which closed a dozen "quack" medical colleges. He was also instrumental in breaking up the notorious "Egan's Rats" gang of murderers and robbers; in helping to convict "Boss" Tom Pendergast, and in defeating the Ed Crump machine in Tennessee, which resulted in the election of Senator Estes Kefauver. He was commentator for the combined television networks during the Kefauver hearings.

Mr. Brundidge was one of two Americans who were first to reach Tokyo after the capitulation of Japan, and he helped ferret out and convict Tokyo Rose. In 1952 he went to London to organize a Far Eastern Bureau for International News Service.

Recently resigned as an editor of *Cosmopolitan*, he is now associate editor of the *American Mercury*.

Nana Lit the Beacons

BY RALPH J. BUNCHE

I FEEL more than a little self-conscious about trying to elucidate my personal, private creed. For, after all, when a person strips down all the way to his innermost beliefs—and in public—he stands awfully exposed. Nevertheless it strikes me as a very useful experience to sit down with oneself and seriously think through one's beliefs and convictions.

The trail of my beliefs and their development leads back to my childhood. I was reared in a deeply religious family. It was a sort of matriarchal clan, ruled over by my maternal grandmother, "Nana"—a name, incidentally, which I had given her as a tot in trying clumsily to say "Grandma." Nana, a strong and devout personality, beloved and respected by all who knew her, guided the family by simple but firm beliefs.

Foremost, she believed in God. In worldly matters, she believed that every person, without regard to race or religion, has a virtually sacred right to dignity and respect; that all men are brothers and are entitled to be treated as equals and to enjoy equality of opportunity; that principle, integrity, and self-respect are never to be worn as loose garments. For each of us in that family these beliefs, almost automatically, came to be part of our very being. For me, this was particularly so, since Nana became both mother and father to me when in my early youth I lost both parents.

In my youth, I had what many would consider a poor and hard life. But as I recall it, I was never unhappy; rather I enjoyed my youth immensely. For I had been taught how to appreciate and get the most out of very little, and that happiness in any circumstance is primarily a matter of control over one's state of mind.

I find that most everything in which I now believe stems from the simple lessons I learned at the knee of Nana. The beliefs I acquired, quite unconsciously and unthinkingly, in those early years, the lessons on how to approach life and its many problems, have been my unfailing guideposts.

Like Nana, I have an implicit belief in a Supreme Being and a Supreme Will beyond the ken of mortal men.

I hold that it is right to believe in one's self, but it is wrong ever to take one's self too seriously. For a keen sense of personal values and that humility which accompanies a balanced perspective are indispensable to congenial adjustment to life in society.

I believe that no man can be happy within himself if he ever surrenders his dignity and self-respect. I have faith in people, in, collectively, their essential goodness and good sense; granted that there will be individual mavericks on every human range.

I believe that men can learn to live together in harmony and peace, in the international community as in domestic communities, and I am unfalteringly devoted, therefore, to the historic effort of the United Nations toward this end.

I believe, also, in looking always on the brighter side of things; in the ability of right somehow ultimately to prevail; in never pressing time or fate; in taking life philosophically and in stride— both the good and the bad—and I have had an ample measure of both.

These are some, at least, of my beliefs. They are, for me, imperative beacons without which life would be utterly lacking in direction or meaning.

⋖§ RALPH J. BUNCHE, educator, humanitarian, and Nobel Peace Prize winner, is currently the principal director, Department of Trusteeship and Information from Non-Self-Governing Territories of the United Nations. Born in Detroit, Michigan, in 1904, he was educated at the University of California and at Harvard, where he majored in government and international relations.

Dr. Bunche entered an academic career and in 1929 became Chairman of the Department of Political Science at Howard University in Washington. In 1936 he acted as co-director, Institute of Race Relations at Swarthmore College. During the last war he served the Government in the State Department and in the Office of Strategic Services.

In the post-war period, Dr. Bunche has been active in the affairs of the United Nations. He is best known, perhaps, for his noteworthy mediation work in Palestine during the period 1948–9. He is holder of over thirty honorary degrees.

Antidote for War

BY BEN LUCIEN BURMAN

I BECAME a philosopher early. I had to become a philosopher. I was rather badly wounded in the First World War at Soissons, France, when I was twenty-two and as a result I was flat on my back for a long time. It was either get a philosophy or crack up.

My code of living is simple. It consists of three parts. One, never be cruel; two, always be artistic; three, never lose your sense of humor.

Number One I don't believe requires much explanation. Never be cruel means, of course, always be kind. I believe that kindness is the natural human instinct, not cruelty. I have no illusions about humanity. I know its faults, its frequent blindness, its capacity for making terrible mistakes. But my work as a writer takes me among all kinds of men and women, often the very rough and the very poor. Everywhere I have found generosity and nobility; men who would have gladly given their lives for me because I had done them some slight kindness. The vast majority of human beings will do the basically good thing if they are given half a chance.

By the second point in my code, always be artistic, I mean that whatever I do I try to do with as much grace as possible. If I write a book, I want to make it as beautiful as I can. If I were a shoemaker, I would want to make shoes the same way, as perfect as possible. In our madly commercialized and mechanized world we have lost our sense of the beautiful. I believe we need beauty in our lives just as much as we need food on our dining room tables. A world where beauty flourishes is a happy world—a world at peace.

The third part of my code, as I said earlier, is never lose your sense of humor. I don't like pomposity. I don't like stuffed shirts. I'm glad I was born in a small town. It's a wonderful antidote for smugness. I remember years ago when I had a little success in

28

New York with one of my first novels. There was the usual round of autograph parties and literary lunches and I was feeling rather pleased with myself. About this time I happened to go back to my home town in Kentucky and I saw an old fellow I had known as a boy standing on a street corner. He looked me up and down a long time and remarked lazily, "How are you, Benny? You been away a while, ain't you? You still teaching school?" That reduced life to its proper proportions.

I was over in Germany not long ago, in the ruins of Berlin, and a reporter asked me to give his paper a thought for the day. That was a bit of an order for me, who had been in two wars against the Germans and had very definite physical souvenirs from both. I reflected on what I could tell the Germans under these circumstances. And then I wrote: "When all the peoples of the world remember to laugh, particularly at themselves, there will be no more dictators and no more wars."

❦

⊷ BEN LUCIEN BURMAN, the author of a long list of best-sellers, sold his first story only after it had collected forty-four rejection slips. Within ten days after its acceptance he had sold $8,000 worth of other stories.

Mr. Burman was born in the river town of Covington, Kentucky, in 1895. He attended Harvard, fought in World War I and worked for New York, Boston and Cincinnati newspapers before becoming a writer.

His first novel was published in 1929, but it was the publication of *Steamboat Round the Bend* in 1933 that won him his important place in contemporary American writing. It was followed by the prize-winning *Blow for a Landing* and several other best-sellers, the latest of which is *The Four Lives of Mundy Tolliver.*

A short, soft-spoken man with a pleasant Kentucky drawl, Mr. Burman spends most of his time traveling. He is often to be found roaming through the byways and backwater towns of the Mississippi in search of new material.

Bread Across the Waters

BY EDDIE CANTOR

I'LL NEVER forget my first pay check. I went out and bought a dinner of all the things I had heard about but never could afford. The fancy dishes were too much for me. After a bad attack of indigestion, I concluded simple foods were best. So it has been with life. I suffered mental and spiritual indigestion until I stuck to staples: work—family—faith.

It's been a winning combination for me. My family was the inspiration for my work. My work has been a success because of my partner. In show business, I'm known as a "single act." This is not true. Every step of the way, I walked hand in hand with faith.

This partnership began, I think because, as a child, we only had one book in the house—the Bible. I took every word literally. If Little David, with God's help, could slay the giant, Goliath, it would be an easy matter for me to overcome poverty and lack of education.

I tried to follow all the precepts of the Good Book, but one in particular appealed to me—perhaps because of its practical aspects: "Cast thy bread upon the waters and thou shalt find it after many days." I made it my guide. In October of 1949, when I had the choice of doing a guest shot on radio or playing a benefit for refugee children, at Grossinger's Hotel in the Catskills, I referred to my guide and chose Grossinger's. My "bread" came back to me—not "after many days," but that very night. I found Eddie Fisher—a boy who added much to my shows, and brought me great personal happiness. He was one of the biggest hits ever to play the Palladium in London—even winning the plaudits of the Royal Family. It was during this engagement that Eddie cabled me, offering to fly back for one day to appear on my thirty-ninth wedding anniversary television show. If that isn't "bread coming back across the waters," I don't know what is.

One time, when I was starring in a Ziegfeld show, opening night fell on Yom Kippur—a high holy day for the Jews. I could not open. Did I suffer? No. A Jewish organization applauded this decision by sending a check to my pet project—Surprise Lake Camp, where poor children are given a holiday in the country.

And that reminds me of another story. Just about five years ago, in Houston, Texas, where I was raising money for "The March of Dimes," I thanked one man for his exceptionally generous contribution. He said, "Eddie, this is my way of thanking you. You see, I was once a Surprise Lake Camp kid."

I could go on and on. My life has been a series of proofs that the Bible is not only a literary masterpiece, but a workable theory for living.

Running a close second to this book with all the answers, has been my family. In an often insecure world, this was my haven— the one element I knew was unchanging. In good times, their pride in my accomplishments was a never-ending source of joy; in bad, the inspiration to push forward. I'll never forget 1929. Everything I had was swept away. My spirit might have gone with my assets, if it hadn't been for my wife and children. Their confidence in my ability to succeed again, made me ashamed to settle for less. This is only one instance. In my forty years of marriage, my wife has never failed me. Each of my five daughters is a person I'd be proud to know if she were not my child.

I've been happy most of my life because of these things in which I believe: work—family—faith.

⌁§ EDDIE CANTOR was born Edward Israel Iskowitz on the lower East Side of New York City. His father, a violinist, and his mother, both Russian immigrants, died when he was two; his grandmother worked to support him and, as a youngster, Eddie sang and clowned for pennies on street corners. He followed the path of success from Carey Walsh's saloon at Coney Island, where a boy named Jimmy Durante played the piano, to the top of vaudeville, musical comedy, motion pictures, radio and television. He is indefatigable both as a comedian and as a humanitarian. Despite a heart ailment and his sixty-two years, he has flown from one end of the country to the other "wheedling, cajoling, serenading and joking the American people" out of hundreds of millions of dollars for charitable and patriotic causes. His marriage to Ida Tobias over forty years ago and their five daughters are not unknown to Americans.

31

Eskimos Know Best

BY WILLIAM S. CARLSON

THE LURE of the Arctic is of little concern to a generation that looks upon flights to the Pole as a daily routine, and dreams of exploration in terms of Buck Rogers, space ships and rockets to the moon. Many of the values that come from roaming to the far ends of the earth have been lost. On the other hand, the years I spent in the primitive north, satisfying a youthful curiosity, gave my life a sense of direction.

During one long, lonesome winter I lived and traveled with an Eskimo family of five, the head of which was a noble character named Andreus. Their honesty, sincerity, coolness in the face of danger, thoughtfulness for my comfort and welfare, and generous help in attaining my scientific objectives, roused my respect and deep liking.

The members of the family were not only amiable, there was about them a refinement of body, manners and mind. They were a closely knit unit; the relationship between Andreus and his wife Ewa was a kindly and sympathetic one, while the two children were cherished by both. Parental affection was reciprocated by the children. They loved one another in a helpful, tender, but not sentimental way. Nor were the aged and infirm neglected. Andreus' mother, an ancient crone, lacked nothing in the way of comforts and was treated considerately and respectfully. Here, as elsewhere, I learned that it is the civilized man who could emulate the so-called savage to advantage.

I found they knew infinitely more than I did about life and living. They knew when to think, when to eat, when to play and be joyful, in just amount. Above all, they saw that all others got a fair chance to use their gifts to the full. As heathens they practiced the Christian virtues. They were not just Eskimos, but people I knew in their strengths and weaknesses, friends and neighbors and others who were indifferent to me, but in any case a part of my life. Among them I soon came to the realization that I do not belong to a superior race after all; it was only so in my thoughts.

And so, during the long months I lived their life, eating their matak and seal meat, cramped in a hut, using their boats and dog sledges—as thoroughly cut off from the twentieth century as they— they taught me enduring lessons in social conduct: the ideal of democratic brotherhood, and the sanctity of the family.

Living in semi-isolation, I expected to be lonely and was half surprised at finding myself lonely so little of the time. Over-long absence from loved ones teaches patience and makes one introspective. Patience, a virtue in a citizen, seemed to demand of me fantastic concessions; introspection taught me the need of systematic self-evaluation and the worth of the method of science in the ascertainment of truth.

The brotherhood of man, the virtue of patience, the need of self-evaluation, the unity of family, the method of science—these are beliefs I hold most dearly. In my present work, education, I advocate these beliefs as a way of life that can be grasped and adopted by the humblest citizen.

Finally, I believe that not only educators, but all who live in the realm of ideas, owe it to themselves and their fellow men to deal with the positive in modern life and point out those numerous paths of hope by which the world's men and women may work themselves out of their present unhappy predicament. I am confident we will. I look to the future with hope and eagerness for I believe the spirit of man is in the image of God.

◄§ WILLIAM S. CARLSON, educator and explorer, is President of the State University of New York. As a graduate student of geology at the University of Michigan, he made two expeditions to Greenland. His experiences during long periods of solitude in the North—as related in his book, *Greenland Lies North*—have profoundly influenced his own creed.

During World War II, Dr. Carlson was a special consultant on Arctic problems to the commanding general, U.S.A.A.F.; he rose through grades to colonel in the Air Force, serving on plans boards in many theatres, and receiving the Legion of Merit.

For the past twenty years—apart from his war service—Dr. Carlson has devoted his life to public higher education, as teacher and administrator at the Universities of Michigan and Minnesota, and in the presidency of the Universities of Delaware and Vermont, and the State University of New York.

Wisdom at Cribbs Creek

BY CARL CARMER

OFTEN, AFTER a man has reached his mature years, he has experiences that seem, like sudden shafts of sunlight, to illuminate and give meaning to events of his past.

Such a revelation came to me beside mud-yellow Cribbs Creek when I first saw an Alabama Sunday-baptising. A one-armed Negro in a white robe, waist-deep in the current, was preaching the sermon and I found myself spellbound by a miracle of talk packed with homely but poetic phrasing, with deep and passionately felt wisdom. Somehow the man's words stirred a memory of myself, a small boy on my weekly Sunday afternoon walk with my gentle, child-loving father in upstate New York. The man in the water had suddenly made me understand those walks with my father as I had never understood them.

Each Sunday we visited an old man. One was white-haired Mr. Coan, who had seen bears among the trees in front of the very porch on which we sat, and had known Indian chiefs who still talked of destroying whites who had stolen their lands. Another was town florist, French-born Monsieur Duquette, who had joined the Union Army during the Civil War and whose valor grew ever brighter and more dramatic as he reported it. A third was short, bald and merry Jerry Simpson, editor of the town weekly, who explained as well as he could what a saturnine man named Eugene V. Debs had meant when I had seen him harangue, between trains, a dozen depot idlers on the hardships of the American working-man.

Unsatisfied with formal education, my school-superintendent father had wanted me to know the wisdom of the people—wisdom that had been recognized, sifted, polished, handed down by generations of undistinguished but thoughtful humans. He wanted me to realize that from such succinct, simple folk-proverbs as our

Sunday hosts often used, may come such beauty and truth as even our greatest wise men have seldom expressed.

Since that Cribbs Creek episode, I have long sought for expressions of the wisdom of the folk, formulated from their own journey through time. Though mountains and deserts have even psychic effects on the man who lives on them, though cattle herding or accounting strongly color a man's mind, it is something more wonderful than these that brings him wisdom.

I call friend a man who, at nineteen, committed a serious crime. He is now a wise and cultured and good companion. He became the man he is through nineteen years of the worst environment man has created for man, a high-security prison.

Some men deny the authority of worldly experience and turn the bread-and-water fare of a literal or figurative imprisonment into the spiritual wine of freedom. Such men as they, are the true miracle workers. Granted as much of godhead as each of us they use it nobly, sure that dying for one's convictions is never loss of the battle. To them and millions like them, unknown and undistinguished, belongs the truest wisdom, the wisdom that grows in mankind.

❦

CARL CARMER, writer and lecturer, is best known among his many works for the popular *Stars Fell on Alabama*, which was a Literary Guild selection for 1934. He was born in Cortland, in up-state New York, in 1893, and educated at Hamilton College and Harvard, at which he took an M.A. During World War I he served as a lieutenant of Field Artillery, and, later, became Professor of English at the University of Alabama. After six years in that chair, he left to become a columnist on the New Orleans *Item-Tribune*, and there he married Elizabeth Black who, incidentally, has illustrated five of his books for children.

Mr. Carmer is at present editor of the "Rivers of America" series for which he wrote *The Hudson* and has just completed *The Susquehanna*. Well known also are his *Listen for a Lonesome Drum* and *Dark Trees to the Wind*. His network radio writing has included the widely heard *American Scriptures*, in collaboration with the late Carl Van Doren.

Affect the Farthest Star

BY HARLAN CLEVELAND

WHAT I believe is not some series of fixed principles, but rather a constantly changing set of ideas—ideas that I'm willing to do something about. If I were not prepared to do something about them, they would be merely theories, not beliefs.

My mother repeated two precepts so often that we remembered them. "Never stop learning," she would say; and "Don't ever get the feeling you've arrived." So what I believe is mostly aspirations for the future.

It's hard to say whether the beliefs I now hold were cause or effect; before the war I chose to be associated with a program to help low-income farmers in this country; during and after the war I got into relief and reconstruction work in Europe and the Far East. In any case, whether cause or effect, this is what I believe: that I should do what I can to maximize the morale of the greatest possible number of individual human beings.

Surely the most basic aim of social action is the morale, or sense of well-being, of the individual person.

As I see it, any individual's morale is measured by the degree of satisfaction of four basic wants. A man wants a sense of security, a sense of achievement, a sense of justice, and a sense of participation in the decisions that directly affect his own living and his own destiny.

My own sense of achievement is greatest when I feel that I'm doing something practical about these basic wants. The underlying belief here is that progress is natural and good, and practicable— a relatively recent arrival in the history of ideas. It is combined with the very old Christian idea that the individual—not the family, or the group, or the State—is the important unit.

I have come to believe that even in our culture, steeped though we are in the philosophy of rationalism, there is both rational and instinctive evidence of God.

My son, almost since he has been able to talk, has been asking me unanswerable questions about infinity. He comes by it naturally. I have always been engrossed by two facts about the universe that seem to me self-evident. One is the remarkable degree of order that we are able to ascertain—in natural law, in musical harmony, even in the relations of one person with another. The other fact is the interwoven continuity of everything and everybody with everything and everybody else. When I was very young I learned something I hope is true: that if I wiggled my little finger, it would affect the farthest star. Occasionally, when walking by myself, I would wiggle my little finger, just to keep that farthest star on the alert. What is true in space must also be true in time: what I do now will live on in its effect; what I am cannot be destroyed by death.

The God of this orderly and continuous cosmos is also a personal God. The evidence here is that at the critical moments in his life a man in trouble instinctively prays.

I didn't learn this by going to church, even though I was a minister's son. When I was twenty-one I spent a night on a damaged liner that was listing badly after being hit by a tidal wave, trying to ride out a hurricane in the middle of the Atlantic. Seated on a bunk, trying to hold rigid between my knees the broken neck of an elderly woman whose survival depended on me, I prayed for the first time without feeling self-conscious about it.

∙⊰§ HARLAN CLEVELAND, executive editor of *The Reporter*, came to this post after a long and varied career of public service which culminated in the assistant directorship for Europe of the Mutual Security Agency. He had joined the Economic Cooperation Administration, forerunner of MSA, in 1948, as consultant on the China program, of which he later became director, and then deputy assistant administrator in Washington.

A graduate of Princeton and a Rhodes Scholar, Mr. Cleveland's career in government included work with the Department of Agriculture, the Board of Economic Warfare, and the Foreign Economic Administration. He served as acting vice-president of the Allied Commission in Italy, as deputy chief of UNRRA in Italy, and as director of UNRRA in China. For his work in Italy he was awarded the U.S. Medal of Freedom, and he has also been decorated by the Italian and Chinese Nationalist governments.

The Chase

BY ARTHUR J. CONNELL

I BELIEVE that in every man there is a preponderant potential for good. I believe that for all living and for each life there is a purpose which is God's, and that every human being is possessed of the reason and the will to achieve it. I believe that total happiness and total understanding are beyond mortal grasp, and that success in life lies not in realizing these goals but in reaching for them.

These beliefs I base upon personal acknowledgment of both the mastery and the mystery of Divine Law.

Self-control, self-criticism and a remorseless urge for self-improvement are the indispensable virtues. Upon these foundations, the individual can build useful achievements. Apart from them, there is no good way to initiate or evaluate personal success.

Perhaps the most difficult of all problems is to draw the line between what is ordained for us and what we can and should ordain for ourselves—between submission to Divine Will and the expression of our own will.

My wife and I in 1943 suffered the loss of our only child—a daughter about whom our very lives revolved. For us it was a shattering experience, and it left a long and teeming wake of doubt and depression and questions which seemed to pose neither answers nor escape. In the larger sense, of course, there was and is no escape; but there was a reason, and if the wisdom and justice of it remained veiled from our view, it was also true that the God who gave us our greatest blessing might rightly reclaim it. All I ask, however, of this life is that, with the grace of God, I shall so conduct myself that some day I shall have earned the right to walk hand in hand with my daughter through eternal life.

The individual's title to happiness is at best insecure; his right is in the chase, not the catch. To attempt to limit one's aspirations by the measurable results achieved is the easiest and most futile of follies; for it assumes a power we do not have, and squanders the power that we do have.

All that I have been taught by a mother and father who lived their faith—a mother who was the apostle of devotion and understanding; a father, foresighted and industrious, who believed in education, honesty and industry—all that I have learned from personal experience has supported one fundamental fact: life is worth living for those who live true to themselves and to their God. This I believe!

ARTHUR J. CONNELL, of Middletown, Connecticut, is National Commander of the American Legion for 1953–54, to which post he was elected unanimously. A Navy veteran of World War I, he rose through the ranks of the Legion, starting as post commander. In September 1952 he officially represented the national organization at the Memorial Building Dedication in Suresnes, France, and the Pilgrimage to American Military Cemeteries in Europe. In addition to his other interests, he heads the firm of Connell's in Middletown.

Born in Boston, in 1898, Mr. Connell was educated at Exeter Academy and received his B.A. degree from Harvard, where he also studied at the Graduate School of Business Administration. His many public welfare interests and affiliations include the vice-presidency of the Greater Middletown Community Chest and the Secretaryship of the Connecticut Veterans' Home and Hospital Commission. He is also an Incorporator of the Middlesex Memorial Hospital.

Music Is My Weapon

BY HENRY COWELL

I BELIEVE in music: its spirituality, its exaltation, its ecstatic nobility, its humor, its power to penetrate to the basic fineness of every human being.

As a creator of music I contribute my religious, philosophical and ethical beliefs in terms of the world of creative sound—that sound which flows through the mind of the composer with a concentrated intensity that baffles description, the sound which is the very life of the composer, and which is the sum and substance of his faith and feeling. When he offers a composition one should remember that it is complete, concrete, and full of dynamic force in his mind and consciousness; and that a performance is only a run-through of the music for the benefit of those who listen, those who the composer hopes will respond. Yet this presentation will, if successful, so impregnate the listener with the philosophy of the composer that it is shared both in the realm of feeling and that of intelligence.

Since I am more used to expressing ideas in music than in words, I find that the latter seem inadequate, and do not have the drive, positiveness and persuasiveness that I should hope for in a musical presentation; but here are what words I have: My belief is that the Golden Rule is the supreme guide in human relations. I do not believe that any race or people is better or worse than any other.

I believe that each human being should have the liberty to be an individual, and that everyone who wins the right to act in his own way must, in return to society, behave ethically. I used to be almost totally uninterested in politics; but it becomes increasingly clear to me that ethical individualism cannot flourish under radically extreme political conditions. Thus I abhor communism, under which individualism is impossible and expression of liberal thought is punishable; and I abhor its right-wing counterpart under which innocent liberals fear persecution and reprisals of various sorts if they express their sincere ideas for the betterment of the government. My own belief is in a regard for individual rights according to the letter and spirit of the United States Constitution. This I fight for by creating music which I hope will reach and touch all who listen so that they will be thereby encouraged to behave according to their own highest possibilities. Unexpected inner response to the power of music dedicated to human integrity might reach dictators more easily than an atom bomb.

In any event I believe that a truly devoted musical work acts to humanize the behavior of all hearers who allow it to penetrate to their innermost being.

This is why I am a composer.

HENRY COWELL, one of America's leading composers, began his career as a professional musician in 1912 at the age of sixteen. He made his debut in San Francisco, playing his own compositions for piano. Since 1923 he has made five European concert tours and an annual American tour. Since 1928 he has been on the faculty of the New School for Social Research in New York, and is now also on the faculties of Columbia University and Peabody Institute.

President of the American Composers Alliance he received the award in composition conferred by the American Academy of Arts and Letters in 1948.

Mr. Cowell, whose works have won him wide acclaim, is the author of several books on music and more than eight hundred compositions, including eleven symphonies. He has done much to advance the cause of good music throughout the world. His home is in New York.

Nature of the Species

BY SIR CHARLES G. DARWIN

I RECOGNIZE fully that the appeal of things in life will be different for different people, and I can only say what I have found the most important things in life for myself. I count as one of the most important things in the world the understanding of the world. I have spent most of my time working at the physical sciences, and I count myself fortunate in having lived through the heroic age of physics when—what with relativity and the quantum theory —our understanding of the nature of inanimate matter has been as much revolutionized as it was three hundred years ago in the days of Newton.

This has been the science I have most studied, but I have always had a lively interest in biological subjects too, and these have much affected what I believe. Among such subjects one is the question of human nature, and this has colored my view of what will happen to mankind in the future. I believe that a great deal of what is now being attempted for our betterment is doomed to fail, and I don't share the particular enthusiasms of many of the would-be benefactors of humanity.

It is true that there have been immense improvements in material conditions during the past century, but they are quite external and they leave man's fundamental nature no better than it was before. So too the intellectual triumphs of recent years don't signify that man has become any more intelligent than he was in the preceding dark ages. I see no safeguard for us against a relapse into conditions like those exemplified in the sad records of past history.

The main hope of bringing about any real betterment in mankind depends on a different thing; it must be based on applying the idea of heredity, a science that is already understood in its principles, though hardly yet in many of its applications. Holding this, I believe intensely in the importance of the family as the *continuing* unit of human life. When the science of eugenics has been more fully developed, there may be a hope on those lines of really bettering humanity.

These are the things that for me are consciously of the chief importance. But underlying them there are others. The great philosopher Kant once said that there were two things that continually filled him with wonder: the starry heavens above him and the moral law within him.

Like him I too continually wonder at the moral law within me, which dictates my conduct, or perhaps I ought to say the ideals of conduct which I wish I could fulfill. But I am entirely lacking in the thing which so many people seem to regard as their mainstay in life, a mystical sense of religion. This I lack, and I am perfectly content to be without it.

&§&

Sir charles galton darwin, k.b.e., m.c., sc.d., f.r.s., is the grandson of the author of *The Origin of Species* and is a relative of the famed eugenicist, Galton. It is appropriate then that Sir Charles is himself both a physicist and a eugenicist.

After graduating from Cambridge, he was associated with Rutherford at Manchester and therefore concerned with some of the earliest work on nuclear physics. From 1914 to 1918, he served with the Royal Engineers and with the Royal Air Force. Following the war, he was successively Tait Professor of Natural Philosophy at Edinburgh University, Master of Christ's College, Cambridge, and Director of the National Physical Laboratory.

His work during the Second World War included supervision of "Mulberry," the artificial harbor for D-Day, and membership of the famous "Tube Alloy" Committee which was directing Britain's atomic research. Numbered among Sir Charles's publications are *The New Conceptions of Matter* and *The Next Million Years*, published in 1952.

43

Ten Black Seconds

BY ARCHIBALD T. DAVISON

OF THE many passages in the Bible which have for me a deep personal significance, none is more closely allied to my own experience than the story of the sons of the prophets in Second Kings. Elijah is trying, with merciful evasion, to spare Elisha the knowledge that their final parting is at hand. Elisha knows what must happen; but he is not to be allowed to bear his grief in silence, for at every stopping place on their journey, the two travelers are greeted by the sons of the prophets who keep asking Elisha, "Knowest thou that the Lord will take away thy master . . . today?" And Elisha, out of the sickness of his heart, must each time answer, "Yea, I know it; hold ye your peace." That, in a way, is my story because many, many years ago, for one tragically unforgettable moment, I stood among the sons of the prophets.

On a bitter winter's day, a man—and I still remember that he wore neither overcoat nor gloves—came to the door of my father's house and asked if he might shovel the snow from our steps and sidewalk. In silence, and looking at him fixedly, I began slowly to close the door. Seeing what I was about to do without even a courteous word of refusal, there came across his face no look of resentment or of surprise, but rather, one of complete resignation as though he would have said, "I know it; I am shabby and almost a beggar and I mustn't expect a small boy who lives in a prosperous-looking house to wonder if I'm hungry and cold and in need of what little money I can earn at this sort of work."

Child that I was, and perhaps none too sensitive, I was suddenly smitten by that look which has never left me; and of the many things that I have done, the remembrance of which now grieves me, none has remained more vivid in detail, none has so plagued my imagination. Many a night, lying in the dark, I have looked into that man's eyes and have literally sweated with longing to be a child again and to atone for those ten black seconds of time.

But that experience of my childhood was not all loss, for from the shock of it I unconsciously developed not a novel philosophy of conduct but, I believe, a salutary and a comforting one, embracing all animal as well as human life. It has made me infinitely careful to avoid inflicting the small hurts that so often grow into bigger ones. I try—though probably not always with success—never to speak a sentence which may affect the peace of mind of another without first quickly putting myself in his place, weighing the chances of a misunderstanding or the possibility of giving pain. This is not laborious nor does it make me over-meticulous in my dealings with others. It is purely automatic and arises from an instinctive dread of repeating in some form that cruelty of my youth.

I doubt not that, to many, my reactions to that childhood incident will seem abnormal; that were I just plain sensible I would long ago have dismissed the matter from my mind as of little importance and something not at all foreign to childish behavior. For myself, I am glad that that moment, in spite of its depressing consequences, has continued to live with me. It is so easy to be a son of the prophets. Certainly, there are few more tragic experiences in life than by wounding to be wounded, and to hear always afterward those words, even if unspoken, "Yea, I know it; hold ye your peace."

ARCHIBALD T. DAVISON, affectionately known to Harvard students as "Doc," has left a stamp on the musical life of his country. For it was by his work as conductor of the Harvard Glee Club, and later the Radcliffe Choral Society, that he helped bring to life the present nation-wide interest in choral singing and set a standard of performance by amateurs that is now maintained in many parts of the country. He also is a specialist on church music and studied organ with Widor in Paris, and was Harvard's Organist and Choirmaster for thirty years. He has written a variety of books on musical subjects, all educational, and has been given honorary degrees by Oxford, Harvard and Washington universities and Williams College. He is a Fellow of the Royal College of Music, London. His Harvard services have extended over a span of forty-five years, and he now is James Edward Ditson Professor of Music, emeritus.

"Success" Is a Failure

BY DONALD DAY

I BELIEVE in dynamic democracy.

By this I mean a democracy broad enough to encompass all human relationships, from the individual to the eternal, in a framework that keeps always in sight, regardless of momentary success or failure, liberty, equality and brotherhood.

I reject what Francis Parkman in the 1850's called "the national disease: rising in the world," or what is more commonly known as "success." I cannot live in dignity and in peace with myself if my goal is to be so narrow and restricted. I don't believe anybody can.

That does not mean that I should not do things nor have things. Far from it. It is a challenge to make what I do and what I have the means and not the end. I must control the doing and own the having, rather than let them control and own me.

As a man, I believe in living with a woman in happiness and creative fulfillment, and I believe just as sincerely that the woman I live with has the right to expect the same. I believe that the man and woman should have a separate life, so that their life together can be greatly enriched.

I believe that the same basic relationship of an individual to his wife should be broadened and extended to the community, the state, the nation and the world. I believe the rule should be not "rising in the world" but "rising with the world."

Only in this way are the fundamental and glaring faults in American democracy to be corrected. Surely they cannot be cured by totalitarianism or dictatorship, which are indeed scientific and selfishly perfected "rising in the world."

I believe that "rising in the world" has made the United States the most materialistic, the most prosperous and the most uncomfortable nation on earth. It has led innumerable men, women and even children to think that the highest aim in life is to get and not to give—surely the road to sterility, decadence and eventually to materialistic poverty. I see "rising in the world" creating jungle-fanging tactics expressed in showy houses, expensive automobiles, "the ten best-dressed women," paunchy men in plush clubs, and countless other neuroticisms. I see women made pawns and men pawnbrokers. If this is to be the yeast with which the loaf of democracy is baked, the rest of the world will find it soggy eating.

On the political side, I believe "rising in the world" has made of American governments the instrumentalities for individuals and groups to use for selfish aggrandizement, rather than basic umpires with laws and rules to insure the greatest good for the greatest number. I recall that on November 11, 1918, Woodrow Wilson warned that the United States "must hold the light steady" until the war-torn world recovered its equilibrium. Instead, the United States rushed back to "normalcy"—another word for "rising in the world."

In the spiritual field, I believe "rising in the world" has created creeds and churches competing with each other by giving comfort and solace to men and women too selfishly employed to rise "*with*" the world on weekdays. If money-tithing could be changed to time-tithing, with the dynamic democracy of Christ as a guide, I believe there might be fewer massive and glittering churches but more glowing hearts.

These are some of the demands of dynamic democracy, which I believe is the only way to defeat the jet plane "rising in the world" of totalitarian enslavement.

◄§ DONALD DAY was born in Millseat, Texas, thirty miles from a railroad. In his lifetime, he finds, he has lived through the fundamental life experience of the United States as a whole. He grew up from the Texas self-sufficing farm and ranch to see more of his country and to take his doctorate at the University of Chicago. He wrote *Big Country: Texas* for the American Folkways Series, and was co-editor of two Texas Folklore publications, *Backwoods to Border* and *From Hell to Breakfast*. He was also editor of *Franklin D. Roosevelt's Own Story*, *Woodrow Wilson's Own Story* and *Uncle Sam's Uncle Josh*, a biography of Josh Billings. After close association with Will Rogers, editing *The Autobiography of Will Rogers* and the humorist's book, *How We Elect Our Presidents*, Mr. Day counts as the leading authority on the American cowboy philosopher. He has been editor of the *Southwest Review* and editorial representative of *Reader's Digest*. His most recent book is *The Evolution of Love*.

Vote for the Angels

BY ARTHUR DEAKIN

I BELIEVE in man. I believe every human being has the power to serve his fellows, the duty to render this service and the right to do so in the way commanded by his own conscience. I believe every human institution, religious, social or political, and every human action, must stand judged by the extent to which it helps or hinders the individual in this task.

Perhaps, as you listen, you are saying to yourself, "Only a fool would claim such a belief today, when all around us lies the dreadful evidence of man's inhumanity to man." I do not forget the evidence. But I do not forget, either, how often in the past, men living through the dark moments of history must have come near to despair of themselves, yet lived to see humanity triumph. And in our own time we have seen our fellow-men give the lie to those who preached the doctrine of mankind's steady deterioration.

All my adult life I have worked with and for the laboring men of my own country—the men whose place in our society, and whose share in our common heritage, has been the last to be recognized; and it is upon them my belief is based. I know their courage, their loyalty, their deeprooted sense of fair play, and their dogged endurance when the need arises. These are the men from whom I learned, and I know these qualities belong to all mankind, not to any one nation, race or class.

> "The rank is but the guinea's stamp:
> The man's the gowd for a' that."

Because I believe in man, I believe he ought to be free to make his own decisions on matters of principle and conscience. He is not free, if poverty and ignorance chain him; he is not so free, if he is shackled by dogma and blinkered by lies or partial truths;

48

he is not so free, if force or fear shuts him off from enquiry and experiment; he is not so free, if he has not the right to dissent.

These beliefs, clumsily and haltingly though they are expressed, are to me a touchstone and a way of life. Because of them, I have striven and shall continue to strive to raise the physical standards under which men labor and live; for no man can reach his full stature if he is denied the decencies of life, as they are understood in his age and place. Because of them, I can neither accept a society which excludes some men from full participation in its duties and privileges, nor seek to change such a society by means which are themselves unjust. Because of them, I reject any theory of society which denies to a minority the effective right to be heard, even if in such a society the ruling class were actuated by the best of intentions. Because of them, I cannot agree that the end can ever justify the means, in our dealings with our fellow-men.

Well . . . there it is. Ill-stated and confused enough. But I think it is essential to decide whether man is, basically, an ape or an angel. Like Disraeli, I'm on the side of the angels.

⋘⧉⋙

ARTHUR DEAKIN, English labor leader, inherited from Ernest Bevin the General Secretaryship of the Transport and General Workers' Union. He is one of the "Big Four" leaders of the Trade Union Movement in Britain, and was Chairman of the Trade Union Congress.

Mr. Deakin is the son of a Warwickshire cobbler who died when the boy was a child. His mother went into domestic service and the boy, at thirteen, began work in the steel mills of South Wales. His story is one of a steady rise to power.

In the internal controversies within the Labor Party, Mr. Deakin has always supported Clement Attlee against Bevanite criticism. The *London Sunday Times* has called him "probably the most forceful personality in the trade-union movement." He has an intense hatred of Communism. His intimates know him as affable, at times a trifle wistful, and at others almost formidably playful.

We Do Not Choose Our Parents

BY HUBERT T. DELANY

I WAS once invited by a clergyman to address his congregation during Brotherhood Week. He warned me that though we were of the same religious faith, his congregation might not receive me cordially because I happened to be of a different race and color than they.

This warning caused me to ask myself: Who am I that people who did not know me, and had never seen me, should choose to be hostile toward me? I answered this question in my own mind. When I went to the church, I introduced myself to the audience as follows:

"I am an individual, just like each of you, who had nothing whatsoever to do with choosing who my parents would be. I, like you, did not know whether I would be born of parents who were rich or poor, black or white, Jew or Gentile. I did not know whether I would be born in America or on foreign soil, or whether my parents would speak English or Hottentot. I, like you, did not know whether I would be born of parents who were the owners of a large mansion, or would be living in a slum tenement, unfit for human habitation. I, like you, did not know whether I would be born of parents who were drunkards or high priests. As a matter of fact, I had nothing whatsoever to do with deciding whether my parents would be married at all."

In this somewhat unconventional way, I introduced myself. At the close of the religious services, people came up to me and said they had never realized before just how—but for the accident of birth—anyone of us might be the other. They told me this gave them a new, and a broader point of view.

And my own awareness of who I was and who—but for the accident of birth—I might have been, strengthened my faith in the conviction that all human beings are the children of one Creator, and that the Creator of this earth intended that all of the peoples who inhabit the earth should share together the benefits and blessings of the earth to their full use and enjoyment. I also believe that all men were created equal, and that any differences in the physical or mental capacities of man today, or of the skills and initiative with which man uses his talents, are due either to environmental factors, or are the by-products of man's inhumanity toward man, in what has become a struggle by some men for more power, and for the possession of more worldly goods than they need to enjoy the benefits and blessings of this earth.

Applying these beliefs to everyday life, it seems clear to me that people who really believe in democracy as a way of life can no longer tolerate one measure of justice and equality for some and a different measure for others. This I believe; this I try to practice.

Now, what are some of the specific things I have found important in my own life in this connection? I have found that it is important to follow in my daily life and in the public service, the doctrine common to us all: Do unto others as you would be done by, even if you were unlucky enough to be in the shoes of those who are compelled to appear before you at the bar of Justice. Each day as people appear before me, I am concerned not so much with being known as an erudite judge as with being known as a human judge—as a defender of the rights and liberties of all the people. Each day as I open court and look upon those who come before me seeking justice, I say to myself: "There, but for the grace of God, go I."

Ƨ HUBERT T. DELANY was born in Raleigh, North Carolina, the son of Nanny James Delany and the late Bishop Henry B. Delany. He attended college in New York City, graduating from the New York University Law School in 1926, and being admitted to the New York State Bar. A year later he became Assistant United States Attorney for the Southern District of New York. When Mayor LaGuardia took office in 1934, he appointed Mr. Delany a Tax Commissioner for the Borough of Manhattan. In 1942 LaGuardia named him Justice of the Domestic Relations Court of New York.

Justice Delany is a member of the Board of Directors of the National Association for the Advancement of Colored People. He is also on the Board of Talladega College; the YMCA; New York Tuberculosis and Health Association; the Mayor's Committee on Child Care; and the Lay Advisory Board of Harlem and Riverside Hospitals.

An Honest Doubter

by ELIZABETH DEUTSCH

At the age of sixteen, many of my friends have already chosen a religion to follow (usually that of their parents), and are bound to it by many ties. I am still "free-lancing" in religion, searching for beliefs to guide me when I am an adult. I fear I shall always be searching, never attaining ultimate satisfaction, for I possess that blessing and curse—a doubting, questioning mind.

At present, my doubting spirit has found comfort in certain ideas, gleaned from books and experience, to form a personal philosophy. I find that this philosophy, a code consisting of a few phrases, supplements, but does not replace, religion.

The one rule that could serve anyone in almost any situation is, "To see what must be done and not to do it, is a crime." Urged on by this, I volunteer for distasteful tasks or pick up scrap paper from the floor. I am no longer able to ignore duty without feeling guilty. This is "the still, small voice," to be sure, but sharpened by my own discernment of duty.

"The difficult we do at once, the impossible takes a little longer." This is the motto of a potential scientist, already struggling to unravel the mysteries of life. It rings with the optimism youth needs in order to stand up against trouble or failure.

Jonathan Edwards, a Puritan minister, resolved never to do anything out of revenge. I am a modern, a member of a church far removed from Puritanism, yet I have accepted this resolution. Since revenge and retaliation seem to have been accepted by nations today, I sometimes have difficulty reconciling my moral convictions with the tangled world being handed down to us by the adults. Apparently what I must do to make life more endurable, is to follow my principles, with the hope that enough of this feeling will rub off on my associates to begin a chain reaction.

To a thinking person, such resolutions are very valuable; nevertheless, they often leave a vacuum in the soul. Churches are trying to fill this vacuum, each by its own method. During this year, I have visited churches ranging from orthodoxy to extreme liberalism. In my search for a personal faith, I consider it my duty to expose myself to all forms of religion. Each church has left something within me—either a new concept of God and man, or an understanding and respect for those of other beliefs. I have found such experiences with other religions the best means for freeing myself from prejudices.

Through my visits, the reasoning of fundamentalists has become clearer to me, but I am still unable to accept it. I have a simple faith in the Deity and a hope that my attempts to live a decent life are pleasing to Him. If I were to discover that there is no afterlife, my motive for moral living would not be destroyed. I have enough of the philosopher in me to love righteousness for its own sake.

This is my youthful philosophy, a simple, liberal, and optimistic feeling, though I fear I shall lose some of it as I become more adult. Already, the thought that the traditional thinkers might be right, after all, and I wrong, has made me waver. Still, these are my beliefs at sixteen. If I am mistaken, I am too young to realize my error. Sometimes, in a moment of mental despair, I think of the words, "God loves an honest doubter," and am comforted.

❧✿❧

More than two hundred schools in the United States have taken up the study of "This I Believe" and have encouraged students to write their own creeds. The kind of result this study can produce is exemplified in the statement written by ELIZA-BETH DEUTSCH. She was born in Vienna, Austria, and came to the United States when she was two years old. She is now a senior, seventeen years old, at the Shaker Heights Senior High School, where she is active in sports, on the school newspaper and on the Student Council. During the summers she has worked as a counselor in a girls' camp. She twice won first place in New York *Herald-Tribune* book report contests; and in April, 1954, she was the first prize winner in the student division of the Cleveland *Press* "This I Believe" contest, winning a trip to New York during the Easter holidays.

A Friend Fights

BY PAUL H. DOUGLAS

LIKE OTHERS, I am continually forced to make decisions as to how much I should rely upon the forces of love and good-will which are in the world and deep within men, and how much I should seek to protect both myself and the nation from the malicious who seek to injure and to maim.

I was in my twenties when, upon reading the Journal of John Woolman, the Quaker tailor of the eighteenth century, I first felt intensely the power of active good-will to awaken similar motives in others and to transform hatred into love. This led me to a fresh appreciation of the real meaning of Jesus' life and works and to deeper admiration for such noble spirits as St. Francis of Assisi, Tolstoi, and our own Jane Addams. The task of Christians seemed to be to transform the world by personal deeds and spirit into a fellowship of friends. That still seems true to me.

But as I saw at first hand Lenin and Stalin, and then Hitler and Mussolini, try to take over the world, I could not believe that these principles would of themselves melt the hearts of either the communists or the Nazis, or alter the policies of their governments. For the rulers of those countries prevented any effective appeal by others to the better natures of their peoples and by their control of the schools, press, radio, armies and secret police, shaped men's thinking in hostile ways. To turn the other cheek was interpreted by them as a sure sign of weakness, and yielding brought the danger ever closer.

When the attack finally came upon a country, the vast majority of those who had previously put their faith in good-will would resist, but since their resistance would be belated, it would be ineffective. Only the saints would practice the doctrines of Matthew: 5–7, and these by definition would be few. A glacier of tyranny would descend upon us and the free world which might not melt for centuries or millennia. Seeing all this, I decided that

54

one must resist with the weapons of the flesh this onsweep of tyranny, and when the time came, I tried to do so in an appropriate manner. Now the same principle is involved in the attempt of the communists to take over the world. Their tyranny is just as bad as was that of the Nazis, and is indeed more hypocritical.

I believe forcible resistance to their aggression is as necessary now as it was in the case of the Nazis, fifteen years ago.

Does this mean then that the hope of a fellowship of friends bound together by mutual trust and affection must vanish and be replaced by brutal struggle? That would be a terrible prospect. Rather, to my mind, it intensifies the need for us to practice loving kindness within the family, the community, our country and the whole free world. Indeed, while we resist the aggression of the communist world, we should not hate the people over whom the communist hierarchy rules, but should rather be charitable and understanding in our judgments. We should, in fact, feel friendly towards them and seek their ultimate good. Thus we should not let our use of the weapons of the flesh destroy our faith in and practice of the reconciling influences of goodwill.

The same principle should apply in politics. The only Christian way is to regard one's opponents as being basically potential friends, and to treat them with dignity and respect so that men may seek a common way for dealing with the issues of our time.

◄§ PAUL H. DOUGLAS has been United States Senator from Illinois since 1948. A man of broad culture and warm human sympathies, his great specialty is economics. Educated at Bowdoin and Columbia, where he took his M.A. and Ph.D., he also studied at Harvard. He taught economics at the University of Illinois, at Reed College, Portland, Oregon, and at the University of Washington. Since 1925 he has been professor of economics at the University of Chicago. Throughout the 1930's he served on many committees for the study of unemployment and social security.

Mr. Douglas has a distinguished war record. In World War II, he enlisted as a private in the Marine Corps, advancing to lieutenant-colonel while overseas. He fought with the First Marine Division, was wounded on Okinawa and decorated for "heroic achievement in action" at the battle of Peleliu. He has written extensively on economics and employment problems.

Liberty Is Over

BY WILL DURANT

I FIND in the universe so may forms of order, organization, system, law, and adjustment of means to ends, that I believe in a cosmic intelligence, and I conceive God as the life, mind, order, and law of the world.

I do not understand my God; and I find in nature and history many instances of apparent evil, disorder, cruelty, and aimlessness. But I realize that I see these with a very limited vision, and that they might appear quite otherwise from a cosmic point of view. How can an infinitesimal part of the universe understand the whole? We are drops of water trying to understand the sea.

I believe that I am the product of a natural evolution. The logic of evolution seems to compel determinism, but I cannot overcome my direct consciousness of a limited freedom of will.

I believe that if I could see any form of matter from within, as I can see myself through introspection, I should find in all forms of matter something akin to what in ourselves is mind and freedom.

I define virtue as any quality that makes for survival; but as the survival of the group is more important than the survival of the average individual, the highest virtues are those that make for group survival—love, sympathy, kindliness, cooperation. If my life lived up to my ideals I would combine the ethics of Confucius and Christ—the virtues of a developing individual with those of the member of a group.

I was a Socialist in my youth, and sympathized with the Soviet regime until I visited Russia in 1932; what I saw there led me to deprecate the extension of that system to any other land. Experience and history have taught me the instinctive bases and economic necessity of competition and private property.

I am not so fanatical a worshiper of liberty as some of my radical or conservative friends. When liberty exceeds intelligence it begets chaos, which begets dictatorship. We had too much economic liberty in the later nineteenth century, due to our free land and our relative exemption from external danger; we have too much moral liberty today, due to increasing wealth and diminishing religious belief. The age of liberty is ending, under the pressure of external dangers; the freedom of the part varies with the security of the whole.

I do not resent the conflicts and difficulties of life. In my case they have been far outweighed by good fortune, reasonable health, loyal friends, and a happy family life. I have met so many good people that I have almost lost my faith in the wickedness of mankind.

I suspect that when I die I shall be dead. I would look upon endless existence as a curse—as did the Flying Dutchman and the Wandering Jew. Death is life's greatest invention, perpetually replacing the worn with the new. And after twenty volumes it will be sweet to sleep.

WILL DURANT, now a resident of Los Angeles, California, was born in North Adams, Massachusetts, in 1885. He received his bachelor's degree from Saint Peter's College, Jersey City, and his doctor's degree from Columbia University. After teaching Latin and French for a time, he returned to Columbia to teach philosophy. In 1935, Dr. Durant became Professor at the University of California.

Although he began writing at the age of eighteen, he did not publish any of his works until he was forty. Among his many books are *The Story of Philosophy* and *On the Meaning of Life*. He is now engaged in writing the monumental "Story of Civilization" Series and has published to date *Our Oriental Heritage*, *The Life of Greece*, *Caesar and Christ*, and *The Age of Faith*. The fifth volume of this world history, *The Renaissance*, appeared in 1953.

God's Athlete

BY MARTHA GRAHAM

I AM a dancer. I believe that we learn by practice. Whether it means to learn to dance by practicing dancing or to learn to live by practicing living, the principles are the same. In each it is the performance of a dedicated precise set of acts, physical or intellectual, from which comes shape of achievement, a sense of one's being, a satisfaction of spirit. One becomes in some area an athlete of God.

Practice means to perform, over and over again in the face of all obstacles, some act of vision, of faith, of desire. Practice is a means of inviting the perfection desired.

I think the reason dance has held such an ageless magic for the world is that it has been the symbol of the performance of living. Many times I hear the phrase . . . the dance of life. It is close to me for a very simple and understandable reason. The instrument through which the dance speaks is also the instrument through which life is lived . . . the human body. It is the instrument by which all the primaries of experience are made manifest. It holds in its memory all matters of life and death and love. Dancing appears glamorous, easy, delightful. But the path to the paradise of that achievement is not easier than any other. There is fatigue so great that the body cries, even in its sleep. There are times of complete frustration, there are daily small deaths. Then I need all the comfort that practice has stored in my memory, and a tenacity of faith. But it must be the kind of faith that Abraham had wherein he "Staggered not at the promise of God through unbelief."

It takes about ten years to make a mature dancer. The training is two-fold. There is the study and practice of the craft in order to strengthen the muscular structure of the body. The body is shaped, disciplined, honored and in time, trusted. The movement becomes clean, precise, eloquent, truthful. Movement never lies. It is a barometer telling the state of the soul's weather to all who can read it. This might be called the law of the dancer's life—the law which governs its outer aspects.

Then there is the cultivation of the being. It is through this that the legends of the soul's journey are re-told with all their gaiety and their tragedy and the bitterness and sweetness of living. It is at this point that the sweep of life catches up the mere personality of the performer and while the individual (the undivided one), becomes greater, the personal becomes less personal. And there is grace. I mean the grace resulting from faith . . . faith in life, in love, in people, in the act of dancing. All this is necessary to any performance in life which is magnetic, powerful, rich in meaning.

In a dancer there is a reverence for such forgotten things as the miracle of the small beautiful bones and their delicate strength. In a thinker there is a reverence for the beauty of the alert and directed and lucid mind. In all of us who perform there is an awareness of the smile which is part of the equipment, or gift, of the acrobat. We have all walked the high wire of circumstance at times. We recognize the gravity pull of the earth as he does. The smile is there because he is practicing living at that instant of danger. He does not choose to fall.

꿎 MARTHA GRAHAM, a tenth generation American and a direct descendant of Miles Standish, was born in Pittsburgh, Pennsylvania. When she was ten, her father, a prominent physician, moved his family to Santa Barbara, California. She was educated in private schools there and in Los Angeles.

Always deeply interested in the dance, when she was sixteen she attended a dance concert of Ruth St. Denis and, as a consequence, resolved to be a dancer. She started at once to study dancing at the Denishawn school in Los Angeles, and in 1926 made her New York debut.

In 1932 and in 1939, the Guggenheim Foundation awarded her a scholarship, the first dancer to be so honored. Since 1939, she has toured the United States, winning both popular and critical acclaim. Her repertoire includes such brilliant compositions as "Death and Entrances," "Cave of the Heart," and "Appalachian Spring." She conducts a school of contemporary dance in New York and has formed a company composed of former pupils.

Man Made God

BY JOHN GUNTHER

SOME YEARS ago the British novelist E. M. Forster wrote an essay which began with the words, "I do not believe in belief." This pungent phrase reflected the mood of the debunking era. Einstein upset our belief in conventional mathematics and physics. Freud and Pavlov played havoc with the concept of romantic love, and Spengler modified much of our faith in history. Even in the fine arts, my generation grew up in an atmosphere of destruction and revolt. Picasso broke up light, James Joyce broke up language. That some of these men were sublime artists, and that the older, more placid forms thoroughly needed revivification and change, added to the intellectual convulsion of the years in which we grew up.

But, if I may say so without pretention, I have always been able to believe in a good deal even in a world largely bereft of belief. Modern scientists and philosophers have ruthlessly assaulted the old standards, but that does not interfere with what seems to be my own basic belief in the dignity, decency, and should I say educability of man.

I hate cruelty; therefore I believe in humanity and justice. I hate oppression; therefore I believe in freedom. I hate vulgarity; therefore I believe in balance, clarity, and grace. I hate tub-thumping, hypocrisy, greed, and falseface; therefore I believe in order, sequence, moderation. Above all I hate irrationality, distortion, the wanton abuse of truth to achieve ignoble ends; therefore I believe in reason, that is, truth.

But abstractions like these need to be pinned down and defined. This one cannot do in 600 words. I believe very firmly in definition. Also it is quite clear that these abstractions have no meaning outside the enclosing body of one's own self. Logically, before believing in anything else at all, I am compelled to believe in my own self—whatever its manifest imperfections and shortcomings—or my life would hardly be worth living.

I believe it was William James who said that the chief value and virtue of life was to give you a chance to do something that will outlast it. I believe that you have to earn happiness, because happiness—at least for me—lies mostly in achievement, the consciousness of full effort and concentration applied to a task whether the task is successfully completed or not. In other words, though I am one of the laziest of men, I believe in work. Also—let me see—I suppose one must believe in things one likes, such as sunshine, watching tennis, Beethoven, good food, good talk, and the sonnets of John Donne.

I do not have much interest in formal theology but I don't think that I'm irreligious. I have a fairly marked ethical sense, and of course I believe in love, which should be the foundation of all religions. I believe that we are all part of a universe that has certain forms, patterns, interrelations, and compensations, even for the worst of personal tragedies. But I do not know enough to know why I think this. In other words the idea of God is a wonderfully convenient abstraction through which we can satisfy our yearning for order in the universe. And, if things go wrong, the concept of God not only can give us hope and succor, but, since the universe is too big for most of us to comprehend, it also relieves us of some responsibility. Of course I believe in God. But my approach is human, not celestial, in that I think that man made God, not vice versa.

☙ JOHN GUNTHER is a reporter in the most distinguished sense of that term. Since the early 1920's the globe has been his beat, starting as assistant London correspondent, and going on to correspondent in Paris, Moscow, Rome, Berlin, Vienna, and other world capitals. In the course of his work he has interviewed most of the great names of our time. He was war correspondent in London, 1941, and later accredited to General Eisenhower's headquarters in Malta.

Mr. Gunther is best known, of course, for his celebrated "Inside" books. Beginning with *Inside Europe* in 1936, he went on to author *Inside Asia*, *Inside Latin America* and *Inside U.S.A.* In 1949 he wrote the strong and tender *Death Be Not Proud*, following the loss of his only son. A steady contributor to many important magazines, he has also been a network radio commentator on world affairs. Mr. Gunther and his wife live in New York.

Ideals Don't Bend

BY UTA HAGEN

"I KNOW that in an accidental sort of way, struggling through the unreal part of life, I haven't always been able to live up to my ideal. But in my own real world I've never done anything wrong, never denied my faith, never been untrue to myself. I've been threatened and blackmailed and insulted and starved. But I've played the game. I've fought the good fight. And now it's all over, there's an indescribable peace. I believe in Michelangelo, Velasquez, and Rembrandt; in the might of design, the mystery of color, the redemption of all things by beauty everlasting, and the message of Art that has made these hands blessed. Amen. Amen."

These words were given to the dying painter, Louis Dubedat, in George Bernard Shaw's *The Doctor's Dilemma*. It is the credo of an artist, a specific human being; and only a part of the author's credo, whose beliefs are summed up in the entirety of his work. Not being a writer, a prophet or a philosopher, but an actress, I must again employ the help of a playwright to paraphrase my faith. I believe in the ancient Greeks who initiated our theater 2,500 years ago, in the miracle of Eleanora Duse's gifts, in the might of truth, the mystery of emotions, the redemption of all things by imagination everlasting, and the message of Art that should make the untiring work and striving, the inspiration and creation of all actors, blessed. Amen. Amen.

In the other part of my life I feel "guilty" about living up to my ideal, but not so much as poor Louis Dubedat, and of course not for the same reasons. I have in my life to guide me the Declaration of Independence, the Bill of Rights, and above all, the teachings of Jesus, and I believe in them to the letter—to the dismay of some. I, too, can get strength from Michelangelo and Rembrandt, and Bach and Mozart, and Shaw and Shakespeare, and Plato and Aristotle. These great makers and shakers have helped me—do help me—to find reason, majesty and greatness in this world. They have helped me to drown out the frenetic racket made by the compromisers who try to bend ideals to fit their practical needs and personal appetites, and to deprive us of our spiritual salvation.

The knowledge that every day there is something more to learn, something higher to reach for, something new to make for others, makes each day infinitely precious. And I am grateful. One thing makes for another. Shaw wouldn't be without Shakespeare, Bach without the words of Christ, Beethoven without Mozart, and we would be barren without all of them.

I was proud the day I first learned to make a good loaf of bread, to have learned a simple thing which others could enjoy. Or to plant a bulb in the ground and tend it and help it grow; or to give birth to a child and help her reach her own individual freedom; or to make a character in a play come off the printed page and become a human being with a point of view who can help others to understand a little more; all these things, and the effort to do them well, make it possible for me "while struggling through the unreal part of life, and being threatened, blackmailed, insulted and starved, to be true to myself and to fight the good fight."

UTA HAGEN, prominent American actress, was born in Germany, went to school in the United States and in Europe and attended the Royal Academy of Dramatic Art in England. Eva Le Gallienne helped her get the role of Ophelia in *Hamlet* but, although the production was a success, the following winter found her out of work and broke. With one of her last nickels, she phoned for an audition, and triumphed in the part of Nina in *The Sea Gull*. In 1947 some commercial managements said she was finished. She proved them wrong with her portrayal of Blanche in *A Streetcar Named Desire*, and in *The Country Girl* she won the Critics Circle Award and the American Theater Wing's "Tony." In 1951 she gave New York one of the most exciting *Saint Joan's* of the era.

Miss Hagen is devoted to her daughter, with whom she lives an untemperamental life in a New York apartment.

63

Of Sonnets, Symphonies and Socrates

BY EDITH HAMILTON

KEATS SAID, "I see in Shakespeare, the poet, the power of resting in uncertainty without any irritable reaching after fact and reason." What Shakespeare knew, he could not prove by fact and reason. In the truth he was seeking there could not be certainty logically demonstrated or factually self-evident. There can never be that kind of certainty in the things that are greatest and most important to us. To me in the course of my long life, this has become a profound conviction. No facts, no reasoning, can prove to me that Beethoven's music is beautiful or that it is more blessed to give than to receive. No facts can prove to me that God is. There is an order of truth where we cannot have the proved certainties of the mind and where we do not need them. The search for spiritual truth may be hampered by them, not helped. When people are certain they know, the way to more knowledge is closed. But to perceive beauty opens the way to a fuller perception of beauty. To love goodness creates more goodness. Spiritual certainty leads to greater certainty.

The truths of the spirit are proved not by reasoning about them or finding explanations of them, but only by acting upon them. Their life is dependent upon what we do about them. Mercy, gentleness, forgiveness, patience—if we do not show them, they will cease to be. Upon us depends the reality of God here on the earth today. "If we love one another God dwelleth in us." Lives are the proof of the reality of God.

When the world we are living in is storm-driven and the bad that happens and the worse that threatens press urgently upon us, there is a strong tendency to emphasize men's baseness or their impotent insignificance. Is this the way the world is to go or not? It depends upon us.

St. John spoke of the true light that lighteth every man coming into the world. Belief in the indestructible power of that light makes it indestructible. This lifts up the life of every man to an overwhelming importance and dignity.

God leaves us free. We are free to choose Him or reject Him. No tremendous miracle will come down from heaven to compel us to accept as a fact a Being powerful enough to work it. What would that kind of belief do toward making love or compassion a reality? God puts the truth of Himself into our hands. We must carry the burden of the proof, for His truth can be proved in no other way. "Glorious is the venture," Socrates said.

EDITH HAMILTON is both scholar and writer, and one of the foremost interpreters to our generation of the classical civilizations of Greece and Rome. Her career has been pretty evenly divided between teaching and writing. Educated at Bryn Mawr College, she won a European fellowship in 1894, and was the first woman to be admitted for study at the University of Munich. On her return to this country she became Head Mistress of the Bryn Mawr School, a post she held for twenty-six years.

In 1922 Miss Hamilton began her second, or writing career, publishing her first book, *The Greek Way*, in 1930. It has been reprinted many times. Following this came *The Roman Way*, *Three Greek Plays*, *Mythology*, *Spokesmen for God*, and *Witness to the Truth*. She holds honorary Doctor of Letters degrees from both the Universities of Rochester and Pennsylvania, as well as the National Achievement Award for 1951.

Old Creeds in a New World

BY DAG HAMMARSKJOLD

THE WORLD in which I grew up was dominated by principles and ideals of a time far from ours and, as it may seem, far removed from the problems facing a man of the middle of the twentieth century. However, my way has not meant a departure from those ideals. On the contrary, I have been led to an understanding of their validity also for our world of today. Thus, a never abandoned effort frankly and squarely to build up a personal belief in the light of experience and honest thinking has led me in a circle; I now recognize and endorse, unreservedly, those very beliefs which once were handed down to me.

From generations of soldiers and government officials on my father's side, I inherited a belief that no life was more satisfactory than one of selfless service to your country—or humanity. This service required a sacrifice of all personal interests, but likewise the courage to stand up unflinchingly for your convictions.

From scholars and clergymen on my mother's side I inherited a belief that, in the very radical sense of the Gospels, all men were equals as children of God, and should be met and treated by us as our masters in God.

Faith is a state of the mind and the soul. In this sense we can understand the word of the Spanish mystic, St. John of the Cross: "Faith is the union of God with the soul." The language of religion is a set of formulas which register a basic spiritual experience. It must not be regarded as describing in terms to be defined by philosophy, the reality which is accessible to our senses and which we can analyze with the tools of logic. I was late in understanding what this meant. When I finally reached that point, the beliefs in which I was once brought up and which, in fact, had given my life direction even while my intellect still challenged their validity, were recognized by me as mine in their own right and by my free choice. I feel that I can endorse those convictions without any compromise with the demands of that intellectual honesty which is the very key to maturity of mind.

The two ideals which dominated my childhood world met me fully harmonized and adjusted to the demands of our world of today in the ethics of Albert Schweitzer, where the ideal of service is supported by and supports the basic attitude to man set forth in the Gospels. In his work I also found a key for modern man to the world of the Gospels.

But the explanation of how man should live a life of active social service in full harmony with himself as a member of the community of the spirit, I found in the writings of those great medieval mystics for whom "self-surrender" had been the way to self-realization, and who in "singleness of mind" and "inwardness" had found strength to say yes to every demand, which the needs of their neighbors made them face, and to say *yes* also to every fate life had in store for them when they followed the call of duty, as they understood it. Love—that much misused and misinterpreted word—for them meant simply an overflowing of the strength with which they felt themselves filled when living in true self-oblivion. And this love found natural expressions in an unhesitant fulfillment of duty and in an unreserved acceptance of life, whatever it brought them personally of toil, suffering—or happiness.

I know that their discoveries about the laws of inner life and of action have not lost their significance.

◄§ DAG HAMMARSKJOLD succeeded Trygve Lie as Secretary General of the United Nations. "Call me Hammershield," he says. "That's as near as most people get, and it's what my name means." Born in Sweden in 1905, he is 5 feet, 10 inches in height, trim, blue-eyed and the bachelor scion of an aristocratic family of civil servants. His father was World War I Prime Minister of Sweden. A graduate of Uppsala University, he took his doctorate at Stockholm University. At college, friends tagged him "the perfect civil servant"—a good prediction! He speaks English, French, German, as well as Swedish, and is known for his nimble debating and impressive erudition. In 1951 he was Deputy Foreign Minister of Sweden.

Though economics are his great specialty, his interests are wide-ranging and include *avant-garde* poetry, Braque canvases and Matisse and Picasso drawings. His principal recreation is mountain climbing in Northern Sweden.

"Happy Talk"

BY OSCAR HAMMERSTEIN II

I HAVE an unusual statement to make—I am a man who believes he is happy.

What makes it unusual is that a man who is happy seldom tells anyone. The unhappy man is more communicative. He is eager to recite what is wrong with the world, and he seems to have a talent for gathering a large audience. It is a modern tragedy that despair has so many spokesmen and hope so few. I believe, therefore, that it is important for a man to announce that he is happy, even though such an announcement is less dramatic and less entertaining than the cries of his pessimistic opposite.

Why do I believe I am happy? Death has deprived me of many whom I loved. Dismal failure has followed many of my most earnest efforts. People have disappointed me. I have disappointed them. I have disappointed myself. Further than this, I am aware that I live under a cloud of international hysteria. The cloud could burst and a rain of atom bombs could destroy millions of lives, including my own. From all this evidence could I not build up a strong case to prove why I am not happy at all? I could. But it would be a false picture—as false as if I were to describe a tree only as it looks in winter. I would be leaving out an acknowledgment of the many successes that have sprouted among my many failures. I would be leaving out the blessing of good health, the joy of walking in the sunshine. I would be leaving out a list of people I have loved and who have not died. I would be leaving out my faith that the goodness in man will triumph eventually over the evil that causes war. All these things are as much a part of my world as the darker worries that shade them.

The conflict of good and bad merges in thick entanglement. You cannot isolate virtue and beauty and success and laughter and keep them from all contact with wickedness and ugliness and fail-

68

ure and weeping. The man who strives for such isolated joy is riding for a fall. He will wind up in isolated gloom.

I don't believe anyone can enjoy living in this world unless he can accept its imperfection. He must know and admit that he is imperfect, that all other mortals are imperfect, that it is childish to allow these imperfections to destroy all his hope and all his desire to live.

Nature is older than man, and she is still far from perfect. Her summers do not always start promptly on June 21st. Her bugs and beetles and other insects often go beyond her obvious intentions, devouring the leaves and buds with which she has adorned her countryside. After the land has remained too dry for too long she sends relieving rains. But frequently they come in torrents so violent that they do more harm than good. Over the years, however, nature keeps going on in her imperfect way and the result, in spite of her many mistakes, is a continuing miracle. It would be folly for an individual to seek to do better—to do better than go on in his own imperfect way, making his mistakes, riding out the rough and bewildering, exciting and beautiful storm of life until the day he dies.

❦

Oscar HAMMERSTEIN II, who holds a record for hit shows simultaneously playing on Broadway, began his career as a lawyer—and thereby hangs a tale. Inheriting a name which for decades had been practically synonymous with the New York stage, he was persuaded by his father to set his sights on the law office, as being perhaps more secure than the box-office. But, the theater was in young Hammerstein's blood, and his work for the stage began as a student at Columbia, where he wrote one or more of the varsity shows of his day, in the years around 1916.

Today, as the country's best-known librettist, he has authored a long line of successful musicals, including *Show Boat*, in collaboration with Jerome Kern, and in recent years, *Oklahoma!*, and the fabulous *South Pacific*, both to the music of Richard Rodgers. His song lyrics include the sensitive "Ol' Man River," the nostalgic "The Last Time I Saw Paris," and the ebullient "O What A Beautiful Morning!" His latest musical is *Me and Juliet*. He lives in Bucks County, Pennsylvania.

Adagio Penseroso

BY ROY HARRIS

I BELIEVE that a Divine Intelligence conceived the Universe and Universal Law which governs it; and that Universal Law is too vast and intricate to be understood by human mentality, which is itself such a small and ever-changing part of the Universe.

I count on the infallibility of Universal Law as it governs my own life—on the law of gravity which holds me and my fellow men on this revolving planet; on the consistent nature of matter and energy; on the miracle of life and regeneration. I count on Universal Law which determines the rhythm of my heartbeat and breathing—the delicate strength of my senses.

I believe that man's struggle to understand and use Universal Law is clear evidence of kinship to Divine Intelligence.

I believe that Divine Intelligence conceived matter and energy as integral parts of precise patterns of Universal Order for Ultimate Purpose; and therefore, man's discovery of the chemical-physical nature of matter and energy is only the smallest and most discernible fraction of the total comprehension of matter and energy.

I believe that man is making the same error of fractional discovery about himself as a part of the Universe, and is therefore slow to comprehend the limitations of his own rational processes and the danger to himself of his own incomplete comprehension and short-range outlook. I am convinced that power, separated from its Universal Purpose, is evil. I fear that man, in ignorance and in blind egotism, could succumb to the lure of releasing power over which he has no control; that man's only hope of fulfilling his destiny is receptivity to Universal Intelligence, wherein man's intuitive faculties can be awakened, strengthened, and guided toward a larger and clearer understanding of Universal Law.

For this reason I believe that the theologian, the philosopher, the artist, the lover, the parent, the friend, is sometimes able to gain a clearer vision of Universal Order through creative intuition than is the scientist within the scope of the empirical method. Certainly my experience as a composer has taught me that an objective use of acquired technical skill, without the subjective impulse of intuition, yields neither the drive nor depth of creativity.

It seems to me that intuition may be as old and wise as mankind's total evolution in the scheme of Universal Law, but that individual rationality can only be as wise as the perceptions of the individual in life experience.

I believe, then, that an inescapable consequence of man's struggle to understand and use Universal Law must be an eager willingness to be used by it as an instrument for it; that understanding of Universal Law can only lead to a scrupulous fidelity and personal responsibility to Divine Intelligence of which the Universe was created and, within it, mankind—so headstrong, so impotent, so eager, so faltering, so loving, so selfish, so promising.

⌘

ROY HARRIS, distinguished and distinctively American composer, is composer-in-residence at the Pennsylvania College for Women, Pittsburgh. (His wife, Johana Harris, is pianist-in-residence.) As a musical pioneer, Mr. Harris has helped free American music from the domination of European musical culture; and he is, in fact, to many younger composers, a musical emancipator. (Coincidentally, he was born on Lincoln's Birthday, in a log cabin in Lincoln County, Oklahoma.) He is justly proud of his pioneer background.

Mr. Harris has composed a large number of works, including half a dozen symphonies, six concertos, and some twenty-five other orchestral scores, as well as chamber, choral and piano music, and three ballets. Nearly every symphony orchestra in the United States and Europe has performed his works. Serge Koussevitsky said of him: "I think nobody has expressed with such genius the American life, the vitality, greatness and strength of this country."

That Look You Get

BY JOSEPH C. HARSCH

EVERYONE, I suppose, tends to define his own beliefs in terms of what he has found in his own experience to have highest value; those being the things which cause him to go on working, rather than quit and give up and just vegetate. I never did much vegetating. When I tried it, I got bored. I have kept working. And that means that I did believe in a number of things during my younger years when I wasn't overly conscious of what I did believe in. Now that I try to sort them out, I think they fall in this order. I have found two separate and distinct sources of satisfaction in life. One is the satisfaction of being in forward motion. It has not mattered so much how far I got as that I did get along. This process of being in motion has something to do with the kind of society in which we live. I think I have figured out what makes it valuable to me. Our western society is marked above all by its diversity of peoples, and forms of government, and ideas. I have been moving, with personal satisfaction, in a diversified society. I like it. I am happy moving among people who frequently disagree with me, and who lead very different lives from mine. Therefore I conclude that there is virtue of both material and spiritual kind in a diversified society of diversified man. My political instinct is therefore to aid and to abet in what small way I can the further evolution of diversified man. I believe that it is good, healthy and stimulating to do this, and that the doing of it is as good a way as any I know to show respect toward the Deity whom I conceive to be a diverse concept itself manifesting activity in diversity.

Then there is the memory strong in me of the occasions when I have seen a glance of surprised appreciation in the eyes of another person. Don't misunderstand me. I never did anything spectacular in the way of kindness for others. But sometimes we do do things which spring from an understanding of the needs and feelings of others. People always seem so surprised when you do that sort of thing, and so very grateful. And that look you get is a vast reward. It is the other great source of satisfaction. It comes from being considerate, even in very small ways. So from that sort of experience I have evolved a belief that there is virtue in being considerate, in being kind, in occasionally remembering the Golden Rule. And what does that prove? To me it proves that there is something decent in this thing we call the human spirit. It's a good thing; it must be, because it brings a little light into human eyes. Why is that good? I suppose it's because the ability to give kindness and receive appreciation in return is the one thing which really proves that man has climbed up out of the jungle and gotten hold of something higher than just the satisfaction of survival.

The net of this is that I know that I do believe in several things. I believe there is merit in life. I believe there is particular merit in the way diversified western man lives. That seems to me to represent progress. And I believe that because men have learned to give kindness and receive appreciation that there must be something higher leading us on to more compassion and more consideration for others within the context of human activity. In short, the process of thinking through this exercise has made me realize that I really do believe in the existence of that something we are all groping for when we use the word God.

◆§ JOSEPH C. HARSCH rates as a journalist's journalist and a commentator's commentator. That means that his colleagues recognize his insight and knowledge, trust his information and respect his judgment. As foreign correspondent, he wrote one of the best war books, *The Pattern of Conquest* (1941). He made a name for himself as commentator on CBS and NBC and as one of the regular speakers on the BBC's American commentary.

Mr. Harsch filled in as chief Washington representative of the *Christian Science Monitor* during Roscoe Drummond's leave of absence with ECA in Paris, and established himself as one of the most perspicacious of the Washington political columnists. After Mr. Drummond left the paper, he became a regular on the *Monitor's* first page. He does considerable public speaking on current events and is a frequent contributor to magazines on topics in this field.

Faith Takes Practice

BY ELLA MAE HOWEY

I BELIEVE I can live an abundant life, so am dissatisfied with an adequate life; I believe I can be constructively creative, so am not content with some accepted ruts of living. I believe these things are possible for me because I believe in a personal, loving God.

Six years ago I could not have understood that, let alone say it. I never thought or wondered about a belief. Then I learned I had a physical handicap that usually became progressively worse. Self-confidence and inner strength were conspicuous by their weakness and self-pity took over.

There are times in a life when knowledge of other heavier burdens is little consolation and comparisons are futile. At thirty-three, with a considerable life expectancy and a husband and sons whose love and respect I cherished, I soon realized two things: I would have to manage this problem or else *it* would manage me, and *what* happened was unimportant but *how* I accepted, faced or overcame what happened was very important. A new eagerness to learn joined my established feelings of inadequacy and doubts.

An intensive search that was objective and wary began. What I discovered replaced the air of catastrophe in my life with an air of personal revolution. Developing convictions grow stronger and deeper each year.

I believe:

that an all powerful God created the universe with a plan, easily observed in nature, that includes man;

that as a human spirit I enjoy, or suffer from, a distinctive ability to choose;

that God's plan is the most exciting, satisfying way to live, and requires self-development plus outgoing work;

that it calls for unfamiliar self-disciplines but results in expanding horizons and greater happiness;

74

that to pray for my will to be done is presumptuous and impractical, but to pray for God's will, and be willing to accept it in my life, is realistic and right;

that (try as I may to avoid it, and I have tried) any improvement must start within me;

that to perform good works in public and win ego-comforting praise is meaningless, unless my family receive the best of my kindness, patience and love;

that the alternative is to discount God, for believing these things I can find no straddling position.

To practice and study for physical and mental skills or artistic techniques seems very logical, but I admit it surprised me to learn that an understanding and awareness of God takes the same kind of consistent practice and study. But soon, it too made sense.

My continuing choice of God's will and unending search to understand God better, have helped reveal unsuspected abilities and strength in my own life. Recent achievements, though insignificant to the world, surpass anything I would have dared outline for myself. This indicates to me the potential power and possibilities available within all human spirits waiting only for faith, initiative and energy.

These six years have been demanding, yet joyous. And after a glimpse of the dynamic living and potential accomplishments in a life, I could choose no other way.

Is it any wonder that I anticipate the second half of my life with awe? I'm just beginning.

ELLA MAE HOWEY is a housewife with two sons, fourteen and nine. She was born in Alabama, graduated from high school, and settled down to family life in Cleveland, Ohio. When she was thirty-three years old, she was afflicted with deafness. She faced her difficulty by working out new ways of thinking and living. She says she found that bitter disappointments and struggles with compromise involved steady effort; detours, never before confronted and falteringly passed, exacted constant disciplines. She discovered that the belief she formed was a vigorous, challenging participation in life. She reacted to her own loss of hearing by learning to write creatively and to speak to adult education groups on hearing problems. In the spring of 1954, the Cleveland *Press* conducted a contest for its 300,000 readers, awarding prizes for the outstanding statements entitled "This I Believe." Mrs. Howey entered the contest, and this statement of her creed received first prize.

A Sunset in Your Hand

BY DAME LAURA KNIGHT

I BELIEVE that belief in something is essential to everybody.

We've all got to have our ideals, but to set one's own down in cold blood is rather apt to sound pompous I'm afraid. However, I have never conformed to any creed, but find that trying all the time to do your job well means a lot and gives you a grand feeling, even if you don't succeed in doing much.

What I would like to be able to do is to learn to see with real understanding and show to others the beauty that can be found even in ordinary things, say the footprints of a bird or a human creature in the snow, or even the black converging wheel-tracks of the car ahead of you when snow is beating against your windscreen. Oh, what lovely half-circles the wipers make and how the green, red and amber traffic lights, like a cluster of jewels, first show and then vanish.

I am sure that in whatever walk of life, the real thing is to try and clear away ignorance and prejudice. I don't mind growing old a bit. Nowadays there are lots of things I see and love that I would have never even glanced at in the days when youth's pride over-balanced one's judgment.

To learn to see is so important to an artist. And what a job trying to be an artist is! Sometimes you think you know a little, but when you are confronted with those messy tubes of paint, and that great bare canvas, you find you know nothing.

Here's the sunset. What a marvel! That red, purple and gold! What hope has one of expressing in paint that emotion—that change from light to darkness—immensity—myriads of stars that roll in space like our own world?

Turner could do it with his magic brush and give it to you to hold in your hand. Think of the great Milton who in metaphor of verse put Creation itself within our ken. As for Rembrandt and

Shakespeare, they not only gave us sympathy with the lame, the halt, the beggar and the blind, but with the King himself in all the unease of his heavy crown. By their insight, these men all left the world the richer for their being here.

In one's own small way, perhaps one may help to keep the flag flying until great genius is born afresh. I am proud to be allowed to bear my little flag, my ideal.

That is what I believe.

Do whatever one's gift it is to do, however humble it may be, and do it with all your might hoping that in some small way you may not only pay for the privilege of being here, but what matters even more, have served the Purpose, call it Divine if you will, that to us is not revealed.

‍⋙⋘

◆§ DAME LAURA KNIGHT is a leading British painter. Now in her late seventies, she has behind her half a century as exhibitor in the Royal Academy and an equal period as partner in a notable marriage. Both she and her husband, Harold Knight, have won international acclaim as painters and are the only husband-and-wife Royal Academicians.

Dame Laura (she was made a Dame of the British Empire in 1949) was born in Nottingham, Derbyshire. Her people were poor, and she was cradled in a drawer pulled out of the kitchen dresser. Romantically enough, she met at thirteen, in art school, the man she was later to marry.

Dame Laura's canvases show her preoccupation with gypsies, the theater, the circus and the ballet. She has a gentle, benign, rather sweet appearance which belies the fact that she is actually a tough and determined fighter, with a great zest for art and life.

77

We Were Not Skeptical Enough

BY JOSEPH WOOD KRUTCH

I was born in what was called "An Age of Unbelief." When I was young I took that description seriously, and I thought that I was an intellectual because of the number of things I did not believe.

Only very slowly did I come to realize that what was really characteristic of myself and my age was not that we did not believe anything but that we believed very firmly in a number of things which are not really so.

We believed, for example, in the exclusive importance of the material, the measurable, and the controllable. We had no doubts about "what science proves" and we took it for granted that whatever science did not prove was certainly false.

When, for example, "science proved" that man had risen from the lower animals, we believed, as I still do, that this is a fact. But when science found it difficult to define, or measure, or deal with the ways in which a man's mind, and character and motives differ from those of the lower animals, we believed that there was no important difference between them. The trouble was not that we were skeptical but that we were not skeptical enough.

We studied man by the methods which had proved fruitful for the study of animals and machines. We learned a great deal about his reflexes, animal drives, the ways in which he could be conditioned to behave. And then, because our methods did not permit us to learn anything else about him, we came to the conclusion that there was nothing else to be learned.

We came to believe, to take the most familiar example, that love was "nothing but" the biological impulses connected with sex. What is even more important, we came also to believe that his thinking was "nothing but" his power of rationalization and that his ideals and values were "nothing but" the results of his early conditioning. We began to assume that what he believed to be his free choices were not really anything of the sort; that he was not the captain of his soul but only what the dialectic of society or perhaps his infantile fixations had made him. He was, we tended to believe, not a cause but an effect.

Seldom before in the history of civilization has the world been in so parlous a state and not often before have men seemed to believe less in a God who would save them. Yet it is at this moment that we have lost faith in man himself as a prime mover of events.

What I believe in most firmly is *man himself*. And by that I mean something quite specific. I believe that he descended from the animals but that he has powers which animals share but little, if at all. I believe that he is something in himself. I believe that he can will, and choose and prefer.

That means, for example, that society is what he makes it, not that he is what society makes him. It means that he can be permitted to think, not merely conditioned by good or bad propaganda. I believe, therefore, that he can be freed, and that means a good deal more than given the vote or permitted civil liberties. The difference between a totalitarian and a democratic society is the difference between those who believe the individual man capable of being the captain of his soul and those who believe that he is merely the creature of the society in which he lives.

I believe that we cannot set the world free until we believe that the individual himself is free.

◄§ JOSEPH WOOD KRUTCH, author, teacher and dramatic critic, retired in 1953 as Brander Matthews Professor of Dramatic Literature at Columbia University. Born in Knoxville, Tennessee, he was educated at the University of Tennessee and at Columbia, which conferred a Ph.D. upon him in 1924. He has been a life-long contributor to leading magazines and has written some fifteen books, mostly literary history, biography, and criticism. These include studies of Samuel Johnson and Henry David Thoreau.

He also contributed the introduction to the American edition of Marcel Proust's *Remembrance of Things Past*. In 1940–41 he was president of the New York Drama Critics Circle.

Out of his hobby, which is natural history, have come several works, notably *The Desert Year* and *The Best of Two Worlds*. A widely discussed book, *The Modern Temper*, published in 1929, was succeeded in 1953 by a reassessment called *The Measure of Man*. He now lives in Tucson, Arizona.

The People Know

BY ALFRED M. LANDON

I BELIEVE in people. Their accomplishments as members of the society created through centuries of courageous trial and heartbreaking errors merit belief in individual thinking and the right to do so.

Mankind has made astonishing progress in a few millennia. It may be that not all of our boasted progress has been of real value.

It may be that we have tried to purchase material well-being at a price too high spiritually. Even so, with all our woes, the civilization of the twentieth century—where it prevails—gives greater opportunity for the Good Life for all the people than did any of the so-called golden ages of the past, when the powerful few regarded the great masses as little better than mere beasts of burden.

I believe social and political progress does not "just happen." We cannot too greatly honor and revere the great men of history—the great reformers, the great leaders. However, it is a sad fact that there have always been as many false prophets as true prophets, as many powerful self-seeking demagogues as selfless, patriotic statesmen, as many ruthless exploiters as benefactors.

The race has made progress only so far as the people have developed the ability to distinguish the false from the true and the will to follow the truth at whatever cost.

Two thousand years ago, the world had great philosophers, great culture, great and powerful empires. Then came a meek and lowly man of Judea. The learned and the great rejected Him, but "the common people heard Him gladly." The whole course of human history was changed by their acceptance of His teachings.

I believe in the people—not that they are infinitely wise, but that in the main they instinctively believe in fair play, in decency, in justice.

Necessarily, man must live with others and learn to get along with them—first in the family, then in the clan, the tribe, the nation and ultimately the world.

In the family a sense of justice, of trust, of loyalty, and—foremost of all—affection are imperative. It is these traits which give validity to democracy and which are the basis of our faith in the final decisions of the people.

The civilization which we cherish today and in defense of which we will wage uncompromising war, rests upon the ideals of democracy. Democracy, if it be a vital force, must be in the hearts of the people—an instinctive and irresistible demand for liberty and justice for all. Democracy cannot be bestowed upon a nation. When the people—the common people—are ripe for it, they just naturally take it as the natural inalienable right.

I believe that instinct is in every human heart.

Alfred M. Landon, two-term Governor of Kansas, was Republican nominee for President of the United States in 1936 running against F.D.R. Born in Pennsylvania, he was educated at Marietta (Ohio) Academy and the University of Kansas. He was a bookkeeper in a bank in Independence, Kansas, until 1912 when he became associated with the oil-producing business, in which he has made a fortune.

Mr. Landon has been an influential delegate-at-large at the past several Republican Conventions and today enjoys the status of elder statesman in Republican councils. A man of innate modesty and warm and friendly personality, he has carefully avoided the national limelight of recent years, preferring to live quietly at home in Topeka. He smokes a pipe, plays bridge, likes the movies and, for exercise, does much horseback riding.

Pondering in Prison

BY WILLIAM T. MANERS

To DISTINGUISH between what I believe and what I would like to think I believe is the prelude of distinguishing between the thoughtful and the thoughtless. And between these there can be no compromise. I believe, in the words of Shakespeare, that "there is nothing either good or bad but thinking makes it so," and that we are not the creatures of circumstances, but circumstances are the creatures of ourselves, our thoughts.

I began my real thinking in the summer of 1952, while recovering from a self-inflicted wound incurred in a tragedy that took a very close and cherished life. My pondering brought me to see that I exist in the consciousness of my thoughts and beliefs, and that they are my most powerful God-given possessions. I see that these thoughts and beliefs are my origin and the source of all things gained or lost. They mold my character, affect my health and determine my success or failure. Everything that I do comes from this generating force of thought.

I know this is a power. If I ignore it, I am easily persuaded by what I see or hear. If I believe in the power of my own positive thought, and act on it, I overcome all the hostile influences like fear, anger, selfishness and weakness. For these are not present if not first manifested in my thought.

Paracelsus said that men who are devoid of the power of spiritual perception—what I call thought—are unable to recognize anything that cannot be seen externally. I come into this condition of awareness when I find myself. I am sure that I have learned this much, not by intellect or scholarly attainment, but by pondering and, in pondering, discriminating. I discriminated, not between creeds or religions, but between true and false, important and unimportant, right and wrong, selflessness and selfishness.

It is by discriminating that I find I am able to rid my consciousness of the past errors and mistakes in my life, though only as I progress in understanding. And I also have noted that I cannot progress if I continue to hold these mistakes and errors in my consciousness. What I aspire to is a final understanding of myself and my relationship to God, and I am aware that I have much to learn.

I find I am rewarded by giving, not necessarily material things, but myself, even in giving myself an opportunity of giving to others. In this way I have found an abundance of love, understanding and selflessness among my fellow men.

It helps me in my relations with others to divide them in two groups, those who ponder and those who have not had the occasion to do so, have not yet experienced the compassionate desire to learn. This classification has given me the best rule of tolerance I have found so far.

Now, in my second year of life imprisonment, I begin to realize how little I have come to comprehend. But I have grown in the faith that with God all things are possible. And I have concluded that neither Heaven nor Hell are locations, but are conditions of mind, a state of awareness in which I live.

This I have learned and this I believe.

～⧈～

WILLIAM TANNER MANERS had twenty-three years of distinguished service in the United States Navy. When fifteen, he left a broken home to enlist, and spent the next nine years aboard destroyers. With the *U.S.S. Plunkett,* he served on escort duty in the North Atlantic and the Mediterranean. Skipping two ranks to be the ship's communications officer, he participated in the invasion at Salerno and at Anzio. He became electronics officer of Atlantic Fleet destroyers, then served for four years with the Atomic Weapons Project, and finally, was assigned as radar officer to the staff of NATO. The termination of this Lieutenant Commander's brilliant career was sudden and tragic. In July, 1952, while under severe emotional strain, he acted in violence, a life was destroyed, and he was tried and sentenced to the penitentiary.

He wrote this statement in his second year of a life sentence, "to help others avoid both my own and less serious experiences."

Laugh, Love and Lift

BY MARY MARTIN

WHEN I was five and people asked me what I wanted to do when I grew up I quickly said, "To sing and dance on the stage in New York and to be happily married and have two children."

When I was ten I experienced two memorable moments that have helped guide me ever since. In the Episcopal Church in Weatherford, Texas, when I told the minister my dreams he said: "God has given you a giving talent. Each of us is a vessel, a medium of expression. You must have faith to sing and dance. Just believing you can do these things is not enough, studying and working for them you will do them. Faith is the most powerful means in the world."

The second moment came when my schoolteacher spoke a verse and then gave me a card with the words printed on it. They were:

"I would be true, for there are those who trust me;
I would be pure, for there are those who care;
I would be strong, for there is much to suffer;
I would be brave, for there is much to dare;
I would be a friend to all—the foe—the friendless;
I would be giving and forget the gift;
I would be humble, for I know my weakness;
I would look up—and laugh—and love—and lift."

I was told these things at a wonderfully impressionable age and they have never left me. I have been happily married for fourteen years and we have two healthy, happy children. I sing and dance on the stage. But there have been great tests of my faith.

Once during a performance of *Annie Get Your Gun* in Oklahoma City I suddenly couldn't sing. Not a sound came out. All the doctors I saw that night and the next day said I must not sing or speak for weeks, or I might never sing again.

We were to open in Los Angeles in less than five days. I consulted a throat specialist there. Could I open? He wouldn't say, but immediately he began treatments, three times a day. The afternoon of the opening, I asked him again, could I perform that night? He said only I could answer the question. We went to the theater. I stood on the stage and sang a scale, the first sound of any kind I had made in four days. They said they could hear me in the last row of the top balcony.

Shaking, I went to my dressing room and lay down. In the quiet darkness I was able to clear away the suspense, the doubts and fears. The doctor had given me every help. People who had faith in me depended on my opening that night. Now I felt a moment of the greatest joy and a new strength came. I breathed deeply and held each moment of strength within me. Long before my cue, I knew I had much to give that night, and within me, I knew, was more than enough of the necessary health and happiness— to give.

I have met many people—some smile or doubt or deride any attempt to give expression to a faith. Yet, I have known that there are those who trust me, those who care; there is much to suffer, much to dare; I know my weakness, my friends and the friendless. I know the joy of giving and I have been given to beyond wishes or dreams. I want to look up and laugh and love and lift. I have had faith from an early age. My faith, only my faith, has made my every wish come true. This I believe—this I know without exception.

⁎§ MARY MARTIN, star of stage and screen, burst into overnight Broadway fame warbling "My Heart Belongs to Daddy" in *Leave It to Me.* Before playing the fabulous trigger girl in *Annie Get Your Gun,* she had been seen as the wistful heroine of *Lute Song,* and as the highly decorative animated statue in *One Touch of Venus.* As the original Nellie Forbush in the Rodgers and Hammerstein musical, *South Pacific,* she danced, sang and washed her hair on stage for 1300 performances. After appearing in *Kind Sir* on Broadway, she starred in *Peter Pan* in 1954.

Miss Martin is adored by audiences and co-workers alike for her great warmth as a human being, as well as her unmatched talent. Born in Weatherford, Texas, she was educated at the Ward-Belmont School in Nashville, Tennessee. She is married to Richard Halliday.

A Doctor's Concern

BY DR. CHARLES W. MAYO

ALL PHYSICAL substance, animate and inanimate, as well as all activity, instinctive and contemplated, has purpose. I believe there exists an all-wise, all-powerful plan which is not inconsistent with happenings of the past, the present or those to come in the future.

Sound study of events of eons and eons in the past discloses nothing that is in opposition to any religious belief of reasoning man. Knowledge of evolution, and of other refinements which have occurred progressively throughout history, makes me more keenly aware of the wonder of all things and more conscious of a feeling of Divine guidance.

A whole is made up of parts. Just as the body is made up of millions of individual cells which are integrated into related groups, so I feel we each have a part in a mammoth plan with a personal role and an obligation of service—so-called self-existence with a purpose above self.

Problems of a personal nature should be expected and met. More distant problems, but equally realistic ones by the very nature of things, are those relationships of an international scope. Time, combined with tolerance, and especially with knowledge and un- biased consideration of the particular problems of others, no mat- ter who they are or what their race, their culture, religion, native laws, economics or methods of living, should result in a better understanding among all peoples of the world. To bring this about, not only should we appreciate our failure *actually* to know these people and their problems but also more especially should we take into consideration their inability and their lack of opportunity to know our problems; these matters should concern us. At present, our great fault seems to be to ignore basic principles. We should not lose thought of our personal responsibilities to ourselves as well as to others.

There is a definite purpose behind the inanimate and the animate, and the birth, life and death of all living things. Man will never be successful in taking unto himself controls that fall only within the knowledge and competence of the Almighty.

Honest thought and action, consideration for details, and the passage of time are most important factors in the solution of all problems. However, although life is serious, I believe it must be balanced with a lighter side. For me, life without humor and time to relax from care would be dull indeed. The crux of any fun should be that it not be had at the expense of others. I believe that we must be mindful that service to others and search for truth should be our unfailing obligations.

CHARLES W. MAYO, as surgeon of the world-famous Mayo Clinic at Rochester, Minnesota, and Professor of Surgery at the Mayo Foundation Graduate School, University of Minnesota, stands at the very top of his profession. However, unlike most men who have attained eminence in his field, Dr. Mayo has found, or rather made, time to interest himself importantly in national and world affairs. Thus, as Alternate U.S. Delegate to the United Nations General Assembly, he demonstrates that he is also an outstanding citizen of this country and of the world.

Dr. Mayo, who is a son of one of the founders of the Mayo Clinic, has been decorated by several foreign countries. He belongs to a score of medical associations, and is a member of the Board of Regents, University of Minnesota, and the Medical Advisory Board, American Legion. On the personal side, he is short, easy-going, somewhat rumpled in his dress, and has a gay and twinkling smile.

The Crossword Puzzle

BY HARRY S. McALPIN

BASIC IN my life have been these beliefs: that there are some things for which I am not responsible, some I cannot change, some I can. Around recognition and acceptance of these facts I have tried to build a philosophy by which to live in our complex society.

Forty-six years ago I was born a Negro in America. For this, of course, I was not responsible, though I am proud of it. I have traveled around the world, and have learned from experience that I would rather be an American with an inalienable right to fight against discriminations and prejudices and injustices, than to be any other nationality with a pseudo-equality, in slavery to the state, unable or afraid to express or even think my dislikes or disagreements, as is the case in Russia and other communist-controlled countries.

I had a father who regrettably died when I was fifteen years old and a senior in high school. He was a man of great principle. He abhorred injustice. He believed, in spite of the handicaps he suffered because of his color, that all men were created equal in the sight of God, and that included him and me. He instilled me with his beliefs.

To live by these beliefs I have found it necessary to develop patience, to build courage, to pray for wisdom; but despite my fervent prayers, I find it is not always easy to live up to my creed.

The complexities of modern day living, particularly as I must face them day to day as a Negro in America, often put my creed to test. It takes a great deal of patience to accept the customs of some sections and communities—to try to fit into the crossword puzzle of living the illogic of a practice that will permit me to ride on the public busses without segregation in seating, but deny me the right to rent a private room to myself in a hotel; or the illogic of a practice which will accept me as a chauffeur for the

88

rich who can afford it, but deny me the opportunity of driving one of the public busses I may ride indiscriminately; or the illogic of a practice which will accept me and require me to fight on the same battlefield, but deny me the right to ride in the same coach on a train.

It takes a great deal of courage to put principles of right and justice ahead of economic welfare and well-being, to stand up and challenge established and accepted practices which amount to arbitrary exercise of power by petty politicians in office or by the police.

Trying to live up to my beliefs often has subjected me to both praise and criticism. How wise I have been in my choices may be known only to God. I firmly believe, however, that as an American, as a man, and as a Christian, I have been strengthened and life about me has been made better by the steel-hardening fires through which my creed and my faith have carried me.

I shall continue to pray, therefore, a prayer I learned in the distant past which I now count as my own—"God give me serenity to accept the things I cannot change, courage to change the things I can, and wisdom to know the difference."

❧ ❦ ❧

HARRY S. MC ALPIN is a Louisville, Kentucky, attorney who turned to the practice of law from a distinguished career as a journalist and government official. A graduate of the University of Wisconsin, where he played varsity baseball, he became the first Negro correspondent to be accredited to the White House. He served during the administrations of Roosevelt and Truman, representing 51 newspapers of the Negro Newspaper Publishers Association.

During World II, Mr. McAlpin traveled 30,000 miles around the Pacific islands, as Navy war correspondent with the rank of Lieutenant Commander (the first Negro to hold that rank in the Navy). For this work, he was awarded a Certificate of Commendation from the Secretary of the Navy. In 1947, he became Director of Information for Sugar Rationing Administration of the Department of Agriculture (still another "first" for him as a Negro). He is married and has a daughter who graduated from Howard University in 1954.

God Wasn't Fooling

BY J. P. McEVOY

I BELIEVE in work. When God told Adam: "In the sweat of thy brow shalt thou eat thy bread," He wasn't fooling.

I believe in prayer. Not as a dog is taught to sit up and beg for a bone, but as a respectful effort to make contact with a Superior Being—and a two-way communication, if possible. I do not believe that prayer is dialing "Information" for God when you are in trouble, or calling "Operator" to complain about the service.

I believe with Hamlet there are more things in Heaven and Earth than are dreamed of in our philosophy. So it doesn't bother me any more that philosophers disagree with each other—because I reserve the right to disagree with them. I know they are smarter than I am, but I console myself with the thought that none of them has come back from the Other Side with the Answers.

I believe in Democracy—when that means equal opportunities for all—but I believe just as steadfastly in the aristocracy of intelligence, taste and character. I believe there will always be leaders and those who yearn to be led; burden-bearers and free-riders. Since there will always be more of the latter than the former I don't believe that wisdom is a monopoly of the majority. Leaders, too, can be right—history proves it—and we shouldn't be beastly to them, unless they lead us in the wrong direction.

I believe in Liberty—not just something precious to die for in far-off places, but something equally precious to live for at home. Many brave men have fought abroad to preserve liberty, only to come home and find it nibbled away by ducks: officious bureaucrats, bullying bosses, nosey neighbors, nagging wives, interfering in-laws.

I believe we have been bewitched into believing that committees, organizations, clubs, campaigns and drives will solve our problems. I believe if householders plant vegetables in their back yards and flowers in front all neighborhoods will be lovely and there will be no need for garden clubs. Likewise, parents must train and discipline their own children and not abdicate responsibility to the schools, police and juvenile judges.

The late W. C. Fields, explaining his raffish approach to life, told me: "Lots of people believe in Reincarnation. They think they are coming back here—but *I* know I'm going through here only once."

I wonder! We have been solemnly warned—the sins of the fathers are visited on their children. In short, you can't get away with it. The Hindus call this Karma. They believe we are doomed to keep coming back here in one form or another until we have paid all our debts in full; righted all the wrongs we have committed; made complete restitution. Call it Karma, the Sins of the Fathers, or the Last Judgment: it gives one pause!

I believe so long as we thrill to the words of Homer, the art of Michelangelo, the music of Beethoven, these great spirits will be immortal. So long as any of us remember the inspiration of our fathers and mothers, they, too, will never die. And we in turn may achieve such immortality.

Finally, I believe if you have the choice it is better to be kind than to be clever. I believe Epictetus: "Lead the good life and habit will make it pleasant." And I believe Virgil: "Happy is he who can search out the cause of things, for thereby he masters all fear, and is throned above Fate."

J. P. MC EVOY is a literary virtuoso, one of America's most prolific and versatile writers. Born in New York City, he began his career some forty-three years ago as a cub reporter for the South Bend, Indiana, *News*. Later gravitating to Chicago, he covered sports for the *Record Herald*, and afterwards turned to the writing of greeting-card messages. In his own words, he has been a "wall-motto writer, children's book editor, and advertising slogan thinker-upper." He has written five novels, several books of short stories, a volume of verse, and ten Broadway productions. These last include three editions of his successful musical revue, *Americana*.

Mr. McEvoy has also worked for Hollywood studios, written radio serials and, not least, is the creator of the comic strip "Dixie Dugan." Since 1942, his chief occupation has been to keep traveling as the roving editor of *Reader's Digest*. He now lives in Havana, Cuba.

A Man in Solitude

BY ELMORE McKEE

WHAT A MAN really believes is shown by what he thinks and does in solitude.

I shall try to set down some things that keep coming to me in those rare moments when solitude becomes creative—and comes with the assent of all three avenues to reality that are given me: my reason, my feeling, my intuition.

First, I discover there is a core of being deep within me, where either creative or destructive forces are constantly taking possession of me. I believe that here, the Creator either gains or loses ground in terms of his specific purposes for me. And I find that I am held responsible for what happens in this solitude; as, for instance, when five years ago I made the radical decision to become a layman after having been an Episcopal minister for twenty-five years. I find this freedom to make choices and to be held responsible for them an essential, if sobering, experience.

I am reminded of some German friends who, as a committee, were struggling in 1947 to plan a laundry for our Quaker neighborhood center in Frankfort. One day they came to me exclaiming, "We have just discovered what democracy means!" Then, with surprise written all over their faces, they added, "It means that each member of our committee must take responsibility."

Next, I have learned that this inner core of my being is definitely the Creator's outpost, not my private preserve. And there's a lift in admitting this. It has saved me—in the uncertain days when I have been making a fresh start—from taking myself too seriously. Nothing is so exhausting as mentally to carry oneself around all day—not to mention the wearing effect it has on others. I shall never forget Dwight Eisenhower saying to his friends on the night of his election: "Always take your job seriously, never yourself."

These two discoveries lead me to a third. I see my neighbor in a special light. For the Creator is trying to do the same kind of business within him as within me. So I have learned to knock on doors expectantly. Sometimes I find the person who opens the door is willing to risk even slackened production to express his basic and often, perhaps, buried instinct for mutuality.

I had a friend who constantly gave expression to this instinct, the late colorful, greatly human vicar of St. Martin's, Trafalgar Square, London, Dick Sheppard. I found he had a curious habit, whenever he left a hotel room, of praying for the next person who would occupy the room, that he might make a better go of things in life than he himself had. He saw humanity in a special light, as bound together in and under God.

And there has come this final insight. Sometimes life slaps me down hard. At such times I must try at all costs to forgo the luxury of self-pity. So I try to get my thoughts and my fingers quickly onto the next constructive job. This puts the fresh hoof-prints of creation over the danger spot where I am tempted to enjoy the contemplation of my own miseries.

Uniting each of these four insights is a single creative principle that acts as a steady, difficult-to-heed pressure away from self. Its theme is this: real life always lies in giving, never in taking.

A noble Jew named Jesus once let himself be wholly mastered by this theme. In so doing he pioneered and occupied new spiritual ground. If we ignore His victory, I believe we ignore our destiny. I have found in all effective solitude that I cannot escape Him.

ELMORE MC KEE originated "The People Act" radio program and directed the educational and civic movement which grew out of it. This was the culmination of a decision reached several years earlier when he resigned from the rectorship of a prosperous church and later from the Episcopal ministry. Contributing to this choice was his experience in Germany as the head of a Friends' relief mission. His resignation from the clergy did not mark any diminution in the religious spirit which brought Mr. McKee to the chaplaincy of Yale and later to the outstanding rectorships of prominent churches in Buffalo and New York City. On the contrary, he has extended its scope and is pursuing his long-time concern with the "religiousness of the so-called non-religious person."

Mr. McKee is a lean, athletic man with gray, deep-set eyes and an equally deep-set sense of humor. He lives in New York.

A Tick of the Clock

BY AGNES E. MEYER

I BELIEVE that the universe is purposeful as the gradual evolution of man and his natural environment indicates. This implies the existence of a Central Force conscious of itself and its creation. It also suggests that man should seek to collaborate with nature rather than to dominate it.

When we think that man's conscious efforts to transcend himself are recorded for only some 5,000 years, this period represents but a tick of the clock in comparison with the millions of years of instinctive striving toward the humanization of mankind which preceded it. If we see man's recorded history against this long primitive background, it seems obvious that we have only just begun to explore the latent capacities of human nature and that it is man's highest duty to replace his deeply imbedded archaic heritage of fear, superstition and other atavistic survivals with beliefs which conform more closely to our accumulated knowledge and the actual problems that confront us today.

Thus I believe with the German poet Lessing that man's worth lies "not in the truth he possesses or he believes he possesses, but in his sincere effort to win to the truth." Through this eternal quest are developed those powers in which man's ever-increasing perfection consists. It is the source of his cosmic dignity.

That is the reason why liberty is man's greatest need, for without it he cannot freely pursue the truth and fulfill his moral imperative to grow in mental, emotional, and spiritual stature.

I believe democracy is the highest form of government because it seeks more arduously than any other to establish a human society in which freedom can prevail and encourages all its citizens to self-enhancement and the pursuit of truth.

The harmonious progression of the universe also teaches us that an orderly society is essential to human liberty because the absence of friction leaves the mind free to develop and become creative in every field of endeavor. Order makes possible the highest human relationships which are the principal source of man's education. Disorder keeps people apart, creates mutual antagonisms and prevents the interchange of ideas so essential to human progress.

The effects of a disorderly society are vividly illustrated in our country today. The egotism of man is encouraged when society disintegrates; his vision of the good life in which all share alike and to which all can contribute is obscured.

I believe it is now my duty and the duty of every American to help reestablish an orderly society as the basis of security, free communication and the sense of brotherhood without which democracy is meaningless.

Democracy will prove indestructible as long as it keeps the music of men's lives in harmony with the music of the spheres by opening new and broader avenues to the development of individual capacities and aspirations.

It will become the world over a fighting faith which sees in the security that arises from orderly government not an aim in itself, but the means to freedom, to love and compassion, to international amity and to the untrammeled pursuit of man's destiny here on earth.

AGNES E. MEYER, journalist and social worker, is a remarkable woman in her own right, quite apart from her role as wife of Eugene Meyer, chairman of the board of the Washington *Post–Times Herald*. She has five children and eleven grandchildren.

Educated at Barnard College (of which she is now a trustee), at the Sorbonne, in Paris, and at Columbia University, she has spent her life in public and women's affairs and in welfare work. Her abilities were recognized by committee appointments by both Presidents Hoover and Roosevelt; and she was named a member of President Truman's Commission on Higher Education in 1946.

Author of several books and pamphlets, and contributor to leading American magazines, she recently published her autobiography, *Out of These Roots*, the record of a full and productive life. As one reviewer of this book says, Mrs. Meyer "is a scrupulous plugger of American rights who keeps the dust of hysteria out of her eyes."

A Shameless Old Woman

BY JAMES A. MICHENER

I BELIEVE that all men are brothers. I really believe that every man on this earth is my brother. He has a soul like mine, the ability to understand friendship, the capacity to create beauty. In all the continents of this world I have met such men. In the most savage jungles of New Guinea I have met my brother and in Tokyo I have seen him clearly walking before me.

In my brother's house I have lived without fear. Once in the wildest part of Guadalcanal I had to spend some days with men who still lived and thought in the old stone age, but we got along together fine. In the South Pacific, on remote islands, I have sailed and fished with brown men who were in every respect the same as I.

Around the world I have lived with my brothers and nothing has kept me from knowing men like myself wherever I went. Language has been no barrier, for once in India I lived for several days with villagers who didn't know a word of English. I can't remember exactly how we got along, but the fact that I couldn't speak their language was no hindrance. Differences in social custom never kept me from getting to know and like savage Melanesians in the New Hebrides. They ate roast dog and I ate Army spam and if we had wanted to emphasize differences I am sure each of us could have concluded the other was nuts. But we stressed similarities and, so long as I could snatch a Navy blanket for them now and then, we had a fine old time with no words spoken.

It was in these islands that I met a beat-up, shameless old Tonkinese woman. She would buy or sell anything and in time we became fast friends and I used to sit with her, knowing not a word of her curious language, and we talked for hours. She knew only half a dozen of the vilest English obscenities but she had the most extraordinary love of human beings and the most infectious sense of this world's crazy comedy. She was of my blood and I wish I could see her now.

I believe it was only fortunate experience that enabled me to travel among my brothers and to live with them. Therefore I do not believe it is my duty to preach to other people and insist that they also accept all men as their true and immediate brothers. These things come slow. Sometimes it takes lucky breaks to open our eyes. For example, if I had never known this wonderful old Tonkinese woman I might not now think of all Chinese as my brothers. I had to learn, as I believe the world will one day learn. Until such time as experience proves to all of us the essential brotherhood of man, I am not going to preach or scream or rant.

But if I am tolerant of other men's prejudices, I must insist that they be tolerant of me. To my home in rural Pennsylvania come brown men and yellow men and black men from around the world. In their countries I lived and ate with them. In my country they shall live and eat with me. Until the day I die my home must be free to receive these travelers and it never seems so big a home or so much a place of love as when some man from India or Japan or Mexico or Tahiti or Fiji shares it with me. For on those happy days it reminds me of the wonderful affection I have known throughout the world.

I believe that all men are my brothers. I know it when I see them sharing my home.

❦

❦ JAMES A. MICHENER is, of course, best known as the author of the Pulitzer Prize-winning novel, *Tales of the South Pacific,* on which the fabulously successful musical, *South Pacific,* was based. Before being thus catapulted into world-wide fame, he had traveled, taught school, been a businessman, and an able-bodied seaman. It was while on duty with the Navy in the Pacific Theater, that he gathered the material for, and wrote, his best-seller. Since then, he has become one of America's most illustrious writers. His most recent novel is *Sayonara.*

Mr. Michener was born in New York City and was educated at Swarthmore and the Colorado State College of Education. He also did graduate work at the University of Pennsylvania, Harvard and St. Andrews, in Scotland. His home is in Bucks County, Pennsylvania.

The Clear Channel

BY ROBBINS MILBANK

I BELIEVE it is very easy to build God in your own image. And very hard to rebuild Him when you crumble. I was born to see and experience the love of God. I saw Him in my father, whose kindness and wisdom led me through a thousand anguishes of youth. I saw Him in my wife, especially in her. I told my father about her when I was nine years old. "We are going to marry," I said. He smiled, "I'm glad you feel like telling me. I hope you'll always want to tell me things like this." For many years I was rich, seeing and loving and touching these children of God. I knew what I believed because I believed in them and they in me.

They died. First my father. Then my wife.

Why do I still arrange my desk-work in neat piles? Why do I straighten a piece of furniture? Why do I try to arrive at appointments a minute early? Why do I lie down to sleep or get up in the morning? Have you ever wandered through an empty house looking for a purpose? You do a lot of little things, automatically.

I'd like to talk about my house. It talks to me quietly in the night, of the love it still shares, of the garden that still surrounds it, of the laughter of our children and grandchildren and our pride in them. I lie on my bed, pulling words around, trying to understand their meaning. Words like "I believe."

This I know: I believe in The Lord's Prayer. All of it, but particularly where it says, "Thy will be done." For me, that's one clear channel to God. That one belief "Thy will be done" carries me through each act of each day. It teaches me to live with all that is given me, and to live without what is taken away. It rescues me from the idea that happiness for myself is either important or desirable. But it doesn't at all destroy happiness as a gift I can give miraculously from an empty vessel.

I believe I am held here in trust. That I have no right to violate that trust through negation. No right to turn inward or away from people or jobs I can do. What if I do start through habit and finish in a half-dream? The belief suffices, "Thy will be done."

I believe there is nothing passive, yielding my will to God's. It keeps me very busy, using the brain He gave me to study the fields that need plowing, using the heart He gave me to remember these fields belong to His people, using the faith He gave me to pass up self-satisfaction for doing something I want to do anyway.

If you believe what I believe, you may notice something. You may notice something quite wonderful in most everybody you meet. Even in those who annoy you or frighten you. For each, in his way, is *truth*—neither to be rejected nor run from. If you believe, "Thy will be done," there is less temptation to run away from yourself. You can't escape, anyway.

ROBBINS MILBANK is a successful free-lance writer, living in Burlingame, California. After working for six years as a logger in British Columbia, he left the Canadian woods for the modern world of advertising. In this vastly altered milieu, he spent twenty productive years, mostly in the San Francisco office of one of the country's important advertising agencies. In 1952 he resigned his position as vice-president and creative supervisor to write documentary drama for television.

Mr. Milbank, in his own words, "suffers from what our family doctor calls 'compulsion neurosis.'" Symptoms: recurrent activity in Community Chest, Red Cross, church vestry, and other public and community affairs. As a further outlet for his energies, he busies himself in the work of several advertising associations. He is a Trustee of Smith College, a Trustee, Katharine Branson School, and consultant to the Committee for Free Asia and a member of its Executive Committee.

Note of Human Passion

BY AGNES MOOREHEAD

"WHAT YOU ARE to be you are now becoming." How often these words echo in my brain as the years fly by. It was a favorite saying of the president of my college.

My life has been ruled by my belief. I am a fundamentalist and believe in the efficacy of prayer. I believe that one should work for the glory of God and not for personal glory. I believe that great joy comes when one hungers after self-improvement. Of course it is human to enjoy fame but, strangely enough, I believe that anonymity contributes to such joy.

"As a man thinketh so is he." Man's thoughts are his feelings. I believe that one should not entertain false ideas about himself. I believe in having the moral courage to say and do what one thinks is right. One can be semi-starved for truth. I believe this truth is his inner spring of vision and action. What is more honorable than having clear sight and the courage to maintain it? I believe such clarity is very rare. "Beauty is Truth" but truth is only one of the elements of one's ultimate aim. I believe that one cannot create nobility without being noble. I am in a creative profession—a creative art that is not stimulated or inspired by drudgery or vileness or meanness. An actor's life is difficult. It requires study and work of many kinds. It requires bravery, forbearance and self-sacrifice. The punishment for transgressions is great. I believe the partaking of the spirit, this inner spring of truth, the clarity of thought, the hunger for self-improvement, courage and integrity are vital to the artist in his ability to reach man's heart. As all arts have a bearing on our time and will live beyond it, so a creative artist must sound the notes of human passion which are common to all mankind. Who knows but that sound will echo and re-echo across endless time.

The theater is not merely a place of amusement. It is a living power and should be used for good and not evil. I believe it can be a great educational medium, teaching an audience many things that would otherwise be lost to them. It widens the sympathies and broadens the intellect and sweetens the heart.

I believe Life with all its pain and sorrows is a beautiful, precious gift and I believe I must strive to reproduce its beauty by holding fast to this ideal by doing my duty without regard to personal ambition.

I believe that in the course of living a life, of embarking on a goal and the certain truths that go with honest living—after these precepts have been formulated—then one must set out alone, single-handedly, uncompromisingly in these tenets. No one else can do it for you.

It is difficult to place this analysis within the framework of a single sentence. I once saw it summed up in a tableau over a proscenium arch in a theater in Chicago. It said, "You yourself must set flame to the torches which you have brought."

❧ AGNES MOOREHEAD is one of America's best and most versatile actresses of stage, screen and radio. She is also one of the best grounded in the theory as well as the practice of her art, in which her experience is uniquely broad. Born in Clinton, Massachusetts, she attended Muskingum College, the University of Wisconsin, and the American Academy of Dramatic Art. Thereafter she taught public speaking and later, dramatics at the Dalton School, in New York. Her many successful appearances on Broadway brought her to the notice of Hollywood, and she has three times been nominated for Academy Awards—for *The Magnificent Ambersons*, *Johnny Belinda*, and *Mrs. Parkington*.

Millions of listeners thrilled—and chilled—to Miss Moorehead's brilliant radio *tour de force* of murder, *Sorry, Wrong Number!* She has been acclaimed most recently for her magnificent reading of Shaw's *Don Juan in Hell* and her one-woman show, *That Fabulous Redhead*. Above all, she is a warm, sympathetic human being.

At the Frontier

BY EDWARD P. MORGAN

WHEN I WAS a small boy, I believed in God the same way I believed in Santa Claus: my mother told me it was so. The process of growing up—of sorting out mature convictions from the world of make-believe—this has been a painful thing for me.

I still have my guard up against what might be termed professional religion. It is so easy for us to press ourselves into a pattern—to learn to say pious things self-righteously without really believing in them or acting upon them. How can I profess a belief in what we call a Supreme Being without showing an honest faith in the human being—the ordinary mortal?

Of all times, I think, now is the time when men must believe in men, or they can believe in nothing. If I cannot believe in the man next door and recognize and respect the human dignity which is his birthright as intimately as his skin, what valid connection can I claim with a Presence in whose image I am supposed to be cast? But if I believe in humanity, then I come to know, inevitably, that there is something bigger than myself.

If I couldn't figure this out in the spinning urban world where life is swift and often ruthless, I like to think that a kind of instinctive humility would come to me as I, a man, walked along, say, in a deep green forest. Past the temples of trees, through the canyons of rocks and beside the avenues of shining rivers. Perhaps that is the time when a man's mind can best reach out and grasp the stars.

I have a feeling that the world is bigger than we imagine—that we are on the brink of great discoveries—not only in science but in people.

We are only at the frontier of humanity. We are just beginning to poke into the fascinating recesses of the consciousness and attempt, somehow, to measure that non-dimensional organ called the human soul. In other words, we are on the verge of discovering ourselves. This excites me. This will prove that the world is not only big—it is also small, a cozy place where people can extend their minds, as easily as they extend a hand, and touch each other with understanding.

I believe people must have nourishment for their minds and spirits, just as we need pork chops and potatoes and vitamin C for our bodies. Malnutrition of the mind means a warped character as surely as rickets mean puny bones. There is a certain rich sustenance of beauty which has helped me overcome this disease. For me, beauty is one of the most important things in life. Or perhaps I mean an awareness of beauty. It is everything from the warm, sensuous beauty of woman, who is life itself, to the liquid rhythm of music, the fragile, fleeting loveliness of daybreak, the terrible majesty of a storm. A picture, a poem, the open look of a child.

In our frenetic existence today, these things seem like a blur glimpsed through the window of a speeding train. Our very velocity adds to our uneasiness—uneasiness about ourselves. About how long we are going to live. About death. But the good things are there, I think, if we pause to find them. And I believe that as for himself, a man lives in the faces and the hearts of his children, and in the friendships and the memories of his friends. I believe that all the permanence I need is floating there, on the stream of life.

❧❦❧

EDWARD P. MORGAN, news commentator for the Columbia Broadcasting System, has been a reporter for over twenty years. He started with the Seattle *Star* in his native state of Washington, later joining the United Press as night bureau manager of the Honolulu office. While UP manager in Mexico he covered the story of Leon Trotsky's assassination. During World War II he left UP to join the foreign service of the Chicago *Daily News*. In this capacity and later, as free lance writer, he covered the liberation of Rome, the Nuremberg trials and the founding of Israel. He first came to CBS in 1946, took several years out as correspondent for *Collier's*, and now devotes his journalistic skills to radio and television. He was the first editor-producer of "This I Believe."

Thoughtful, intense, but rarely solemn, Mr. Morgan is a painter by avocation and a New Yorker by adoption.

Having Shed Illusions

BY PAUL SCOTT MOWRER

I AM BY NATURE devout. I worship life. Whatever adds to the dignity and fullness of life is good.

I do not know whence, why or whither. But in this great universe of sand and stars, of life and death, there must be some kind of plan; therefore, a planner; therefore—well, people who recognize this call it, each in his own way, God. A God, however, who can be known only intuitively, in those mystical soul-moments when we suddenly feel ourselves at one with creation.

I have suffered great blows, like everyone, and known great happiness. I believe that, within limits that change according to circumstances, my will is free. To this extent, I mould my own fate. Yet even in the worst that happens to me, there seems to be some good, and in the best, some bad.

I began to lose my illusions at seventeen, when I got my first newspaper job. People were not at all as I had been taught to believe. The shock was tremendous. Since then, in two big wars and several smaller but not less gruesome ones, I have seen man at his best and worst. I like people, all sorts. But I expect little of them. And expecting little, I am often very agreeably surprised.

I have read, gradually, the literature of the ages, and lived in many lands. There is a great deal of wisdom, solace and pleasure available in men, books, nature and art.

Our material progress has been marvelous. It has not made men happier. Skills, knowledge and culture can be accumulated through the generations. Virtue cannot. Morally, every man starts fresh, and happiness comes from within.

To what is the obvious moral deterioration of the last fifty years due? The wars? Perhaps. But perhaps also to the arrogant attempts man has been making to put himself creatively in God's place.

I recognize my enormous debt to society. I will obey the laws, defend my country, my friends, stand up for what I think right, and say my say. But I have no wish to force my views or tastes on others.

Having shed, I believe, most illusions, I live now by faith and hope: the faith that life is its own justification; the hope that I shall continue to find it so.

I have feared death, terribly, in war. But the fear was physical, not mental, and so controllable.

Is this life all? I try to live fully, as if it were. But I am open-minded. I know that, one day, as a good newspaperman, I shall have to accept the assignment, and go find out for myself.

❧❧❧

PAUL SCOTT MOWRER, newspaper-man and poet, has been writing verse since the age of about fifteen. In the midst of a busy and distinguished career of travel and public affairs, as foreign correspondent (Pulitzer Prize, Sigma Delta Chi National Scholarship Award), a war correspondent (Officer, French Legion of Honor), and as editor of the Chicago *Daily News* (Honorary LL.D., University of Michigan); and finally as European Editor of the New York *Post*, he has never lost his lyric feeling for the varying aspects of man and nature. His first volume of verse, *Hours of France*, was published in 1918; his second, *The Good Comrade*, in 1921; his third, *Poems Between Wars*, in 1941. His latest is *On Going to Live in New Hampshire*.

Today, Mr. Mowrer lives in Chocorua, New Hampshire, where he spends his time in writing and, as he says in one of his poems, trying "each trouty brook."

Lesson from History

BY JOHN U. NEF

I BELIEVE in reason and imagination at their best and purest; I believe in the supreme moments of happiness and sorrow, of joy and suffering, of affection and gratitude sometimes vouchsafed us, because I believe that these are human attributes and experiences which transcend the earth and unite us to God. Love and marriage, dedicated however imperfectly to Truth, have brought me to this belief.

In terms of the lives we lead here, what is the value of this hope, which I share with so many across many centuries of time, in redemption through Christ, in the salvation of the individual soul and body?

The Christian faith is the guarantee that our honest, disinterested strivings towards perfection are more than personal urges based on illusions which will disappear once we die. Belief in the perfect wisdom and goodness of the Source beyond matter, space, and time, reinforces our best instincts and enables us to attach ourselves with more profound fidelity and joy to those we rightly love on earth. As a historian, I am convinced that the remarkable, in many ways the unique, achievements of Christian peoples have basic roots in the ways the search for beauty, for moral perfection and for scientific knowledge have been guided by this belief.

Efforts to make over the material world by art, in accordance with a transcendental design more perfect than that of nature, have been responsible for the great variety, the depth and the pervasiveness among the Christian peoples of works of art, from the Romanesque churches to the compositions of Bach, Mozart and Beethoven, and from the paintings of Giotto to those of Rembrandt and Cézanne. The belief that creative intuition leading to this transcendental design is a gift of God, in Whose image man is made, accounts for the incomparable richness of Western art. The beauty in the surroundings which resulted, and which penetrated human hearts, provided a common language for understanding among the peoples of Europe and America.

The limits on war between nations and on violence and cruelty within them, which prepared the ground for the unparalleled quantitative progress since the Napoleonic Wars, were made possible also by increasing tenderness in manners from the seventeenth down to the late nineteenth century. The gentle civilization into which we were born was part of a great effort, lasting for generations, among men and women in all branches of the Christian faith to live a Christian life.

Industrial civilization itself, with its machinery and power, is based in part on a scientific revolution which owes much to this belief. The great scientific innovators, such as Galileo, Kepler and Harvey, were strengthened in their search by confidence in the capacity of the human mind to reason, dimly and imperfectly, as God reasons, to examine the physical and the biological universe, as it were, with His eyes.

Believing all these things, and in the knowledge that the forces of evil and destruction have often threatened to overwhelm men and societies, and certainly threaten them as much now as in times past, I believe the faith that I hold is no less vital for the future of civilization than for our salvation.

❧⟨⟩❧

❧ JOHN U. NEF is considered one of the foremost authorities in the world on economic history, a reputation based first on his study of the rise of the British coal industry published in 1932. He is professor at the University of Chicago, and is chairman of its Committee of Social Thought. Professor Nef has been visiting professor at the Institute of Political Studies of the Sorbonne and temporary professor at the Collège de France, and was a vice-chairman of the American Council of Learned Societies.

Professor Nef's father was a native-born Swiss and professor at the University of Chicago. He himself studied at Harvard, took his Ph.D. at the Robert Brookings Graduate School, in Washington, D.C., and continued his studies in Europe, especially in Montpellier, London and Paris. His books include, *War and Human Progress, The United States and Civilization, Industry and Government in France and England* and a work in French on the birth of industrial civilization.

Not from a Cloud Alone

BY ALFRED NOYES

As A YOUNG student reading Darwin on evolution, I found his most vital sentence, "This grand sequence of events," he wrote, "cannot be due to blind chance. The understanding revolts from that conclusion." The fact that we cannot get plus from minus is my first postulate. But evolution is often made to mean what no real thinker can accept. In the beginning we have a nebula, a cloud or gas within whose chemical changes there has emerged the human race, Beethoven, Shakespeare, the towering cities, the great cathedrals, and all that these imply. But it took far more than a gas to do it. The materialist is like a man who should explain the Ninth Symphony by faithfully tracing the pedigree of the catgut in the violins, but omitting to mention the unseen composer, whose mind speaks to us through those instruments.

I have found real help in Galileo's answer to those who thought that his astronomical universe made an end of the idea of God's care for the least of his creatures. "The sun," he said, "with all those planets moving round it, can ripen the smallest bunch of grapes as if it had nothing else to do. Why then should I doubt His power?" I believe there is a mass of evidence drawn from the inner life of man to support the first postulate of reason and a rightly ordered society. Namely, people believe in the existence of an eternal and Supreme Being, our Origin and End. The nature of that Supreme Being is most clearly revealed in the realm of spiritual values. A child is more valuable than a whole skyful of lifeless matter, and despite Copernicus, is more central because nearer to God.

It is thus in accord with the highest reason to look for our fullest revelation of God in the conscious human soul with its possibilities of love, sacrifice and grasp of things beyond the reach of the senses. The belief of my religion is that the light has thus shone in our darkness, that man in the course of evolution two thousand years ago had reached a point when he was able to meet with a reality of a world higher than that of the beasts that perish, that the nature of God was profoundly revealed in the most divine of all personalities, meeting us not through the vague mists of endless time and boundless space, but in history. When death had passed through my doors, it was He who spoke as none other could speak from the eternal center saying, "I am the Resurrection and the Life."

❧❦❧

ALFRED NOYES, C.B.E., the poet, has achieved world-wide fame. At Exeter College, Oxford, he demonstrated a keen interest in literature, and rowing, he comments, became "the most important thing in life." Immediately successful as a poet in the great succession of traditional English verse, his first volume was *The Loom of Years.*

This was later followed by the equally popular, *Drake*. His next memorable success, *The Highwayman*, has found its way into important anthologies. International peace, based on Anglo-American cooperation, has been one of his consistent themes since before the First World War. He delivered the Lowell Lectures in America in 1913, and was visiting professor of English literature at Princeton University, 1914–26.

Mr. Noyes is the holder of many honorary degrees. Other of his published works include *The Torch-Bearers*, *Portrait of Horace*, *Collected Poems*, and, most recently, his autobiography, *Two Worlds for Memory.*

Once a Contented Agnostic

BY FULTON OURSLER

I BELIEVE in the power of faith, and in the power of love. As I see it, all the achievements of man flow from these two great rivers of strength.

I am often asked how faith took command of my life. It is a simple story. For years I had lived as a contented agnostic. Then, on a tour of Palestine, I was suddenly overwhelmed by two thoughts. First I saw that we could never make the world safe for democracy unless and until we had a citizenship of high integrity and character, worthy of the freedoms of democracy. Second, that Jesus Christ was at once the teacher and the Exemplar of the life of integrity. I decided then to write a life of Christ in popular language to reach the masses. I studied hundreds, perhaps a thousand books. All my studies brought me nearer to the Master. Soon my heart was on fire with faith and now the flame is brighter every day.

The various dictionary definitions of faith confuse me. But I have always known, instinctively perhaps, what faith means to me: not a credo but a blessed assurance; neither belief, nor hope, but knowledge. When I was a child, I knew that Father and Mother were good and kind. I did not have to believe that they were; my faith in them was complete, because of my experience with them every day.

So it is with my faith in God. The assurance is complete and, for me, there is no doubt, because of daily experience.

The logician will demand to have the matter proved—with evidence of the laboratory and slide rule. But I am content with Saint Paul's definition of faith: the substance of things hoped for, the evidence of things not seen.

Still, how can I know what I have not seen? There was a man in the Bible who wanted to believe, who almost believed, but was beset by reservations. He made an honest prayer: "Oh Lord, I believe; help Thou mine unbelief."

Theologians tell me faith is a gift. I think it is a gift that can be asked for, as this earnest old Biblical character asked for it. It can be worked for.

As for love, it is for me the open door to faith, the only approach to truth. The practice of love brings me the awakening knowledge and conviction of faith.

How do I practice love? It is so easy for one to give a coin or write a check against people's misery. But love is not giving money. It is giving myself. I must minister with my own hands, reach out and give some personal help to someone, not just occasionally but every day. And I must go out of my way to do it, not in the mood of a Lord Bountiful, but with tenderness. Such love begins with the person who is nearest to me at this moment; it knows no end, anywhere. All living responds to tenderness.

The potency of love and faith has transformed my life. In them lies my only true security. Embracing them I confront the universe unafraid. I know, then, it is a good universe, and friendly. I know this even when disaster overtakes me and sorrow overwhelms me and I feel I have deserved neither sorrow nor disaster. Nevertheless, because my faith in God is a sure knowledge, I trust in Him even in anguish, even without understanding.

So I am strengthened even by misfortune; my sympathy deepens, all of my forces quicken, and I become—or try to become—an even more ardent servant in the good cause, the value and meaning of my life raised to a new level of effectiveness.

◆§ FULTON OURSLER, who died in May 1952, began his career as a journalist and editor and ended as a highly successful author. With a vast output of writing to his credit, he will no doubt be remembered chiefly for those three best-sellers: *The Greatest Story Ever Told*, *The Greatest Book Ever Written* and *The Greatest Faith Ever Known*, which was finished, at his deathbed request, by his daughter, April Oursler Armstrong.

Born in Baltimore, and the holder of two honorary Litt.D. degrees, Mr. Oursler was editor of *Liberty* magazine from 1931 to 1942, and later a senior editor of *Reader's Digest*. He was a trustee of the Andrew Carnegie Fund for Needy Authors, and a member of the Dramatists Guild and the Authors League of America. Another facet of his writing was the publishing of several murder mysteries under the pseudonym of Anthony Abbot.

His wife, Grace Perkins Oursler, is also a successful writer.

Courage To Be Superior

BY GROVE PATTERSON

THROUGH THE YEARS I have been asked many, many times: "What do you believe: What is your religion?" My answer is a simple one. My religion is not complicated by theology, dogma, creeds. I believe in nothing which is not intellectually satisfying. I do not try to force myself to have faith in anything. I could not possibly be an atheist. To believe in the mechanistic theory of the universe, that humankind is here as the result of a fortuitous conjunction of chemicals on the face of the waters countless ages ago, is an affront to my credulity.

I believe the universe was designed and brought into being by a Creative Mind and Power. This Supreme Power operates the universe by means of unvarying natural law. For me, the supreme fact is that I can by thinking, meditation, prayer, come into communion with the Supreme Power. I call this Power God.

I believe the purpose of God in devising a universe was wholly good, and that man, the highest form of life so far developed, is meant to live in harmony with the Great Power and improve, both in this world and in future manifestations of life. I believe in immortality, because I think it unreasonable to suppose that man can come as far as he does on this earth and be snuffed out with no opportunity to reach greater heights.

Prayer is a self-conditioner. Prayer gives man the courage which enables him to adjust himself to all the circumstances of life. Prayer will not enable man to avoid the results of his own mis-doings nor does it provide an escape from the evil prevalent in the world.

"If God is so good," my friend asks me, "why does He permit evil in the world which He created?" It is a stupid question. Man, from the day he developed into man, was given freedom of choice. Otherwise he would have been a mere puppet of God. With that freedom of choice, he has gone on through the ages, making bad choices. He is responsible for evil in a universe which God created. He has violated natural law. He has made a mess of things but the more he senses his privilege of contact with the Supreme Power, the better he will do, the less evil he will produce.

Because I believe the universe is governed by natural law, I think it useless to pray that natural law be set aside for anyone's personal reason. Devout men sometimes pray for rain, but rain will come only when proper atmospheric conditions bring it about. Men seek by prayer to have their loved ones spared from the consequences of the violation of natural law. Such prayer is not the prayer for courage and for strength, in which I believe. The most pious person is as likely to be burned to death with his family in a tragic fire or destroyed at the railroad crossing as is the most worthless tramp.

Peace of mind for which we long in these jittery days does not come through escape. It will not come through withdrawal from a world of contacts. Rather, it is the product of courage and of an inner poise. It is part of my religion to believe that when one reaches the place in his daily thinking where he knows, come what may, he can take it, his worries and fears will drop away. The most profound courage that one needs, as Newton D. Baker said, is "the courage to be a superior person." It is the courage that comes from prayer.

I know that in trouble I can turn to the Great Power. It is there and it works. I have tried it. That is my religion, and in it I have complete faith. This I believe.

Treasury of Hidden Virtues

BY CHARLES H. PERCY

A GREAT AMERICAN industrial statesman, Clarence Francis, once said, "You can buy a man's time, you can buy a man's physical presence at a given place; you can even buy a measured number of skilled muscular motions per hour or day. But you cannot buy enthusiasm; you cannot buy initiative; you cannot buy loyalty; you cannot buy the devotion of hearts, minds and souls. You have to earn these things. . . ."

This, I believe, illustrates a great truth. We can earn human affection and respect only thru understanding. It is our relationship with people—not people in a mass, but as individuals—which makes our own world rich or poor.

I cannot truly understand everyone. But I can learn an amazing number of things about people if, when I look at them, I really see them; if when I listen to them, I really hear them; and if when I talk to them, I speak from my heart.

The most commonplace person becomes extraordinary when we understand him. The gruffest manner may conceal the kindest heart; the most practical man may be the most idealistic; the quietest, the possessor of the most sparkling intellect. The most unlikely exterior may hide the greatest ability. The qualities of charm, warmth, wit, integrity and unselfishness abound in people around us.

During the Battle of Britain we were amazed at the courage and stamina of the British people, who withstood month after month of heavy bombing without a lessening of their morale. People who had never faced danger or discomfort, endured it heroically. Yet their courage was nothing new. They had always had it, but they had never needed to use it before.

I believe that the faith we place in people is seldom disappointed. To expect the best of a man is almost assurance that you will receive it. When I give a man a job to do, I leave that job to him. It is his responsibility—his is the credit or the blame for what he makes of it. Generally, no two people do a thing in the same way. Every man brings to a problem a fresh point of view and a new approach. The value of individual effort and thinking can never be overestimated.

In our company our production workers often have solved problems on the job that management has wrestled with unsuccessfully. Once a man knows that his opinions are respected, that his ideas are valued, his energy and mind are turned to constructive interest in his work. I do not believe in men doing the work that machines can do. Nor do I believe in hiring only the work of a man's hands when he is eager to give his heart and his mind to his job.

I have never known—really known—a man or woman I couldn't like and respect. I hope I never do. Once we recognize the fact that every individual is a treasury of hidden and unsuspected qualities, our lives become richer, our judgment better, and our world is more right.

This I believe—it is not love that is blind; it is only the unnoticing eye that cannot see the real qualities of man.

❧ CHARLES H. PERCY worked his way through both high school and the University of Chicago where he had an exceptionally distinguished undergraduate record. In addition to other achievements, he held the post of university marshal to the chancellor.

While still at the University, he entered the cooperative training program of the Bell & Howell Company, manufacturers of motion picture equipment. Upon his graduation, he joined the company. In 1942, when he was only twenty-three, he was elected to its Board of Directors.

The Second World War interrupted his business career and he served with the Navy, attaining the grade of lieutenant. Returning to Bell & Howell, he was made secretary and then president. In 1949, he was named one of the ten outstanding young men in the country by the Junior Chamber of Commerce. Mr. Percy lives with his family in Kenilworth, Illinois.

No Idle Game

BY RALPH BARTON PERRY

LET ME SAY, first of all, that I believe in believing. Ideas can have no effect on action unless they are believed. Otherwise thinking is an idle game. As far back as I can remember it has been my idea of my own life that I wanted to leave the world a little better for my having lived in it. This has not meant that I believed I could count for a great deal, but only that I could count for *something* on the right side. I believe, furthermore, that we usually know which *is* the right side. This belief and this attitude were in my early years associated with the expectation of entering the Christian ministry. They have been confirmed by my later philosophical studies and reflection, and they have formed the core of my vocation as a teacher.

I have always believed that history is made not by "historical forces," so-called, or by mechanical necessity, or even by a superior being working outside of men, but by human individuals, acting sometimes alone at some critical point, but more often in concert, combining their efforts and their skills under individual leadership. This is the fundamental belief which underlies my political beliefs. In the kind of human society which I like to think of as democracy, individuals form their own opinions on matters of public policy. Because I believe in the creation of public opinion by the inter-stimulation and cross-fertilization of individual minds, resulting in a voluntary agreement, I deplore not only the authoritarianism which imposes opinions from above, but the imitativeness and hysteria by which the individual minds merely echo one another or succumb to the pressure of the mass. If we do not find ways of counteracting this tendency man's last and best hope of life on earth must be abandoned.

I believe that the ideal society is that in which decisions are made by individuals in order that individual men, women, and children may develop what is in them, and achieve happiness. The fundamental right, the right of all rights, is the right of individuals to so much of the good life as their capacities permit. It follows that if I am to be entitled to my happiness I must not only earn it for myself but dispense it. I believe, therefore, that the last word is love—self-love, yes, in the sense of personal effort and self-reliance, but self-love limited by the love of others, and infused with sympathy and good will.

All of these ideas enter into my beliefs concerning the universe at large. Human experience has proved that within limits the physical world can be controlled by mind. The remarkable advances of science have not destroyed, or even restricted, the area of faith. Indeed as the circumference of human knowledge has been enlarged so has the area of unknown possibilities.

And here, I believe, man has every right to believe what he cannot prove, provided it is not disproved, and provided such belief fortifies his moral will. Here he may allow his hope and his charity to dictate his faith—faith in that ultimate cosmic triumph of good which is what he calls "God": a power *in* ourselves that makes for righteousness and perfection.

❧❦❧

⧉§ RALPH BARTON PERRY, long honored as one of the deans of philosophy in America, taught the subject at Harvard for forty-five years, becoming emeritus in 1946. Crowded as his Harvard years were, his life during retirement seems to be a match for them, for he has since given the Gifford Lectures at Glasgow University, and has taught at U.C.L.A., Michigan, Stanford, M.I.T., and elsewhere.

Professor Perry has more than a score of books to his credit. They are divided between philosophy and current affairs. Among the volumes in the first group is *Thought and Character of William James*, a biography which won a Pulitzer Prize, and, most recently, *Realms of Value*, which appeared early in 1954. In the second group his latest book is *The Citizen Decides*. Professor Perry is a Chevalier of the Legion of Honor, and a member of both the National Institute of Arts and Letters and the American Philosophical Society.

I Quit Carrying a Gun

BY ROBERT B. POWERS

FOR MANY YEARS I searched for someone who could answer my questions. I looked everywhere—in faces and books. Lawrence of Arabia had some of the answers, so I read and re-read his *Seven Pillars of Wisdom* as well as his letters.

Everything about Lawrence made him more than a hero to me. He was almost a prophet. There was only one flaw. His latter years distressed me. Why should one of his brilliance, courage, and integrity have had to end his life in obscurity—yes, and anguish—as an enlisted man in the British Air Force?

One day I found myself talking about Lawrence. You know how it is, when you get started and can't stop? But finally, I ended with "Why, why did this have to happen to him?"

There was a long pause. Then a woman said, almost as if she were talking to herself, "His life among the Arabs—he must have known the *Koran*. There is a passage which Muslims believe are the words of God: 'And we desire to show favor to those who were brought low in the land, and to make them spiritual leaders among men, and to make them our heirs.' "

My question was answered. I was no longer troubled. That was seven years ago, and since then I have looked for answers, directions, in the Holy Books of all religions.

In Judaism I found a reverence I'd never known before for Law. And there, too, I became aware of the dramatic effect on my life of the words: "The Lord our God, the Lord is One."

Reading the Gospels with a new eye, I found the criterion—the reference point—for individual behavior and integrity. Whereas I had lived a violent life, I quit carrying a gun, accepting the relaxing concept of non-resistance. In the *Koran* I found the answers to group-living and the meaning of "Submission to the Will of God" in an active as well as a passive sense.

118

From the Zoroasterian writings—"Arise, 'tis dawn! Who riseth first comest first to paradise"—I found new zest for work and living. From Hinduism, I learned to "renounce the fruits of labor."

And from Baha'i—"The earth is but one country and mankind its citizens"—I became aware that my prejudices had always imprisoned, never protected me.

Thus, I came to believe: That man is an impotent, confused creature, except when he develops awareness of the Supreme Being, which awareness expands into love; that power, guidance and security come only through this love of man for God and God for man.

The universe is organized and orderly; yet every least atom is in motion. The very nature of life is movement. Consequently, there must be an organizer and a governor. When I lose my job, when my child is desperately ill, or when a friend turns against me, these incidents are not fortuitous. No, these happenings are, however painful, a significant pattern of life for me as an individual.

Once, as a child, I became tortured with the thought that my father might abandon me in a strange city. I told him. He said, "That's impossible because of love. I couldn't leave you, Rob, if I wanted to. Love is stronger than the trace chains on a twenty-mule team wagon."

Man today is like that child of fifty years ago. He is terrified that God may abandon him. But if mere man's love is as strong as steel trace chains, then God's love is unbreakable. So man—and mankind—are safe! This I believe.

◄§ ROBERT B. POWERS is a veteran police officer and criminologist who has had an eventful and a colorful career. After serving with the New Jersey State Police, and as deputy sheriff in New Mexico and Arizona, he was police chief of Bakersfield, California, for twelve years. During the war, he was chief law enforcement officer, California State War Council. Later he served as consultant to the American Council on Race Relations, and, prior to that, as coordinator of law enforcement agencies, Department of Justice, State of California.

Mr. Powers is co-author of *A Guide to Race Relations for Police Officers*, and he wrote *Crime Was My Business*, which appeared serially in the *Saturday Evening Post* in 1948. Born in Las Vegas, New Mexico, he was a cavalryman in World War I. He is today a free lance writer and lecturer, living in Yuma, Arizona.

Unless Free, I Am Nothing

BY CLARENCE B. RANDALL

BELIEF IS LIFE itself. Without belief, life has no meaning. Unless a man knows what he believes he cannot determine what he wishes to do with his life, and therefore cannot know whether he has lived his life well.

He must have goals and strive to achieve them or he is a mere creature of flesh whose existence is of no importance. There can be no purpose in effort, no way to keep score, unless a man has a scale of values to which he holds fast.

When an airplane flies above the clouds, passengers cannot determine its speed or direction, since there is nothing with which to make comparison. So it is with life.

Until a man knows what he believes, he cannot establish objectives, and therefore cannot measure progress.

It is this fixing of goals that creates our desire to achieve, and that releases the full potential of our talents.

But since our satisfactions in life depend upon these decisions, we must choose standards that are true.

For myself, I would not dare attempt this alone. I must have help. I, therefore, turn to God in order that I may be governed by principles that are proven and eternal.

And as I look to God, I sense that all around me there are other men who are likewise troubled by their own inadequacy, and who, like myself, are seeking with humility to learn what is true and what is good, and to understand the world in which they were born.

That the world has meaning seems much more reasonable to me than the hideous concept that everything which surrounds me came about by cosmic accident. This thought again takes me to God, to the conviction that outside of myself there is a source of strength infinitely greater than any within me. I want my life to be in parallel with that eternal power for good.

Not for a moment, however, do I doubt that I am free to accept or reject God, or to make individual choices as to what is good and what is bad in life. In fact, it is only because I know that I am free to accept God voluntarily that I believe in Him. Unless I am free, I am nothing.

This concept of personal freedom permeates every aspect of my belief. In education, it forces me to recognize the right of honest men to teach that which they sense to be the truth even though I disagree. In our social organization, it causes me to strive to maintain the American concept of political democracy. In our industrial economy, it finds expression in my conviction that the system of free enterprise, based upon private initiative, and policed by the forces of free markets, brings greater happiness to more people than any other system yet devised.

But freedom is privilege, and privilege begets obligation. We must give back to society as much as we receive. The welfare of others must always dominate self-interest.

And freedom must be shared. We must respect the beliefs of those who hold opposing views, and must listen as well as preach.

Lastly, freedom must be preserved. In our day we have seen whole nations lose it. Other Americans have died for it; we must now live for it.

CLARENCE B. RANDALL is Chairman of the Board, Inland Steel Company. A lawyer turned industrialist, he is deeply concerned with civic and philanthropic works. He counts as one of the most articulate of the nation's industrialists, and he has authored many magazine articles. Two of his books, *A Creed for Free Enterprise* (1952) and *Freedom's Faith* (1954), rank him high among the thinkers in the business world. He was chosen by President Eisenhower as Chairman of the Commission on Foreign Economic Policy which recommended the liberalization of American trade practices.

Mr. Randall was graduated both in arts and in law from Harvard, just in time to serve overseas as an infantry officer in World War I. Afterwards, he practiced law until he joined Inland Steel in 1925. He holds half a dozen honorary degrees, and as many trusteeships. His home is in Winnetka, Illinois.

Freedom and a Piece of String

BY CONYERS READ

As I GROW old, I decide not to bother about things I can do nothing about. When I was young I spent much time in search of the key which would unlock all doors. I never found it and have given up looking for it. I do not regret the search. It brought me into close acquaintance with a large company of good and great men and women. But, so far as I am concerned, I find it more fruitful to direct my attention to those elements in this mysterious world around us which are, or may be, subject to human control, those elements in which the creative force is the mind of man. There, if anywhere on this earth, lies the hope of the future. For that reason, I believe, first of all, that it is our business to provide an environment in which the mind of man can enjoy the maximum amount of freedom to think, to exchange thoughts with his fellows, to produce the best that is in him. I admit no distinction between the white mind and the black mind, or the yellow mind or the brown mind, or the mind male or the mind female. Wherever there is a mind there is the potential of great and good things.

Freedom of the mind I put first of all. But I recognize that men live together in society and that social obligations transcend individual interests. No one man's freedom can be allowed at the expense of another man's freedom. What we have to aim at is the maximum of individual freedom consistent with the larger social interest.

I believe that the finest exercise of freedom is in the service of one's fellow men.

I believe that we spend too much of our leisure watching other people work and play, at the ball parks, in the theater, on the screen. In my opinion, the major satisfactions of life proceed from the exercise of our own creative impulses. For this reason I regret the increasing regimentation and mechanization of life as a menace to human growth. It seems to me, as I look back upon my own boyhood, that I got more fun out of a piece of string than my grandchildren get out of their more elaborate and much more expensive gadgets. You can really do things with a piece of string.

I believe in devotion to causes outside ourselves which we recognize as more important than ourselves and in the service of which we are cheerfully ready to sacrifice our individual welfare. This, in its highest form becomes religion, though many men find their God in strange places and in strange company.

I believe that our immortality will be measured in terms of what, through our own works or our own influence, we pass on to those who follow us.

I believe that there are standards of right and wrong, though I think these standards are too often confused with what is socially proper or socially expedient. I believe that these standards can be and should be defined. I regard it as one of the important functions of educators, from the pulpit, in the classroom and on the air, to present, explain and support these standards.

I believe that a life lived in accordance with these standards will be a happy and a fruitful life.

"It is not life that matters, but the courage we bring to it."

✤⧉✤

◅§ Conyers Read, recently retired as Professor of English History at the University of Pennsylvania, is one of America's fine scholars and historians. Dr. Read took his A.B., A.M. and Ph.D. degrees at Harvard, a B.Litt. at Oxford, and was awarded honorary degrees from Ursinus and Pennsylvania. Known as an inspiring teacher, probably his greatest distinction was his election to the presidency of the American Historical Association in 1949. He is also a member of the Royal Historical Society, London, was a Guggenheim Fellow in 1951–52, and is the author of many books, among them a 3-volume work, *Mr. Walsingham and the Policy of Queen Elizabeth* and *The Tudors.* He is currently writing a biography of Elizabeth's secretary, William Cecil.

Dr. Read's family has been in Philadelphia since the early 18th century, the first of his line being John Read, stationer, whose daughter, Deborah, married Benjamin Franklin.

All-Out and a Little Extra

BY PHILIP D. REED

I SUPPOSE every one of us has at some time said to himself: why and for what purpose am I here on this earth? Is this life an end in itself or simply a preparation for another life hereafter? Ought we to behave in a particular way here in order to enjoy some sort of Paradise later; or should we seek to make this life our Paradise?

It is probably fair to say that no one can answer these questions dogmatically, and I would be the last to attempt it. But each of us will answer them for himself based on his background, his religious upbringing, his environment and his intellectual makeup.

Take myself, for example. Much as I hope—and on clear, starry nights on a hilltop, much as I believe—that another and perhaps finer experience lies beyond this life, yet I am persuaded that our presence on earth, here and now, is a mission in itself and that we should make the very most of it. I also believe that the true measure of our success or failure in this life is the fullness, the fineness, the completeness with which we succeed in living it.

Fortunately each of us in this world is different from every other one. Each has certain aptitudes and skills, certain capacities, certain likes and dislikes which, taken together, make us individuals or personalities. We may, and frequently do, have different values, different standards, different ideas of what is important, or useful, or fun. But we are all people with bodies and souls.

I may be wrong, but it has been my observation that the people who seem both to give and to get the most out of life are those who, in addition to all their other qualities, have two things in common.

First, they do whatever they are doing—all out. Whether it be work or play, dull or exciting, little or big, they give the matter their undivided attention and try to do their level best. Without being stuffy about it they have made a sort of creed or habit of being satisfied only with their utmost effort.

The second thing these people have in common is the rather special satisfaction, the deep-down joy they get out of a very simple thing—being helpful to other people. Just to be able in the course of their everyday lives to do something a little extra for a friend, a client, a patient, a customer or perhaps a complete stranger, they have found to be a most rewarding experience.

The kind of people I speak of are all about us, in every walk of life and of every faith and nationality. They are the truly happy people who are making this life gloriously worth living.

And so, I deeply believe that if I concentrate just a bit more on those two qualities—trying to do everything I do a little better than I know how, and making a point of giving a hand to others—I too can get all the joy and satisfaction out of my life that those wise and fortunate people are getting out of theirs.

❦

PHILIP D. REED is regarded as one of America's most able, farsighted and statesmanlike businessmen. Born in Milwaukee, he was graduated in electrical engineering from the University of Wisconsin, going on to Fordham, where he took a law degree. Thus trained as both engineer and lawyer, he rose from a minor legal job with General Electric to become that firm's youngest Chairman of the Board, a post he holds today. During the war, Mr. Reed headed the United States Economic Mission to London, with the rank of Minister; was president of the International Chamber of Commerce, and a spearhead of the Committee for Economic Development. A Commander of the Legion of Honor, and the holder of the President's Certificate of Merit Award, he has combined the career of business and distinguished public service to an unusual degree. Mr. Reed has a son and a daughter, and lives in Rye, New York.

Why Pain?

BY DR. HOWARD A. RUSK

I CAN'T REMEMBER when I didn't want to be a doctor. Even as an adolescent, when I scrubbed floors and ran errands at the local hospital in order to smell ether and go on rounds with the country doctor, surgery did not spell the glamour in medicine to me. It was people—sick people—their suffering, their problems, and their victories that challenged.

It has been a rare privilege to be a doctor in medicine's golden era. Far more scientific advances have been made in the last three decades than in all time heretofore. Man's life span has increased from 18 two thousand years ago to 68 in America today.

But I have found it impossible to ignore the fact that these great medical advances have posed new problems. Crippled children, who in the past would have died early in life, now survive. They want to grow and work and love and be loved.

I have heard old people to whom we have added these years ask, "For what—the shelf to wait for death, or an opportunity to live and work in dignity as long as we are able?"

Millions of veterans throughout the world, who have scarred their minds and given parts of their bodies to war, have more than earned their right to live and love and work and to know that their sacrifice has at least been one small stone that is being used to build a better world.

Sick people throughout the world ask their God, "Why must I suffer?" Possibly the answer comes in the work of the potter. Great ceramics are not made by putting clay in the sun; they come only from the white heat of the kiln. In the firing process, some pieces are broken, but those that survive the heat are transformed from clay into objects of art, and so it is, it seems to me, with sick, suffering, and crippled people. Those who, through medical skill, opportunity, work and courage, survive their illness or overcome their handicap and take their places back in the world, have a depth of spirit that you and I can hardly measure. They haven't wasted their pain.

Because of this experience, they have a desire to share that is almost a compulsion. It matters not whether they be a physician from India, a Zionist from Israel, a Greek veteran or a Pole disabled in a mining accident—all want to share the understanding they have gained through suffering or by helping those who have suffered.

I believe that this basic and inherent desire of man to do something for his less fortunate fellow transcends religious dogmas, political beliefs, and geographical barriers. If we could only use this universal language, we would have a tool to unravel the babel of tongues and an instrument which would penetrate any iron curtain or closed boundary.

It does not seem strange to me that the sick should turn to those who have suffered for the greatest comfort. And so, in a sick world, it is not strange that we turn to those who have been ravaged by suffering and disease for a common language. If we could start to work here together in a program where all of us have the same goals, it is more than possible that, with God's help, we would find the solution for living together in peace. This I believe!

HOWARD A. RUSK, a specialist in the field of physical medicine and rehabilitation, is one of this country's great physicians. Born in Brookfield, Missouri, Dr. Rusk took his medical degree at the University of Pennsylvania. While practising internal medicine in St. Louis, he taught at Washington University and was associate chief of staff at St. Luke's Hospital.

After World War II, in which he served as a colonel in the Army Air Force Medical Corps, Dr. Rusk became associated with New York University School of Medicine, as professor and department head. He also serves as consultant on rehabilitation to the City of New York and the United Nations. He is a recent winner of the Lasker Award, which has been called Medicine's "Oscar." His friends, associates and students know him as both a distinguished physician and a compassionate human being.

My Fellow Worms:

BY CARL SANDBURG

THE MAN who sits down and searches himself for his answer to the question, "What Do I Believe?" is either going to write a book or a few well-chosen thoughts on what he thinks it might be healthy for mankind to be thinking about in the present tribulations and turmoils. I believe in getting up in the morning with a serene mind and a heart holding many hopes. And so large a number of my fellow worms in the dust believe the same that there is no use putting stress on it. I can remember many years ago, a beautiful woman in Santa Fe saying, "I don't see how anybody can study astronomy and have ambition enough to get up in the morning." She was putting a comic twist on what an insignificant speck of animate star dust each of us is amid cotillions of billion-year constellations. I believe in humility, though my confession and exposition of the humility I believe in would run into an old fashioned two or three hour sermon. Also I believe in pride, knowing well that the deadliest of the seven deadly sins is named as pride. I believe in a pride that prays ever for an awareness of that borderline where, unless watchful of yourself, you cross over into arrogance, into vanity, into mirror gazing, into misuse and violation of the sacred portions of your personality. No single brief utterance of Lincoln is more portentous than the line he wrote to a federal authority in Louisiana. "I shall do nothing in malice, for what I deal with is too vast for malicious dealing." Now I believe in platitudes, when they serve, especially that battered and hard-worn antique, "Eternal vigilance is the price of liberty." Hand in hand with freedom goes responsibility. I believe that free men the world over cherish the earth as cradle and tomb, the handiwork of their Maker, the possession of the family of man. I believe freedom comes the hard way—by ceaseless groping, toil, struggle—even by fiery trial and agony.

⌘

CARL SANDBURG, the poet and biographer of Lincoln, is one of America's most revered men of letters. He was born in Galesburg, Illinois, the son of a Swedish immigrant. After serving in the Spanish-American War, he worked his way through Lombard College in Galesburg. In 1913, he began his long career.

As early as 1914 the excellence of his poetry was recognized and he was awarded the Levinson Prize by *Poetry Magazine*. In 1919 and 1921, he shared a prize of the Poetry Society of America. He was honored with the Pulitzer Prize in 1951.

Mr. Sandburg is known now throughout the world for his verse and for his great life of Abraham Lincoln. Among his numerous volumes are *Chicago Poems; Cornhuskers;* a novel, *Remembrance Rock; Complete Poems;* and the recently-published *Always the Young Strangers*. The compiler of *The American Songbag*, he has frequently appeared on the lecture platform, interpreting ballads and accompanying himself on the guitar.

When Children Are Wanted

BY MARGARET SANGER

THIS I BELIEVE, first of all: that all our basic convictions must be tested and transmuted in the crucible of experience—and sometimes the more bitter the experience, the more valid the purified belief.

As a child, one of a large family, I learned that the thing I did best was the thing I liked to do. This realization of doing and getting results was what I have later called an awakening consciousness.

There is an old Indian proverb which has inspired me in the work of my adult life. "Build thou beyond thyself, but first be sure that thou thyself be strong and healthy in body and mind." Yes, to build, to work, to plan to do something, not for yourself, not for your own benefit, but "beyond thyself"—and when this idea permeates the mind you begin to think in terms of a future. I began to think of a world beyond myself when I first took an interest in nursing the sick.

As a nurse I was in contact with the ill and the infirm. I knew something about the health and disease of bodies, but for a long time I was baffled at the tremendous personal problems of life, of marriage, of living, and of just being. Here indeed was a challenge to "build beyond thyself." But where was I to begin? I found the answer at every door. I began to believe there was something I could do toward increasing an understanding of these basic human problems. To build beyond myself I must first tap all inner resources of stamina, of courage, of resolution within myself. I was prepared to face opposition, even ridicule, denunciation. But I had also to prepare myself, in defense of these unpopular beliefs; I had to prepare myself to face courts and even prisons. But I resolved to stand up, alone if necessary, against all the entrenched forces which opposed me.

I started my battle some forty years ago. The women and mothers whom I wanted to help also wanted to help me. They, too, wanted to build beyond the self, in creating healthy children and bringing them up in life to be happy and useful citizens. I believed it was my duty to place motherhood on a higher level than enslavement and accident. I was convinced we must care about people; we must reach out to help them in their despair.

For these beliefs I was denounced, arrested. I was in and out of police courts and higher courts, and indictments hung over my life for several years. But nothing could alter my beliefs. Because I saw these as truths, and I stubbornly stuck to my convictions.

No matter what it may cost in health, in misunderstanding, in sacrifice, something had to be done, and I felt that I was called by the force of circumstances to do it. Because of my philosophy and my work, my life has been enriched and full. My interests have expanded from local conditions and needs to a world horizon, where peace on earth may be achieved when children are wanted before they are conceived. A new consciousness will take place, a new race will be born to bring peace on earth. This belief has withstood the crucible of my life's joyous struggle. It remains my basic belief today.

This I believe—at the end as at the beginning of my long crusade for the future of the human race.

❧❦❧

MARGARET SANGER and scientific birth control are practically synonymous. She was the founder and president of the American Birth Control League from 1921 to 1929. At this time the organization's name was changed to the Planned Parenthood Federation of America which it remains today and of which she is Honorary Chairman. She organized the first World Population Conference in Geneva in 1927. When in India in 1935, on the invitation of the All-India Women's Conference, she was the guest of Gandhi and of the great Indian poet, Rabindranath Tagore.

While she is still a controversial figure to many, Mrs. Sanger has nevertheless been widely and variously honored for her work: In 1930 came the American Women's Award for "integrity, vision, and valor"; in 1936 the Town Hall Award of Honor for "conspicuous contribution to the development and enrichment of life"; in 1949, an honorary LL.D. from Smith College; and in 1950 the Lasker Award.

Let the World Disappear

BY VINCENT SHEEAN

AT THE AGE of fifty-three I have come to hold a certain number of beliefs which, although neither precise nor dogmatic, seem to me justified by innate reason and external observation. I reject any form of materialism, defining materialism as the view of life which considers material relations to determine the whole. I believe instead that a spirit informs the Universe, animates and sustains it. This universal spirit, present as I think in all things, is not confined to the planet Earth or to the human species, but to all that takes form in what would otherwise be chaos. There have been, under my own observation, any number of phenomena which cannot be explained or understood in any other way.

If I understand this world as being a physical garment for an immaterial or spiritual power, I must therefore quite tranquilly face the possibility of the disappearance of the world at any moment. I do.

The new possibilities opened up to us by physical science have tended to confirm, although they did not originate, this view of life.

The earliest examples we know of a statement combining atomic energy with the spiritual essence of the universe comes in the Upanishads, in India, perhaps five thousand years ago. These documents were scattered through the centuries and their exact age is uncertain, but some of them, it is sure, come from the very dawn of recorded time. In various passages of these ancient texts it is clearly stated that life and matter consist of atoms of energy, along with the conviction that this arrangement is the manifestation of a spiritual center or source. It was also the belief of those ancient seers that the clash of atomic energy contained the promise of an eventual extinction of the universe. This was not because of any will on the part of the immanent spiritual reality, but because the opposing energies, classified as good and evil, were in unresolved conflict.

In my own life I have felt the pull of opposing forces and witnessed its effects on the largest external scale. The partial theories and observations, particularly those of the nineteenth century, do not seem to me to fit the facts of human life. The only thing that does seem recognizably true is the proposition of innate knowledge, as in, for example, Immanuel Kant, which means simply the knowledge that comes to us from beyond the stars. This proposition makes us capable of love, art, beauty, patriotism, and all the other aspirations which have no basis in reasonable self-interest.

I may add that the greatest personal influence upon my course towards these beliefs was the late Mahatma Gandhi, whom I knew only slightly and only at the very end of his long life, in 1948. I could not talk to him without realizing the overwhelming power of the soul. He was a very practical man, whose preoccupations in life were ethical and social. But nobody who knew him could doubt that a higher power animated his action.

❧❦☙

❦§ VINCENT SHEEAN is one of America's most distinguished journalists and authors. Ever since the publication of *Personal History* in 1935, his eyewitness reports of the great events and personalities of our time have been among the vital documents of the era. Born in Christian County, Illinois, he was educated at the University of Chicago. He early became a globe-trotter and foreign correspondent, and out of his coverage of the revolt of the Riffs against the Spanish in North Africa came his first book, *An American Among the Riffi*, in 1926.

Besides *Personal History*, his titles, which number some fifteen and which represent sojourns in just about as many countries, include *Lead Kindly Light*, a sensitive biography of Gandhi and an important piece of modern spiritual history. In 1935 Mr. Sheean married Diana, daughter of Sir Johnston and Lady Forbes-Robertson, brilliant star of the English stage.

133

Regard the Past

BY SAMUEL SHELLABARGER

WHAT IS BELIEF? We have *opinions* about many things. But I am assuming that we are here concerned with a central faith, a way of thinking, which is the focal point and mainspring of everything else. Such a trend of thought, I suppose, is inborn rather than acquired. At least that is the case with me. As I look back over sixty years, I can see that the experiences of life have strengthened and enriched but have not substantially altered my original bent, which, at first unconscious, has since developed into a fundamental belief.

This, to express it simply, is reverence for the past, an active memory of what time has revealed as valuable and permanent in the traditions which are our roots and from which we can free ourselves only at the risk of futility. Such a regard for the past does not oppose progress, but it values evolution rather than revolution. To look forward wisely, we must look back.

Central in this belief of mine and, of course, permeating all of it, is the Christian religion. By this, in a few words, I mean the recognition of man's helplessness collectively or individually to suffice unto himself—his dependence on God—and the divine love which has made possible a supernatural life to those who seek it. This seems to me without question the chief legacy of the ages. Together with the ethics and the arts which it has inspired, it represents humanity's highest attainment. And if, in the course of time, it has drawn into itself certain other, originally non-Christian elements, it is all the richer and more universal because of them.

But reverence for the past includes more than religious faith, though it is the genius of Christianity to support and color all traditions that dignify man. From the crucible of the ages, as a residue of human experience, has emerged the recognition of certain values that bear upon every phase of life. It seems to me that the value of order and self-discipline is perhaps the chief of these in its effect upon the concepts of law, freedom, justice, manners, education, and the arts. The values of patience, fortitude, honor, and modesty belong also to our inheritance.

I believe in the supreme importance of this tradition. Man cannot improvise the laws of his nature. He can only rediscover in the end what has been discovered long ago.

Thus, to conclude, I find my opinions on every subject and, indeed, the process of daily living, conditioned by an awareness of the past. It is the mainspring of my thought and action, the source of a philosophy, partly instinctive but also consciously accepted, which has become the guide and rationale of my life.

◄§ SAMUEL SHELLABARGER, who died in March 1954, was the author of a succession of historical novels which couple profound research and authentic detail with swift-moving action. As a result his books reached the best-seller list with remarkable frequency, most recently his *Lord Vanity.*

Dr. Shellabarger was also an educator, and this was his first career. Princeton gave him his A.B. and Harvard his Ph.D., and he served as assistant professor of English at Princeton for some years. Later he became headmaster of the Columbus (Ohio) School for Girls.

Dr. Shellabarger wrote a biography of Lord Chesterfield, and his several historical novels include *Captain from Castile, Prince of Foxes* and *The King's Cavalier*—together selling more than 4,500,000 copies. He also wrote mysteries, and additional historical fiction under the name of Peter Loring.

His home was in Princeton.

Survival Must Be Earned

HANS SIMONS

It is no simple matter to single out those beliefs which I can share with others. I find it easy to talk about my political convictions but hard to tell about the ultimate faith from which they spring.

When I was a young man the events of a turbulent era brought it about that I was gravely wounded and for quite some time expected to die. I had then not attained any of my hopes and ambitions, and it came as a shock that my days and years had been spent in preparation for something which now was never to come. But miraculously I survived. Reason as I would, I simply could not regard having been spared as an accident. I was not just self-centered when I felt that I had received a new lease on life from a source impersonal and indefinable but real and related to me as an individual. My share in it was given me through a conscious experience and with new obligations. With an almost physical intensity I felt my values change. Since this new life did not belong to me only, I sought service in order to justify the happiness of living.

Another experience came when the government of my native country—Germany—rejected me as "nationally unreliable" and threatened my freedom and my very life. I escaped to the United States and there had to re-make myself in every respect. Language, traditions, modes of living and of thought, all were entirely new. Again this was like a conscious re-birth. It confirmed my conviction that what makes our life collective is its divine source, while the earthly goal may be different for each individual. As compared with the totalitarian regime which I fled, and with the physical and political provincialism which so often oppressed me in Europe, I found greater diversity and, dependent on it, a wider liberty in America. I still do, notwithstanding some ominous signs of bigotry and jingoism and quite a few recent instances of pressure for conformity at the expense of tolerance and justice.

So it came about that though I was baptized into the Protestant faith I found my religion through insight as a grown-up person. And though I was born into a narrow nationalism I acquired my patriotism through acceptance from conviction as a mature man.

In this way I learned that life is a trust which must be earned. Its delights are as enjoyable and its hardships as regrettable whether they are mere accidents or parts of a meaningful whole. But they are not any longer disproportionately important if I can relate them to their universal origin, see them fall into my individual pattern, and then in turn fit them into a wider purpose. A real joy which stretches the limits of my nature, a good deed which makes me secure in an insecure world, and a completed thought which gives me serenity amidst worries, they are all evidence of my being endowed from without and beyond myself.

While this belief makes life less fearsome, it does not make its daily demands any less urgent. However, it permits a more detached view of current events and a deeper devotion to those duties which my sharing the mysteries of man's origin and destiny imposes upon me.

HANS SIMONS, educator and author, is President, New School for Social Research, New York City. Born in Velbert, Germany, he took his doctor's degree in law and political science at Koenigsberg. Thereafter he plunged immediately into public administrative work, first as executive director, League of Nations Association, then as director, Institute of Political Science, Berlin, and finally as District Governor, Lower Silesia.

Since 1935, Dr. Simons has been associated with the New School, as professor of international relations, as Dean of its School of Politics, and, since 1950, as President. He was also Consultant, Office of Strategic Services, during the war. He is associated with many foreign policy and political science organizations and associations. Two books and innumerable articles contributed to American and foreign journals of politics, social research and education, further attest to his pre-eminence in his field.

They Got Vicious

BY MARGARET CHASE SMITH

MANY NIGHTS I go home from the office or the Senate floor tired and discouraged. There's lots of glory and prestige and limelight for a United States Senator that the public sees. But there's just as much grief and harassment and discouragement that the public doesn't see.

Of course, like everyone else, I went into public service and politics with my eyes wide open. I knew that any public official is fair game for slander and smear and carping criticism. I knew that ingratitude was to be expected. I knew that fair weather friends would turn on me when they felt I no longer served their purposes. I knew that I would be called all sorts of names from crook on down. I should have known that chances were good that I would even be accused of being a traitor to my country.

These things I knew. But I never knew how vicious they could get and how deeply they could cut.

It is these things I think of when I'm tired and discouraged—and when I wonder if being a Senator is worth all that I put into it. These are the times when I consider quitting public life and retreating to the comforts and luxury of private life.

But these times have always been the very times when I became all the more convinced that all the sorrow, abuse, harassment and vilification was not too high a price or sacrifice to pay. For it is then that I ask myself, "What am I doing this for?"

I realize that I am doing it because I believe in certain things—thing without which life wouldn't mean much to me.

This I do believe—that life has a real purpose—that God has assigned to each human being a role in life—that each of us has a purposeful task—that our individual roles are all different but that each of us has the same obligation to do the best we can.

I believe that every human being I come in contact with has

138

a right to courtesy and consideration from me. I believe that I should not ask or expect from anyone else that which I am not willing to grant or do myself. I believe that I should be able to take anything that I can dish out. I believe that every living person has the right to criticize constructively, the right honestly to hold unpopular beliefs, the right to protest orderly, the right of independent thought.

I believe that no one has a right to own our souls except God.

I believe that freedom of speech should not be so abused by some that it is not exercised by others because of fear of smear. But I do believe that we should not permit tolerance to degenerate into indifference. I believe that people should never get so indifferent, cynical and sophisticated that they don't get shocked into action.

I believe that we should not forget how to disagree agreeably and how to criticize constructively. I believe with all my heart that we must not become a nation of mental mutes blindly following demagogues.

I believe that in our constant search for security we can never gain any peace of mind until we secure our own soul. And this I do believe above all, especially in my times of greater discouragement, that I must BELIEVE—that I must believe in my fellow men—that I must believe in myself—that I must believe in God—if life is to have any meaning.

◄§ MARGARET CHASE SMITH, United States Senator, is the first woman to represent the state of Maine in Congress. A life-long resident of Skowhegan, Maine, she began her career by teaching.

When she was twenty-one, she was appointed a business executive for the Maine Telephone and Telegraph Company. Following this, she was associated with a newspaper, the *Independent Reporter*, and with several business concerns. From 1930 until 1936, she was a member of the Republican State Committee of Maine.

When her husband, Clyde H. Smith, was elected to Congress, she served as his secretary. When he was stricken in 1940, a special election was held and she was chosen to complete his unexpired term. She sat in the House of Representatives for eight years. In 1948, she was elected to the Senate. Among her many awards for distinguished service, Mrs. Smith counts the Freedom Award, presented to her by the Freedoms Foundation, for outstanding Americanism.

Dictators Cannot Kill It

BY HAROLD E. STASSEN

As I WALKED with Dr. Albert Schweitzer through his remarkable hospital deep in the African jungle at Lambarene in French Equatorial Africa and watched his expressive kindly face as he paused and talked with an elderly native patient and again as he looked in on a tiny newborn native baby, the central thought of his philosophic writings came again and again to my mind. "Reverence for life" is the phrase which this great man, now in his seventy-ninth year of life and in his fortieth year in the African jungle, has used to tell the world of his philosophy of life. It is a phrase which occurred to him years ago as he was traveling up the Ogowe river in a dugout canoe en route to minister to an ill family in the jungle. He speaks and writes of all life as having the "will to live" and of each one living in the midst of others with a "will to live." From this beginning he follows with his view that "reverence for life" is the basis for civilization, it is the ethics for a desirable way of life.

Dr. Schweitzer has read and written about most of the philosophers of all history from Socrates and Aristotle to Marx and Gandhi. He is also an authority on the music of Bach and has written a number of volumes of interpretation of Bach's chorals. He played a brief Bach concert for me on his small organ before seven o'clock in the morning.

I believe he has come closer to interpreting the teachings of Christ into a guiding philosophy of civilization than anyone has ever done. Perhaps the combination of his medical practice in the jungle and his musical ability have together had a part in shaping his understanding of this philosophy.

Thus in this modern atomic age with all of its uncertainties and dangers and confusions, I believe that faith in God and in the value and worth of a human being is the solid rock upon which to build a happy and well-spent life.

I hold that every man has within him a regard for the well-being and the dignity of his fellow men. At times this might be pretty well covered over. At times it might be encased in a hard shell built up by bitter experiences or by evil objectives. But I believe it is always there, deep down inside.

This is the "Reverence for life" of which Albert Schweitzer writes from Africa. It is a sentiment inborn in man which even the most ruthless dictators cannot completely wipe out.

Thus I believe that man was meant to be free. Throughout history most of mankind has been ruled and dominated by other men. There have been many cruel and oppressive governments. Even at this time, half way through the twentieth century, one third of the peoples of the world are living under dictatorships. But history also shows that even when people have been dominated for centuries, they continue to have an intense personal desire to be free. I believe this too is an inborn part of man himself.

Above all I believe there is a God. There is a power beyond all of mankind and all of this earth. This faith and this belief are the foundation for America. It is the foundation for a worthwhile life. This I believe.

HAROLD E. STASSEN, at forty-seven, is one of America's leading younger statesmen. He is a lawyer and was three times Governor of his native Minnesota. He first took office in 1938 at the age of thirty-one, becoming the youngest Governor in American history.

He resigned during his third term to take up active duty in the United States Navy, serving on the staff of Admiral William F. Halsey in the Pacific theatre from July 1943 to the end of the war. In 1948 he was placed in nomination for the Republican candidacy for President, withdrawing in favor of Thomas E. Dewey. Until recently president of the University of Pennsylvania, he is now Foreign Operations Director, a post to which he was appointed by President Eisenhower. Thus he is enabled to give practical application to his interest in world affairs.

No Other Rock of Safety

BY ADLAI E. STEVENSON

WHAT DO I BELIEVE? As an American, I believe in generosity, in liberty, in the rights of man. These are social and political faiths that are part of me as they are, I suppose, part of all of us. Such beliefs are easy to express. But part of me too is my religion—my relation to all life, and this is not so easy to talk about.

Religious experience is highly intimate and, for me at least, ready, words are not at hand. I am profoundly aware of the magnitude of the universe, that all is ruled by law, including my finite person. I believe in the infinite wisdom that envelops and embraces me and from which I take direction, purpose, strength. First to my mind there spring those words of the Twenty-seventh Psalm, my favorites, "For in the time of trouble [the Lord] shall hide me in His pavilion, He shall set me up upon a rock . . . I had fainted unless I had believed to see the goodness of the Lord in the land of the living. Wait on the Lord, be of good courage and He shall strengthen thine heart. . . ."

Yes, I believe in and I have experienced His goodness in the land of the living, and I have found no rocks of certainty or safety but His. And if doing is part of believing, I find a great design in the simple counsel of the old Prophet Micah: "To do justly, to love mercy and to walk humbly with thy God."

But having beliefs or at least enunciating them is only part of it. Living up to them, for me, is much harder. For as someone said, "It is easier to fight for one's beliefs than to live up to them." And I wonder if the chief cause of discord in human affairs is not so much the undesirable nature of beliefs as it is the fighting for them, the competitive indoctrination among them.

I believe in liberalism, in individualism, in freedom of conscience. And if there is anything that the whole idea of liberalism contradicts, it is the notion of competitive indoctrination. So I

142

believe that if we really want human brotherhood to spread and increase until it makes life safe and sane, we must also be certain that there is no one true faith or path by which it may spread.

But it is not easy to banish the notion that there can be universal brotherhood just as soon as everybody gives up his faith and accepts ours. That day will never come for the richness of human diversity cannot be abolished any more than Mars or Jupiter. It can be resented and it can be fought but only at what an appalling cost. Difference is in the nature of life, it is part of our moral universe. Without difference life would become lifeless. So I reject the idea of conformity, compulsory or complacent, the faith that is swallowed like pills, whole and at once, with no questions asked.

I believe in helping ourselves and others to see the possibilities in viewpoints other than one's own, in encouraging the free interchange of ideas, in welcoming fresh approaches to the problems of life, in urging the fullest, the most vigorous use of critical self-examination. Thus, we can learn to grow together, to unite in our common search for the truth within a better and a happier world.

The basic faith in liberty of conscience is by no means exclusive with us. But I believe we are its ordained guardians in this age of assault and anxiety, when so many seem to believe their doubts and to doubt their beliefs.

Finally, I should like to live and not just believe these strong words of faith in St. Paul's letter to the Galatians: "Stand fast, therefore, in the liberty wherewith Christ has made us free and not be entangled with the yoke of bondage."

ADLAI E. STEVENSON, the Democratic candidate for the Presidency of the United States in 1952, was born in Los Angeles, brought up in Bloomington, Illinois, and at eighteen enlisted as an apprentice seaman in the United States Naval Reserve. Then came Princeton, Northwestern's law school and the practice of law. He served as special counsel to the Department of Agriculture and, in 1941, became special assistant to the Secretary of the Navy Frank Knox. During the war he headed a Foreign Economic Administration mission to Italy and immediately after the war, he was made an alternate delegate to the United Nations. With no experience in politics, he ran for the Governorship of Illinois in 1948 and won by the largest plurality in the state's history. As a Presidential candidate, with a campaign based on "talking sense to the American people," he won the respect, if not the majority of the votes, of his fellow countrymen.

By Losing One's Life

BY WILLIAM E. STEVENSON

UNTIL 1942, I was a lawyer in New York City and found the practice of that profession absorbing and stimulating. Then, when the war came, I had the opportunity to serve as an executive in the American Red Cross, first in Great Britain and then in the Mediterranean Theater. Broadly speaking, the Red Cross assignment was to do whatever we could to promote the welfare of American troops. In whatever we did, we found that great satisfaction which comes to human beings when they subordinate their personal interests to those of others. As a minister's son, I had heard many times that only by losing one's life does one find it, but it took the impact and grimness of war conditions and the appeal of homesick, dreary, sometimes horribly mutilated men, to bring home dramatically and convincingly the realistic significance of that great truth.

It was because of such experiences that, after the war was over, I decided not to return to law practice, rewarding as it had been, but to turn instead to some new pursuit in which, with my wife who had shared those overseas years with me, I could be of more direct and intimate service to people. Since both my wife and I had come from academic homes, it was natural that we found ourselves in the field of liberal education, which we believe should be dedicated to the maximum development of individual human beings and their powers of reason, conscience and faith, not only for their own sake but also for the benefit of all mankind.

Since 1942, I have increasingly discovered that the answer to the ever-present restlessness, neuroticism, and cynicism of so many people is the fact that it isn't money or luxuries or physical gratification which will cure restlessness and dissatisfaction. Rather, it is the realization—stressed through the centuries by great religious leaders and philosophers and in practice by many noble men and women—that it is by aiding others, and thus increasing an appreciation of the dignity and worth of every individual human being, that we find serenity, peace of mind, and God's true purposes for man.

A year ago, Mrs. Stevenson and I visited India and other Far Eastern countries. Memorable as were so many fascinating places, I find in retrospect that the trip's significant and permanent impact on my life was its confirmation that human beings are the only thing of real importance in this world; that people everywhere are fundamentally the same, and yearn for understanding and acceptance. I believe, too, that all people comprehend, each in his own way, that there is a Divine Being, responsible for goodness and nobility in man.

Our world trip also amply demonstrated that it was those who appreciated their fellow men and stood ready to assist them in a friendly spirit, who were joyous and cheerful—who were finding life's greater meaning and added inner strength and resources in their own lives. It was those who were struggling or conniving for personal gain or advantage, who were restless or dissatisfied.

I am grateful that circumstances have brought me a clearer realization that the more one thinks and acts in terms of the interest of others, the greater will be his own joy in living and hence his own effectiveness as a member of the human race. I believe that liberal education should stress significantly the importance of this basic Divine principle which is so frequently elusive because it is so simple.

WILLIAM E. STEVENSON is President of Oberlin College and his selection for that position was a departure from precedent, as he had been neither a clergyman nor a scholar. Despite its accent on academic standing and religion, Oberlin chose a lawyer from New York. It is true his father had been President of the Princeton Theological Seminary, but his own career had been in law. An exception was the years of World War II when he was in charge of Red Cross work in Great Britain, North Africa, Sicily and Italy, for which both he and his wife were awarded Bronze Star medals. He endeared himself with Oberlin students by encouraging the building of space for their social meetings; and of a field for intercollegiate sports. He had himself been a member of the American relay team at the Paris Olympics in 1924, which established a world record in the 1600–meter relay. He is a graduate of Princeton and was a Rhodes scholar at Oxford.

Action Is the Measure

BY RAYMOND SWING

I USED TO THINK I was especially unfortunate. I had more trouble, inwardly and outwardly, than others I knew. Then I spent a long time studying my troubles and their origins. I came to see that every one of my troubles arose out of something I had done myself. Nobody else was to blame for the start of any trouble. I also found that in each instance my original mistake was not one of willful wrong-doing. It was the result of not knowing well enough what was right. That is, I had to suffer not because I was bad at the start of a trouble but because I wasn't good enough. I say "at the start of a trouble" because, as a trouble developed, I sometimes did do what I knew was wrong. But because I knew, the experience of wrong-doing could become part of my education in doing more right. When at last I learned what had been inadequate at the start of a trouble, that particular trouble ended, along with any wrong-doing it had engendered.

So I came to believe that my failures were basically due to ignorance. I had done the best I knew how to do. And I stopped chiding myself. But to be consistent I had to stop chiding others too. The other fellow also was doing the best he knew how to do. When he was in trouble I had some inkling of what he was going through.

You can see this is a belief in a process that is governed by law and is beneficent. Call the process growing into truth. I believe it is what I am here to do.

I have become aware that there is an inconceivable wisdom that governs all things right down to me and less than me. Because I can become more and more part of it, I see that I have in me a potential of the All-Wisdom. But I also am aware that my part is infinitesimally minute. Some of my troubles come from not knowing at the right time my own importance as part of the Godhood, and at the right time my own insignificance. When I work for truth, when I love and serve others and try to make them free, I am exercising my little portion of the All-Wisdom. When I get obsessed with my success, or with what I am getting out of something, or what others are doing to me, I am being bigger than my size.

I came to see that what I didn't like in others was also in me, which is how I was able to recognize it. So I could stop trying to change others and go to work on myself. I am the one person I can do something about and am responsible for.

I also came to see that the love and freedom I want for myself are to be tested by the love and freedom I give others. I show what I value by what I give. So in my book action is the measure of belief. If I hold a belief and do something about it, I begin to grow out of myself and into the fellowship of man and the fellowship that transcends the understanding of man.

I believe that happiness and suffering are the two sides of the coin of growth into truth. I believe the process is the tragedy of creation itself, and while pain is one side, the two together are merciful, and this is the beauty that underlies all living.

❦

RAYMOND SWING, veteran of American journalism and radio, likes to say that his generation is the first in his family not to produce a clergyman since his Puritan ancestors came to America in 1630. But he had a close call, for he's now Editor of the "This I Believe" program. Like many a clergyman's son, he became a newspaper man, served mid-Western newspapers from the age of nineteen till he became a foreign correspondent at twenty-six, then put in eighteen years writing from Europe.

Mr. Swing is a well-known American broadcaster in international radio, thanks to having originated the American commentary for the BBC, which was shortwaved throughout the Empire for the eleven years he gave it, and to his daily political commentaries for the Voice of America. In this country he was widely followed as a wartime commentator, and has spoken over most of the national networks.

As an avocation, Mr. Swing writes poetry and music.

We Chose Vermont

WILL THOMAS

IN 1946 I decided I did not wish to live in my native land any longer; and that I would take my wife and children to Haiti, where as Negroes in a Negro republic, we would be free of racial prejudice and our opportunities would be limited only by our ability to use them.

I do not believe I need detail the reasons behind this unhappy decision, except to say that being considered and treated as an inferior on every level of life can become intolerable, especially when it is by one's race rather than his individual worth, or lack of it, that he is pre-judged—and condemned.

When I reached this point, I had become an unbeliever in both God and country, for it seemed to me that racial segregation and all that it implied was as rigid on the spiritual as on the temporal plane. And so finally I made the decision to leave my native land— permanently.

However, I did not do it. Love of country, I found, can be very deep, very strong. So I thought to make one final try in my motherland for the equality of status which I considered I had been denied; and I chose Vermont for the experiment. I reasoned that because of its great traditions of personal freedom there was at least a chance that I and my family might find there what we so yearned for, and we did. In the small farming community where we settled, we were accepted on a basis of individuality unqualified by race.

However, it is not that which now seems most important to me. It is, rather, that in such a friendly atmosphere, and amid the quiet of a beautiful countryside, it was possible to think calmly, and gradually to gain understandings by which I believe I can live in peace with other men, and with myself, for the rest of my life.

One of these understandings is that unless one seeks sincerely

148

for whatever it is he most wants, he surely will not find it, and that what I really had been seeking most of my life was not what I wanted but instead was justification for the resentments I felt. This is not to say there was not cause for those resentments, but rather that I had so concentrated upon them I could not see that the picture was not all bad—that in fact, there was considerable good in it.

I had condemned my country and my religion because I viewed only what seemed wrong in both. But when I was able to remove the blinds of my own prejudice, it became clear that these failures, these flaws in church and state, were human failures, human flaws, and not mere self-willed bigotry; and that within each there were, and there always had been, many who had worked and fought for what was right.

I think the core of my earlier bitterness had been the conviction that I had been denied my birthright of human dignity. But I know now that is something which cannot be given or taken away by man.

It has been written that he who seeks shall find, and that to him who asks, it shall be given. And I can only testify that when I did seek, I did find; and that when I asked, it was given to me. And I know that only the God I once denied could bestow such precious gifts.

❧§❦

<§ WILL THOMAS, newspaperman and author, was born in Kansas City and traveled over most of the United States before settling in the little town of Westford, Vermont, where he now lives with his wife and three children. Along the way he went to college, and did a little of almost everything from prizefighting to newspaper editing. His experiences, for this reason, combine the unique with the universal because the Thomases are Negroes.

In his autobiography, *The Seeking*, Mr. Thomas tells of moving his family to Vermont in 1946, and the adjustments made by himself and his fellow townsmen in settling down together within the traditions of New England democracy. The New York *Herald Tribune*, reviewing the book, said: "[No one] can read it without a warm hope that what happened between the Thomases and their Vermont neighbors will some day happen to all men everywhere."

149

I Agree With a Pagan

BY ARNOLD J. TOYNBEE

I BELIEVE there may be some things that some people may know for certain, but I also believe that those knowable things are not what matters most to any human being. A good mathematician may know the truth about numbers, and a good engineer may know how to make physical forces serve his purposes. But the engineer and the mathematician are human beings first—so for them, as well as for me, what matters most is not one's knowledge and skill, but one's relations with other people. We do not all have to be engineers or mathematicians, but we do all have to deal with other people. And these relations of ours with each other, which are the really important things in life, are also the really difficult things, because it is here that the question of right and wrong comes in.

I believe we have no certain knowledge of what is right and wrong; and, even if we had, I believe we should find it just as hard as ever to do something that we knew for certain to be right in the teeth of our personal interests and inclinations. Actually, we have to make the best judgment we can about what is right, and then we have to bet on it by trying to make ourselves act on it, without being sure about it.

Since we can never be sure, we have to try to be charitable and open to persuasion that we may, after all, have been in the wrong, and at the same time we have to be resolute and energetic in what we do, in order to be effective. It is difficult enough to combine effectiveness with humility and charity in trying to do what is right, but it is still more difficult to try to do right at all, because this means fighting oneself.

Trying to do right does mean fighting oneself, because, by nature, each of us feels and behaves as if he were the center and the purpose of the universe. But I do feel sure that I am not that, and that, in behaving as if I were, I am going wrong. So one has to fight oneself all the time; and this means that suffering is not only inevitable, but is an indispensable part of a lifelong education, if only one can learn how to profit by it. I believe that everything worth winning does have its price in suffering, and I know, of course, where this belief of mine comes from. It comes from the accident of my having been born in a country where the local religion has been Christianity.

Another belief that I owe to Christianity is a conviction that love is what gives life its meaning and purpose, and that suffering is profitable when it is met in the course of following love's lead. But I can't honestly call myself a believing Christian in the traditional sense. To imagine that one's own church, civilization, nation or family is the chosen people is, I believe, as wrong as it would be for me to imagine that I myself am God. I agree with Symmachus, the pagan philosopher who put the case for toleration to a victorious Christian church, and I will end by quoting his words: "The universe is too great a mystery for there to be only one single approach to it."

❧

❧ PROFESSOR ARNOLD J. TOYNBEE, world-famous historian, has been director of studies in the Royal Institute of International Affairs since 1925. In addition, he is research professor of International History in the University of London.

A Scholar at Winchester, he later went up to Balliol College, Oxford, where he was again a Scholar. Afterwards, he was a Fellow and Tutor at Balliol and served as a delegate to the Paris Peace Conference in 1919. Returning to England, he was appointed Koraes Professor of Byzantine and Modern Greek Language, Literature and History at London University.

During World War II Professor Toynbee was Director of Foreign Research and Press Service, Royal Institute of International Affairs, and Director of the Research Department of the Foreign Office. In 1946, he was again a delegate to the Paris Peace Conference. Professor Toynbee's master work is of course the monumental *A Study of History*, the first volumes of which were published in 1934 and the last in 1954.

The Precepts of a President

BY HARRY S. TRUMAN

I BELIEVE in a moral code based on the Ten Commandments, found in the 20th Chapter of Exodus, and in the 5th, 6th and 7th Chapters of the Gospel according to St. Matthew, which is the Sermon on the Mount.

I believe a man ought to live by those precepts which, if followed, will enable a man to do right.

I don't know whether I have or not, but I have tried.

I believe that the fundamental basis for a happy life with family and friends is to treat others as you would like to be treated, speak truthfully, act honorably, and keep commitments to the letter.

In public life I have always believed that right will prevail. It has been my policy to obtain the facts—all the facts possible—then to make the decision in the public interest and to carry it out.

If the facts justify the decision at the time it is made, it will always be right. A public man should not worry constantly about the verdict of history or what future generations will say about him.

He must live in the present, make his decisions for the right on the facts as he sees them and history will take care of itself.

I believe a public man must know the history and background of his state and his nation to enable him to come more nearly to a proper decision in the public interest.

In my opinion, a man in public life must think always of the public welfare. He must be careful not to mix his private and personal interests with his public actions.

The ethics of a public man must be unimpeachable.

He must learn to reject unwise or imprudent requests from friends and associates without losing their friendship or loyalty.

I believe that our Bill of Rights must be implemented in fact; that it is the duty of every Government—state, local or Federal—to preserve the rights of the individual.

I believe that a civil rights program, as we must practice it today, involves not so much the protection of the people against the Government, but the protection of the people by the Government. And for this reason we must make the Federal Government a friendly, vigilant defender of the rights and equalities of all Americans; and that every man should be free to live his life as he wishes. He should be limited only by his responsibility to his fellow man.

I believe that we should remove the last barriers which stand between millions of our people and their birthright. There can be no justifiable reason for discrimination because of ancestry, or religion, or race, or color.

I believe that to inspire the people of the world whose freedom is in jeopardy, and to restore hope to those who have already lost their civil liberties, we must correct the remaining imperfections in our own democracy.

We know the way—we only need the will.

HARRY S. TRUMAN, thirty-second President of the United States, was born in 1884, the son of a Missouri farmer and cattle trader. He grew up on the family farm in Grandview and in Independence where his home is today. He entered the Army upon the outbreak of World War I, serving in France, first as captain and later as major in the field artillery. His war record helped bring him his first political office as Judge of Jackson County Court. In 1934 he was elected to the Senate where, in his second term, he was made famous by his committee's investigation of waste in war contracts. In 1944 he was elected to the Vice-Presidency, and when F.D.R. died five months after his election, Mr. Truman filled out the term. Against what appeared to be impossible odds, he was re-elected in 1948.

Mr. Truman, now in private life in Missouri, is over seventy. He is healthy, cheerful, and outspoken on current national problems and is hard at work writing his memoirs.

All or Nothing

BY WALTER WHITE

THE MORE I have thought about what I believe the more certain have I become that it is what I have been taught to believe. I have been blessed with great teachers. The first and greatest of them were my mother and father. As Negroes of quite modest means, in an often hostile environment in Georgia, they were buffeted from both sides because their skins were of such color they could have lived on either side of the racial fence. Through thrift and hard work they had provided for us children a modest but immaculate and attractive home. But neither envy nor hostility of poor whites or poor Negroes ever caused them to deviate one fragment of an inch from the stern code of ethical behavior they had established for themselves and their children.

The second body of teachers were the idealistic, courageous men and women who had given up better and safer jobs in the North to teach in Southern missionary schools like Atlanta University, from which my five sisters, my brother and I graduated. Theirs, too, was a stern moral code. Both my parents and they were devoted to the principle that compromise is not only evil but in the long run does not pay.

I am totally and irrevocably convinced that in personal behavior, political life and other areas of human activities, the seeds of decay begin to sprout the minute a man or nation begins to consider surrender of moral principle to attain a given end, however moral and desirable that goal may be. Naturally I have been assailed countless times for being an "all or nothing" person. I am proud to plead guilty to that charge.

A second article of faith to which I cling is that love of one's fellow human beings can conquer whatever obstacles he faces. In travelling more than two million miles in all parts of the world during the past thirty years, I have seen again and again what misery and degradation of the human spirit hate has brought to mankind. Its corrosive effect on the human mind and spirit, which has found expression in war, religious bigotry and racial schisms, has been so appalling as to convince me that the codes of behavior given by men like Jesus and Gandhi offer the only hope of our survival.

Therefore, I believe that no human being should ever be judged on the basis of race, creed, sex, religion, economic status or place of birth. To measure any man or to accept or reject him as friend by any other standard than his individual worth is to deny oneself the vast benefits which come from knowing fellow human beings as fellow human beings. My own life has been immeasurably enriched by knowing people, both famous and obscure, all over the world.

Finally, I believe it is imperative that we recapture that passion for human equality and justice which inspired the early Christians to create a world of ethical behavior to replace barbarism.

❦

◌§ WALTER WHITE, Executive Secretary of the National Association for the Advancement of Colored People, is one of the great Americans of our time. Born in Atlanta of poor but characterful parents, his first job paid him fifty cents a week. Later he worked as clerk for an insurance company and so helped to put himself through Atlanta University. Shortly thereafter he went to work for the NAACP and in 1932 succeeded as its acting head the late James Weldon Johnson, poet and author.

Because of his features and pigmentation Mr. White early had the opportunity to "pass," as the phrase is. He refused, and cast his lot with the Negro for whom he has fought hard and well throughout his lifetime. Mr. White published a novel in 1924— *The Fire in the Flint*, and in 1929, following a year abroad on a Guggenheim Fellowship, a book called *Rope and Faggot*, subtitled, *The Biography of Judge Lynch*. His autobiography, *A Man Called White*, came out in 1948.

Scholar from Childhood

BY NORBERT WIENER

I AM BY PROFESSION a working mathematician and natural scientist. I was destined to the career of scholar from childhood by my father. He was a scholar in the very different field of philological-historical research, and he imbued me—rather by example than by precept—with the duties and responsibilities of the scholar. These are an unswerving devotion to the truth, whatever it may be and however much it may cost to formulate and to utter it. Joined with this was an iron intellectual discipline which very soon became a self-discipline. It has compelled me to subject my own work to the most rigorous criteria of validity to which I would subject the work of anyone else, and to tear up mercilessly whatever I find to be faulty or insufficient.

I was brought up outside a formal religion, and I have never been able to bring myself to a thorough acceptance of any religion, not even that of the militant atheist. But I have realized through my own experience that no life can be satisfactory to me which does not recognize the intrinsic dignity of other human beings, whoever and wherever they may be, and which does not insist on the recognition of my own dignity by others.

I say "dignity," but what I mean by the word has nothing whatever to do with pomposity and is indeed its deepest enemy. Neither is dignity in any way inconsistent with humor and a cheerful attitude to life. I cannot indeed claim any thorough-going cheerfulness in these days of the external threats of Armageddon and the destruction of civilization, and of the internal threats which tend to put us all in spiritual blinders. It is easy to maintain a calm philosophy of life and a spiritual equanimity in a vacuum, or in an ivory tower. But whatever equanimity is left to us today is one which has to support itself against the shocks and alarms of a spiritual battle.

We are living in a world where there are many powerful forces definitely hostile to scholarship and to human dignity. If, like myself, a scholar happens to work in a field with engineering applications which may pay off in industry or in weapons of war, he is likely to find himself reduced to an impersonal place in a scientific machine which blunders along by its very mass and bulk. I cannot and do not accept such a life, for I prefer the right to make mistakes on a piece of paper and to come out of them with a better understanding of the truth, to the unwelcome privilege of participating in the expenditure of millions of dollars. The goose that lays the golden egg has become a Strasbourg goose nailed down by its feet to the floor of its coop and crammed with information—not cracked corn—to the end that from the degeneration of its brain—not its liver—a profitable commercial commodity may be drawn.

I have no belief in any knowledge of the truth that can be reached without a very real possibility of error, and I claim the privilege of entertaining not only unpopular but even definitely wrong ideas. It is only when I am thus free that I can satisfy myself of their wrongness and come to a belief which is more than a time-serving conformity chiefly prompted by a lust after the flesh pots of Egypt.

◆§§◆

◆§ NORBERT WIENER is nationally— and internationally—known as one of America's leading mathematicians and scientists. He is particularly identified today with the new science of cybernetics, dealing with communications, which he originated and named. Forty-five years ago he was widely celebrated as a child prodigy who was a college freshman at the age of eleven and a graduate student at fourteen. The roster of the colleges and universities at which he has studied, or lectured, is long, and includes Harvard, Columbia, Cambridge (England), Göttingen (Germany) and Copenhagen (Denmark).

Professor Wiener has taught mathematics at Massachusetts Institute of Technology since 1919, and now holds from that institution a roving commission to do any scientific work to which his creative impulse may lead him. He is the author of many books and papers on higher mathematics and scientific subjects. His most widely discussed work, *Cybernetics*, was published in 1948.

No Mortal Answer

BY CHARLES WYZANSKI

SOLITARINESS is the core of every man. And what he believes lies at the core. When overcome by emotion this inner loneliness vibrates, and its secrets can be discharged by love, by prayer, by meditation. But no one can stand deliberately before a microphone and make that intimate revelation from which emerges the understanding peace that surpasseth knowledge.

I can, however, try to give you the atmosphere in which my deeper self dwells. When I pause for reflection, I am aware of bipolar tensions. All the different aspects of me are arrayed on one side and are drawn to one magnetic field. Pulling at the other end are all the forces in the universe that are not part of me. And yet I feel not merely this separateness, but a strong togetherness between me and everything else that is.

I wish I could say that this view of my relationship to the universe had made me humble. Humility is the noblest fruit of introspection. It establishes defenses against pride—that sin which the orthodox church justly stamps as the foundation of all evil. But when I become concerned about the miserable creature that I am, I do not draw closer to God, or to the magnificence of His creation. I am only inflating my own importance in my own eyes.

Yet self-assessment is not self-defeating. Through intimate analysis, man recognizes more clearly that he is weak, and that he lives without protective boundaries, always dimly apprehensive of the impenetrable beyond. If man is to comprehend this further territory he must summon as his guide not reason, but mystic insight. And there is no guarantee that a reliable guide will come when called. Not having had any mystic experience myself, I formerly thought I could overleap the limitations of my knowledge, my reason, and my discernment by developing fortitude. I supposed that by inhibiting my desires and training my will, I could become immune to shock. But self-knowledge and self-discipline did not yield me a Stoic virtue and equanimity.

But experience prevents me from assuming that by mere volition, practice, and restraint, without grace, man can become his own commander. The fickleness of his human disposition stands prey not only to outside disasters, but also to internal pressures that he cannot distribute according to advance order. Nay, the order itself may produce not obedience, but revolution.

Have I then no authoritative answer to the universe's ultimate question? I have none. Indeed, I take it as inherent in the human dilemma that no mortal can have an answer that will fully and permanently allay doubt. And yet I dare to feel confident that to be even partially satisfactory, an answer must bear the seal of religious faith.

And what do I mean by religious faith? Surely more than a creed, a commandment, a metaphysical scheme. It is that inner compulsion persuading us that we are implicated in an enveloping mystery. It is that search for meaning, which though it never reaches its goal, gives life a structural unity. It is that constant nourishment of our own personal and community roots as the emotional source of spiritual courage. It is that inexpressible yearning toward the fulfillment of the undiscoverable purpose of the universe,—a purpose which when we are tuned to our most excruciatingly sensitive pitch, we firmly believe is unfolding before, and, in small part, through each of us.

◂§ CHARLES EDWARD WYZANSKI, JR. is District Judge for Massachusetts. Educated at Exeter and the Harvard Law School, he served as clerk to both Judge A. N. Hand and Judge Learned Hand, who, he says, gave him his professional canons, intellectual standards, and criteria of what makes a useful citizen. In 1933 F.D.R. appointed him a Solicitor of Labor for Secretary Frances Perkins. In 1935 Solicitor General Reed took him on his staff for arguments before the Supreme Court of the U.S. From 1937 to 1941 he reverted to private practice; but, after serving in Washington on the National Defense Mediation Board, he was appointed District Judge by President Roosevelt.

Judge Wyzanski makes annual trips to Europe on behalf of ILO. In 1943, as he phrases it, "I had the incredible luck to marry the happiest, most unspoiled and most lovable girl I have ever met. Living with her makes the whole year Spring."

They Can't Eat Us

BY JAKE ZEITLIN

WHAT I BELIEVE is not a matter of high-flown language; it is an operational problem related to how I try to live with my family, my friends, and my society.

I believe that I must govern my life by reason and I have the wish, which precedes the faith, that reason shall govern other men. I join Jefferson in the belief that tyranny over the minds and lives of men is evil and I try to avoid imposing my will or philosophy on others.

I believe in discipline, but only the fruitful discipline that is self-imposed. Some poets and philosophers have argued that man and his planet are doomed. I do not accept this as a condition of how I should live. If I were sure the world would end in ten days from Friday, I would start to build a house or write a poem.

I believe that I must accept my share of responsibility for what happens to me, including my accidents and mistakes.

I believe in human dignity and that dignity is worth keeping for myself so much that I will not impose indignities on others.

Fear is my direst enemy and next to fear, pride, which is the other face of vanity, and the twin of folly. I remember the old man of my boyhood in Texas who said once, "Boys, they can kill us but they can't eat us." I do not believe in returning the insult of others in kind. They cannot demean me, but I can demean myself. Therefore, I will not be governed by those who would deprive me of my dignity by threats, insults or flattery.

I believe that a good laugh does more good than a long face. Laughter is something I have had to learn from my good Dutch wife, whose ancestors have lived happily under gray skies for many years. It is easier for me to forgive a gay rogue than a serious fool.

My occupation as a bookseller is an expression of my beliefs. My days and nights are spent with books and bookish people.

Whatever brings knowledge to men, whatever raises their minds and emotions, whatever preserves the products of their imagination and their history, has value to me. The written and printed word survives persecution, book burning, censorship and fashions. When I sell a man a good book I am the happy transmitter of a precious thing and I feel I have justly earned my profit.

I believe in the scientific attitude above the unscientific, but I am not of the faith that science will save us. Science can free man from the physical hardships of nature but only a profound respect for the dignity of all humanity can free us from the misery of man.

Lastly, I believe that my wife, my children, and my fellow-workers are my truest judges. I cannot gain credit from them for what I am not. What I believe will have to stand the test of day-by-day living. They will know and, I hope, tell me truthfully.

JAKE ZEITLIN is a well-known dealer in rare books and art, and a former president of the American Antiquarian Booksellers Association, Southern California chapter. He also publishes books under the firm name of Zeitlin & Ver Brugge; and has lectured at the University of California at Los Angeles, and at the California Institute of Technology, on the history and philosophy of science, one of his special interests.

Mr. Zeitlin is the author of two volumes of verse, *For Whispers and Chants* and *More Whispers and Chants*, and has contributed articles to the *Reader's Digest*, the *Saturday Review of Literature* and numerous other periodicals. Born in Racine, Wisconsin, he grew up in Texas, but has lived most of his adult life in Southern California. Politics is another of his hobbies. He is a member of the Los Angeles County Democratic Central Committee, is married and has four children and two grandchildren.

Section II

IMMORTALS

The Beliefs of Twenty Immortals

MOST OF WHAT WE ARE TOLD about the immortals of history concerns their actions and achievements in their own times. We hear much less about their basic, personal beliefs. But they are immortal at least as much because of their beliefs as because of their creative achievements. The two are hardly separable.

What we of "This I Believe" dig for in every guest is his basic belief, since that is the essence of him. So it has been exciting to ask the authorities on our twenty immortals to bring us their beliefs. They have lived with these great men and women as friends, they have known them intimately, have made themselves their contemporaries.

You may wonder how we came to make up our list of twenty. We asked the guests who had appeared on the "This I Believe" radio program which of the immortals of history they would most wish to hear tell their beliefs. We have pretty closely followed their choice. We are not applying a yardstick to greatness and saying that these twenty are the greatest. They just came naturally to mind.

It happens that only two of them are ancients. Confucius and Socrates were shaping the concepts of men three to four hundred years before the Christian era. Next in sequence are Dante and da Vinci. Then follow Queen Elizabeth and Shakespeare. Benjamin Franklin follows; on the clock of history his America is only minutes away. So most of our figures are close to us in time. But however close, they shine already with the light that marks the historic great.

They would be the last to regard their beliefs as original with them. Indeed our oldest immortal, Confucius, taught that he was no more than the transmitter of the wisdom of the ancients. That gives us a hint about the time it has taken to accumulate the wisdom of the race. The trails go back and are lost in obscurity. They come closer and lead straight to the giants who shaped it and handed it on to us.

Most of us, like many of the immortals presented here, are products of the Christian way. Some of the statements made here, by and for the immortals, have been visibly woven of the teachings of Jesus Christ, and indeed the growth of our civilization is so woven. Christ's teaching of love, which includes love of enemies, is a practical teaching, one that helps and serves and forgives. The fatherhood of God must mean the brotherhood of man. "Whatsoever ye would that men should do to you, do ye even so to them."

More than four hundred years before this was spoken, Confucius had said the same thing, only his Golden Rule was in the negative: Don't do to others what you don't want them to do to you. Many of the central beliefs of the world's faiths have this near-identity.

Sometimes beliefs have divided men at terrible costs, and they continue to divide them. But men are more united than divided by beliefs and are more united than they may realize. As the world shrinks in the workshop of modern and practical science, the acceptance of this unity becomes the most urgent need in human affairs.

The great religions all teach the priority of spiritual over material riches. They all teach the worth of the individual and his capacity to grow nearer to God. And they all agree on the principle of unity, the unity of the universe, the unity of the human family. To this unity all men are taught that they belong. To help make progress toward it is a personal contribution that must come from each of us.

Edward R. Murrow

CONFUCIUS

by Will Durant

WOULD YOU LIKE to know what an old Chinese philosopher thinks of the world?

First, let me get rid of other worlds. I believe there are spiritual forces in the universe, but I cannot know the nature of supernatural beings, and this life is so interesting that I give no thought to death or the beyond.

My absorbing interest in life is in human character. Intellect is good, intelligence is better, but it is character that uses the intellect as its servant, and makes a man bad or good, weak or great.

I have tried to train character through education. I taught my students four subjects chiefly: history, that they might be inspired by the achievements of man, and restrained by learning his nature; poetry, that they might have imagination; music, that rhythm and grace might enter their souls; and manners, that they might become gentlemen. For when good manners decay the state begins to die.

I believe in the uncommon man; it is the uncommon man who begets new ideas, and offers new exemplars for our imitation. I do not know how to make all men equal; but if I can make good men able, or able men good, their example will raise the people to integrity and civilization.

I believe that education must do more for the uncommon man; that special training, above all training in character, should be given to the best students, in the hope of producing a higher type of man for human leadership: men who will be anxious to acquire truth rather than wealth or honors; who will be sincere with the facts, and not distort them with partisanship or dogma; who will never fawn upon those above them, nor ever scorn those below them; who will understand with sympathy the problems of other men; and who will never do to others what they would not have others do to them.

166

I believe in the force of example. The wise men of ancient China, when they wished to disseminate the highest virtues among mankind, first ordered well their own states. Wishing to order their states well, they first regulated their own families. Wishing to regulate their families, they first sought to cleanse their own hearts. Wishing to cleanse their hearts, they first sought to be sincere in their thinking. Wishing to be sincere in their thinking, they first extended their knowledge to the utmost.

Reform begins at home, and Utopia is nowhere except in the clean heart and understanding mind.

✦

Profile of Confucius

◄§ CONFUCIUS (literally Sir Foo Kung) was born in 551 B.C. and died seventy-two years later. He was perhaps the most influential teacher of all time, since he molded the thinking of the Chinese people for more than twenty centuries. But he was without training as a professional philosopher or even as a teacher. His own education came largely from his experience in the world of affairs.

His father was a magistrate in the dukedom of Lu, now Shantung. His mother was a peasant. His father died when he was three, and he was reared in great poverty. By the time he reached his majority he became a minor official, and he stayed with the bureaucracy until he was thirty-eight, when he resigned as a protest against the expulsion of the legitimate duke.

It was this act of protest that launched him on his teaching career. He gathered many disciples around him, and continued teaching with increasing success for twelve years. Then he was invited to take office again. He was first appointed magistrate, and after a year in office he was elevated to the highest position in the government open to a commoner. Here he was to run into difficulties due to his strengthening the legitimate authority of the Duke at the expense of the nobility. For this he was driven into exile. So once more he resumed his teaching. He remained abroad for thirteen years, increasing the number of his disciples. And at the age of sixty-seven he was invited back to the dukedom, and could go on teaching till his death. His disciples stayed on to be near his home and his tomb, and this assemblage developed into the first Chinese university, which retained its identity for eight centuries.

Confucius was not a great originator. He was at heart a traditionalist, and he supported the authority of the ancient sages. His teaching of ethics stressed two factors, "*li*"—the rules of proper conduct, and "*ren*"—benevolent love. Li included polite usages, court etiquette, state religious rituals, the code of gentlemanly conduct and ethical principles.

His staunchest belief was in good government, based on uprightness of rulers. If a ruler was good, he taught, his people would imitate him. Then the neighbors in adjoining tyrannies would move into the well-ruled country and it would grow strong. He laid small stress on strength built on military power. He believed in personal rule, as well as the rule of law, and taught that reform rightly should begin at the top. Thus he was a conservative in a feudal world, but his teachings of benevolent love have made his influence timeless.

❧

WILL DURANT's own statement of personal belief, and a short biographical sketch of him, will be found in the first section of this volume.

SOCRATES

by Gilbert Murray

WHAT A CROWD of people come to listen to me! You are as bad as the Athenians. Where do you come from? America: What is that? Found by Columbus; who was he? I never heard of him. A big country in the Atlantic Ocean? Oh, now I understand. We used to call your country Atlantis. It was rather well spoken of in Athens. A very pleasant life, they tell me; plenty of food and a great wish to learn. That is why you come to me? To learn? But I can't teach you anything. Oh, yes I know the oracle at Delphi said I was the wisest of men; but that I explained long ago. We none of us really know anything, but I am wise enough to know that I don't know anything, and other people think they know such a lot when they don't. They don't even know how to live; and they won't learn; and the clever people, the sophists, won't teach them but go off studying all kinds of useless things.

"What things?" Oh, all about the stars and the sun and the beginning of the world and so on. Take my master, Anaxagoras. He worked away, and at last said he had discovered that the Sun was not a god, but just a mass of white-hot metal, frightfully hot and enormously big. I used always to say to him: "Dear Master, all this may be true about the Sun. I don't see how you know, since you have never been there. But anyway you can't do anything about it. Why don't you try to know about men? You can see they don't know how to live. Why, they all say they want to be better, but they don't seem to know what they mean. I ask them, "What do you mean by better?" and they say, "Oh, wiser and braver and more just." And when I follow up with the simplest question "What is justice" or "What is wisdom," they don't know. They talk nonsense and contradict themselves. They used sometimes to say that they really knew, but couldn't quite find the words, because I confused them. So then I gave up their words, and simply looked at their actions. The result was just the same. They did not know how to live. They were constantly doing bad things. Why? Obviously because they did not know what was bad and what good. Men cannot possibly wish to be bad men rather than good; and if they sometimes are, it must be from ignorance, because they don't know.

I always wanted Anaxagoras or some of these very clever people to stop and teach them, instead of studying the sun and the moon. So at last I had to give up my life to trying to teach the men around me; at least, I could question them and make them think, think how they were living, think what they really meant by good and bad, just or unjust. A few understood and did think and were grateful. But most people hated it, and at last put me to death. It was quite unjust to kill me, for making them think and uprooting some of their false beliefs, but they thought it was just and right. They did not know.

"What false beliefs?" Oh, largely about politics. It was the Few against the Many, both very violent. The Few thought, because they were prosperous and successful, they knew best how to govern a city. But of course they did not really know. So they did the worst thing they could, they killed or banished those who had differed from them. Then the Democrats came back, and they did the worst thing they could, by killing or banishing the Few. The Democrats were very proud of themselves, and quite as foolish as the others. They proclaimed that all men were equal—a good man no better than a bad man; an uneducated man just as good as an educated. Indeed they actually held that the right people to manage a state were the masses of poor and unsuccessful people, who had not known how to manage their own lives!

Both sides were equally angry with me, though it happened to be the second which actually condemned me to death. I could have had a much lighter punishment if I had been willing to plead guilty and ask for it. But I was not guilty, so how could I say I was? Then I could have escaped; but that would have been to break the law. I couldn't do that. Besides how was I to know whether Death was a good thing for me or a bad thing? Many wise men hold that the soul is immortal. I reflected that I might very well enter a life much better than this life, and see the great men of the past, saints and heroes . . . and now of course I know much more, and can tell you . . . oh, I am sorry I see my time is up.

❧❦❧

Profile of Socrates

SOCRATES (469–399 B.C.) wrote nothing, and seems to have had a certain dislike of written words which were fixed and could not be changed. He felt that the pursuit of knowledge must be alive and moving, as it is in a spoken discussion. His thinking concentrated on human or social problems. What is wisdom? What is virtue? And how can man attain a good life? He had a great conviction of man's lack of real knowledge of his own nature and surroundings. He himself, he said, really knew nothing; and he delighted in showing that those who professed to have expert knowledge had nothing more than "opinions," and very confused opinions at that. We hear of his wit, his courage and endurance as a soldier, his stubborn refusal to obey an unjust order either from the regular democratic government or from the revolutionary oligarchy.

Socrates gave no lectures, but taught always by question and answer, applying, as Aristotle says, two principles of research: first, Definition and secondly, Induction. He challenged all sorts of philosophers, sophists and politicians, and his conversations became a regular amusement to listeners. He made an immense impression on his contemporaries.

Little is known of Socrates' private life. He married Xantippe, on whom legend has conferred a reputation as a shrew, though on no known evidence.

It is known that some of his leading pupils were involved in two revolutions against the democracy, and though granted amnesty after their defeat, ill feeling vented itself on Socrates. He was accused of "not worshipping the gods of Athens but other strange gods" and of "corrupting the minds of young men." He refused to plead guilty or to give up his lifelong search for truth, refused to ask for a light punishment, refused a plan of escape which his friends prepared. The death penalty was a draught of hemlock, and Plato, in the dialogue *Phaedo* has recorded what professes to be his last conversation with a few friends in the prison, mostly on the problem of the immortality of the soul. With perfect serenity he discusses the problem, reaching no certain conclusion, till the jailer, whom he had always treated as a friend, brings the poison, and his friends, one after the other, break down in tears. "Such was the end," says Phaedo, "of the man whom, of all I have known, I should call the wisest and most just and best."

☙❦❧

GILBERT MURRAY is probably the world's leading Greek scholar, as well as a poet, dramatist and international publicist. He was born in Sydney in 1866, going to England from Australia as a boy of eleven. He attended Merchant Taylors' School and St. John's College, Oxford. When he was twenty-two, he was elected a Fellow of New College, later became a professor of Greek at Glasgow University and then, for twenty-eight years, Regius Professor of Greek at Oxford.

For many years he was chairman of the League of Nations Union and he now serves as joint president of the U. N. Assocation of Great Britain.

In his writings, as in his daily life, he has tempered his devotion to Greek studies with a deep concern for world affairs. In addition to numerous verse translations of early Greek plays and studies of Greek literature, his works include *Liberality and Civilization* (1938) and *From the League to the U.N.* (1947).

DANTE

by Domenico Vittorini

I BELIEVE in courage, patience and faith, for they have always helped me in facing the difficulties of my earthly existence. I am a man without a country, exiled from my beloved Florence, wandering over Europe, from city to city, from court to court, in search of a livelihood. I have tasted how bitter is the bread of other people and I have learned what a hard road it is to go up and down other people's stairways. I am without family and penniless. Before the sad spectacle of history and of daily existence, it is very hard to keep intact one's faith in God. Courage is not enough. We need patience, too, that we may see the whole of the pattern that God weaves out of the passions of men. But only faith has kept me above the muddy waters of life. Ever so often, I have felt resentment and rebellion surge in my heart, my brain, my very throat, almost strangling me. Yet, through faith, I have never lost sight of the luminous peak of Truth, a humble word for God. Man without faith is like a sailor without a compass, plying the waters of an uncharted sea.

I am grateful to have received from the Lord, Father of all men, a stout heart. Somehow, I never feel lost before perfidious men. I disdainfully look at them and my contempt for those who rely on injustice and fraud is almost as great as that which fills my heart when I meet featureless persons of whom I am never sure as to what they really are: good or bad, religious or godless, friends or enemies, men of my party or of that of my political opponents. The world is full of them, and to a man who believes in the ethical nature of life and in the necessity of ethical conduct, nothing is more offensive than to have dealings with such sordid persons. They speak with garbled words, they cover the meaning of their many wicked deeds by accompanying them with a few good ones, thus perverting virtue for the sake of vice. The Lord does not reserve for them a place either in Hell or in Heaven. Whatever good they may have done in life will not be rewarded by His justice, and whatever wrong they may have done will not receive His compassion.

Endowed by nature with an unbending character, I have always made a sharp distinction between right and wrong. To me, the greatest and most hateful sin is that of betrayal. I know traitors of all kinds: of kinsmen, of fatherland, of those who have been received under one's roof, of benefactors, and I shudder whenever I think of the icy coldness that must bind their hearts. Since I am convinced that the evil that man perpetrates is his own punishment, these traitors, I fancy, in the life to come, will be immersed in the frozen waters of an icy lake, just as the tyrants and perpetrators of war will be steeped in the blood which they have spilled.

As part of my faith, I believe, too, that love is the positive aspect of life. I have always carried in my heart my love for a gentle and exquisite girl by the name of Beatrice, whom I worshipped from afar and who died when very young, leaving her image engraved on my heart. Only she teaches me to seek consolation from the soft light of the stars whenever I feel forsaken by men. She has taught me that a noble woman destroys through love all the elements of triviality and even vulgarity that are inherent in our nature. She lifts to a plane of perfection the yearning of the human heart.

Since my exile, I have been engaged in writing the biography of my soul. For years, day by day, I have consigned to this kind of intellectual diary my innermost thoughts and feelings, distilling in it, drop by drop, all my heart and soul. I shall call it *The Comedy*, especially because I want reflected in it life as I know it, with its diverse and baffling aspects. I shall recount, too, my just pride in having lived through it with courage, patience, and faith, taking back to the Lord, untarnished, my belief in Life.

Profile of Dante

⋑ DANTE ALIGHIERI is the greatest of Italian poets and usually is rated among the half dozen greatest poets of all time. He was master of all the fields of learning open to his generation. In writing his chief poetical works in Italian, instead of Latin, he anchored that language for the first time as a great medium of artistic expression.

He was born in Florence, in 1265, of a noble Guelph family in somewhat straitened circumstances. He received an education well-rooted in the classics and in Provençal poetry. He also studied drawing and music. In 1289, he fought at the battle of Campaldino in which Florence was victorious over the city of Arezzo. In 1292 he married Gemma Donati, and had four children by her, two boys and two girls.

He met, when very young, Beatrice Portinari, a girl of a noble and wealthy family, whom he knew but slightly, but for whom he conceived an overpowering love that lasted all his life, independent of and above the dutiful love that he had for his wife. In 1290 he wrote the *Vita Nuova* (New Life), applying to Beatrice the Provençal concept of courtly love.

From 1295 to 1302 he was absorbed in the government of Florence. He was one of six officials who had charge of keeping peace between the two political parties. He had entered politics by passing to the conservative party of the Ghibellines, that in Florence was known as the White Party. The clash of Pope Boniface VIII with Philip the Beautiful of France and Edward of England, in 1300, paved the way for the defeat of the White forces in Florence in 1302, bringing about their exile as well as Dante's.

During his exile he was without his family, penniless, and he was forced to earn his livelihood by serving in various courts in northern Italy in diplomatic missions and as a courtier. During the last years of his life he was at Ravena, where he completed his *Divine Comedy* and died at the age of fifty-six in 1321.

During his exile, he wrote three major philosophical works: *Il Convivio* (The Banquet), *De Vulgari Eloquentia* (About the Vernacular), and *De Monarchia* (About the Monarchy). *La Divina Commedia* (The Divine Comedy) is one of the greatest works of world literature. The original title was merely *The Comedy*, but Dante's contemporaries called it "divine," and so it has been known to posterity.

◄§ DOMENICO VITTORINI was born in Italy in 1892 and was educated at the University of Rome, where he received his Doctor of Letters in 1916. Shortly thereafter, he came to the United States to study and to teach at Princeton, and then at Temple University. For the past thirty-five years, he has taught Romance languages at the University of Pennsylvania. He has been president of the American Association of Teachers of Italian and he is associate editor of Symposium (University of Syracuse) and the *Modern Languages Journal* (University of Michigan). For many years he has led a course on "Great Books" at the Curtis Institute of Music in Philadelphia. Among his works are *The Modern Italian Novel* (1930), *The Drama of Luigi Pirandello* (1935) and *Modern Drama in Italy* (1947). He is also the author of an Italian grammar, an Italian reader, and literary articles on Dante as a thinker and a poet.

LEONARDO DA VINCI

by Antonina Vallentin

I BELIEVE that my destiny was marked at the very outset of my life by a dream I had when still in my cradle. It was of a great bird that flew upon me and struck me several blows on the lips. I became obsessed with thoughts of that bird. I aspired to ride it one day like a swan as it rose from Monte Cecero—Swan-back mountain—near Florence. It would fill the world with amazement as it flew upward into the sky, bringing renown to my birthplace. I went on to study the flight of the birds, the carrying-power of their wings, the nature of air and the eddies of the winds. So I grew to realize that every achievement of man had to be based on a study of the achievements of nature. The genius of a man may make many inventions, using various instruments to accomplish the same result. But he will never discover a more beautiful, more economical, or a more direct way than that employed by nature. For in nature's inventions nothing is ever superfluous.

When I contemplate the human eye I find myself marveling at the work of God. For it is through the eye, as the window of the body, that the soul enjoys the beauty of the world. Through a small aperture comes the vision of the whole universe. The eye measures the distance and dimensions of the stars. The eye is the prince of mathematicians; it inspires the certainty of science. Whoever would imagine such a marvel or explain such a miracle? It has made possible the creation of architecture, perspective, and the divine art of painting.

I came also to realize that God grants his possessions only at the price of great effort. No mastery is greater than over oneself and for that, if it is to be complete, one must become free of all bonds and ties of feeling. In my youth I thought: If there is to be no such thing as love, what is left in life? But now I know that the greater the feeling of the love, the greater the sacrifice.

176

I believe that the desire to know is natural to all men of good will. As unused iron rusts, as standing water fouls, the mind deteriorates without use. Truth compared to untruth is like light compared with darkness. Thus the humblest truth about a familiar object is infinitely superior to the sophistications and falsehoods of lofty speeches on high and vague subjects. Indeed love is the more ardent for knowledge, for it is made more certain by the complete understanding of the elements that make up the thing loved. But if one is to experience mastery he must be solitary. Only if he is alone does he belong entirely to himself. To have the companionship of even a single person is to belong only half to oneself, and this becomes less and less as one's social life is extended. A painter more than anyone should be solitary.

Nor should a painter allow himself to be tempted by material riches. I do not need a great deal of money to provide the things I actually require. If I have a superfluity of money, that is, money I do not use, it is not mine. It is not maintaining me; it is in other hands. I well know the scorn people had for me when they thought I was poor, but I knew that I was poor only if I desired many things. I knew that the desire for material riches meant to be deprived of the desire for wisdom, which is the real food of the soul. The painter-philosopher must have this well in mind.

As for painting let me say that I strongly disapprove of it being consigned—as some are doing—to the mechanical arts. The painter who paints only by rote is like a mirror that reproduces everything put before it, but knows really nothing about it. I believe that painting is the greatest of all intellectual efforts. He is a poor master whose work runs beyond his intellect. When the painter strives for perfection, his intellect towers over his work.

Only God and time can limit true creativeness. I had to learn to be patient. I had to be patient if I cared to go unharmed on my way. Patience protects from wrongs, as clothes do against cold. As one heaps on the clothing against the growing cold, one should add to his patience in the face of great wrongs. In that way even these are made powerless to vex the mind. I believe that the person who feels that what he wants can be had next spring or next summer or next year, is unwittingly courting his own destruction. In utilizing my days I have striven to leave an enduring memory of my having passed through life. In that way I have not lived in vain.

⁌⧉⧉⧉⧉⧉⧉⧉⧉⧉⧉⧉⧉⧉⧉⧉⧉⧉⧉⧉⧉⧉⧉⧉⧉⧉⧉⧉⧉⧉

Profile of Da Vinci

⁌ "Nature cannot again produce one like him . . ."

That evaluation of LEONARDO DA VINCI was given to his family by his favorite pupil, Francesco Melzi, on the day that da Vinci died, May 2, 1519. The great genius of the arts and the sciences, born in Vinci in Italy, finished his work and his days in France. He died in Amboise, historic city on the River Loire, at the age of sixty-seven.

Nature lavished her most precious gifts on Leonardo. He had "the most beautiful face in the world" according to a historian of that day. And the biographer Vassari recorded that Leonardo, "with the splendour of his mien, brought refreshment to every downcast spirit." He had a voice of "captivating tone," and those who heard it could not forget it.

His impressive appearance was matched by his marvelous memory, which retained everything that he saw. Whatever he attempted, he achieved without difficulty. Everything within reach of a creative spirit of his times was mastered by him—painting, sculpture and architecture in its widest range. He designed not only temples of worship, but also prefabricated houses; humble dwellings and sumptuous palaces. He drew plans for entire towns which were to be what he called "companions of beauty."

But the great dreamer was also signally practical. He tried to improve the conditions of life in his time, to shorten the processes of production by designing machines and re-shaping tools. It was an era of wars, so Leonardo had to give attention to the demands of war. He invented explosives and bombs. He drew plans for tanks, submarines, even airplanes.

Leonardo pried into the riddles of nature, delved into the immemorial past of the earth. He learned the laws that govern the universe, he studied the evolution of the sun, the moon and the stars. His curiosity was perhaps stronger than his creative need, and it pressed him to efforts that could not be completed within the span of one human life. An encyclopedic knowledge remained buried in his note-books. The cathedrals he designed were overwhelming to his contemporaries and never erected. Many of his pictures remained unfinished, because he had decided they were not sufficiently beautiful. But the tremendous legacy of art and science that he left gives him now, nearly five centuries later, a stature hardly ever surpassed in history.

❧❦❧

ANTONINA VALLENTIN is a cosmopolitan. She was born a Pole, lived half her life in Germany, half in France, and has become even better known as biographer in the United States than in Europe. Her first work to win world renown was her biography of Stresemann. She had become intimately informed about Weimar Germany as correspondent for German and foreign newspapers in Berlin, and her Berlin salon became a political center. Later she moved to Paris, where she married the French playwright, Julien Luchaire. Here she continued her literary and political work. Her biographies of Heine and Leonardo da Vinci followed and brought her further recognition. The one on Da Vinci was a Book-of-the-Month selection at its publication. She remains active in French affairs as editor of *L'Europe Nouvelle*. She is a master of languages, speaking and writing in English, French, German and Italian.

QUEEN ELIZABETH I

by John E. Neale

I WAS BORN a child of the Reformation and trained by the best scholars of the English Renaissance. I passed through a stern school of experience. My mother's execution I was mercifully too young to grieve over; but my brother's reign brought further tragedy, and under my Catholic sister my position as the hope of the Protestant cause placed me in constant peril and brought me near to the block. This experience, and my womanly nature, have bred in me a desire for tolerance, clemency and peace.

When I came to the throne I was expected to reign, not rule. Statecraft was considered no business for women. I was aware of this prejudice, but I knew my own qualities. I had a longing—the greater for being a woman—to do some act that would make my fame spread abroad in my lifetime, and afterwards occasion memorial for ever.

Europe was torn with religious conflict. My country was small, impoverished, but of vital strategic importance. If Protestantism could have been destroyed in England, the Counter-Reformation might have prevailed everywhere. In consequence my throne and my life have been repeatedly threatened by plots at home and dangers from abroad.

My councilors and parliaments, in defense of faith and country, have clamored for inquisitions and extreme penalties against my Catholic subjects. While nourishing ardent loyalty, I have constantly resisted fanaticism. My guiding principle has been to open no windows into men's souls.

My reign has not been easy, but my trust has ever been in God. There liveth not any that may more justly acknowledge themselves infinitely bound unto Him than I, whose life He has miraculously preserved, beyond my merit, from a multitude of perils and dangers. As for religion, if I were not persuaded that mine were the true way of God's will, God forbid I should live to prescribe it to others.

Under God, I have placed my chiefest strength and safeguard in the loyal hearts of my subjects. There is no jewel which I set before this: this I count the glory of my crown, that I have reigned with their loves. It is my most inward joy that no prince ever governed a more faithful, valiant and loving people; to whom I wish, that they that wish them best may never wish in vain.

To be a king and wear a crown is a thing more glorious to them that see it than those that bear it. For myself, I was never so much enticed with the glorious name of a king as delighted that God had made me His instrument to maintain His truth and glory and to defend this kingdom from peril, dishonor, tyranny and oppression.

Experience has taught me that a sovereign must sacrifice personal affection when the safety of the kingdom is in question. I have denied myself the normal consolations of my sex: romance and children. I have had to consent to the execution of those whom I would rather have spared: in particular, my cousin Mary, Queen of Scots. But neither fear nor malice has affected my judgment. I know I am but mortal; and so I prepare myself to welcome death whensoever it shall please God to send it. We princes are set upon a stage in the sight and view of all the world: a spot is soon spied in our garments, a blemish quickly noted in our doings.

This kingdom has had many noble and virtuous princes. In love, care, sincerity and justice I will compare with any prince that ever it had or shall have.

Profile of Queen Elizabeth I

⋑ ELIZABETH I, Queen of England, was the daughter of Henry VIII. She succeeded to the throne in November, 1558, at the age of twenty-five, after the short but troubled reigns of her brother, Edward VI, and her sister, Mary. She died in March, 1603, in the forty-fifth year of her reign. She has given her name to an age, which from her own time to the present has been regarded as perhaps the most brilliant in English history.

William Shakespeare, Francis Bacon, Spenser, Sir Philip Sidney, Drake, Hawkins and Raleigh are immortal names—bright stars in a dazzling galaxy of great men. Drake's circumnavigation of the globe and the defeat of the Spanish Armada are highlights in an epic story of achievement. The tragedy of Mary Queen of Scots and the meteoric rise and fall of the Earl of Essex are the most dramatic episodes in a reign crowded with drama.

The Queen herself was the central figure of her age, the inspiration of all its brilliance. As "England's Eliza" and "Gloriana" a cult grew round her in her own lifetime, and after her death she passed into national legend. For well over a century the day of her accession to the throne was celebrated by English Protestants as the Birthday of the Gospel; and to this day tales are told about her which are pure folk-story.

Her personality has always baffled historians. In earlier days, before the emancipation and higher education of women, scholars were apt to attribute the amazing success of her policies to her able statesmen— as her statesmen themselves were apt to attribute it to miracle. Recent research has transferred the responsibility and credit to her.

Hers was a revolutionary age, dominated by the clash of rival ideologies—Catholicism and Protestantism—troubled by passion and fear, persecution, civil and international wars, an age very like our own, even to the menace of a "cold war" and a "fifth-column."

If, at the opening of the reign, an impartial observer had attempted to prophesy about the future, he would have considered it doubtful whether her Protestant regime could survive in so weak and petty a kingdom. That she would humble the greatest power in Europe— Spain—and become the most renowned sovereign of her time would have seemed incredible.

JOHN ERNEST NEALE is a leading British historian whose knowledge and understanding of the first Queen Elizabeth is recognized by scholars to be unexcelled. He was born in 1890, was educated at Liverpool and London Universities. In 1925 he became a professor of modern history at Manchester University and, since 1927, he has been Astor Professor of English History at London University. His recent works include *The Age of Catherine de Medici* (1943), *The Elizabethan House of Commons* (1949), and, published last year, *Elizabeth I and Her Parliaments 1559–1581*. He was Ford's Lecturer at Oxford 1941–2 and Raleigh Lecturer at the British Academy in 1948. He is a member of the American Academy of Arts and Sciences, a member of the Editorial Board, History of Parliament Trust, and a trustee of the London Museum. His biography, *Queen Elizabeth*, published in 1934, was awarded the James Tait Black Memorial Prize.

WILLIAM SHAKESPEARE

by Ivor Brown

I BELIEVE that a man should rise in the world, adventure in new things to the top of his bent, and not stay profitless at home. Yet it were well that he should come back at last and end where he began. I left Stratford because my ambition drove me and a hard blow it was for my parents, my wife and my children when I was resolute to join the players and hazard all in so hazardous a calling. But I believed in myself, as a man must. I went, I wrote, I conquered. I could soon come back to the big house I had bought for my own people and to the lands beside the Avon that I own and love. I had proved that my belief was just. It is not an ugly vanity to have self-confidence. There can be no vigor of life, no creation of fine things, unless a man trust in himself.

We must all return to our roots, on the earth before we die and under the earth thereafter. I shall hope for burial in my parish church of Stratford. I have held to the new reformed religion of my time. My mother was of the Old Faith. But I care not greatly for the names and divisions of creeds. It is the broad way of life and not the narrow point of credence that makes and marks the man.

I believe in degree, authority, and order. In reading the chronicles of my country in order to make plays out of those happenings, I saw England torn by rebellions and civil wars. I saw the sceptre of monarchy turned into the rod of tyranny. I saw murderous division and brother killing brother. But under the Tudors there was order imposed and security won. A man could be safely master of his own, live at peace, and reap where he had sown. So I believe in the power of the Crown to check the bloody dissensions of the nobles and to be a firm example to the slippery commons who run from one idol to another.

I have seen rank abused and crimes pardoned in the rich that were fiercely punished in the poor. I have seen the robes of white fur cover the black heart of guilt. I have spoken of these vices in my plays, even when they were acted in the Court. But I suffered no harm. I have believed in justice, and not in vain.

I have loved the great city of London where I was poor at first and prospered later. I have loved the plays and the players, and the power of poets to sway the minds and hearts of men. I have loved work and I have worked, often through the long, hot nights of the city, until my brain was beating and my body vexed. I have believed in loyalty. No other writer stayed with one fellowship as I did. For twenty years I was their man, in acting, in writing, and in counsel. In all our disputations, for artists will ever be quarrelers as well as comrades, I have believed in Dick Burbage and my companions of the craft; and they, I can say with pride and gratitude, have believed in me.

In London I was sometimes wanton with those wantoning. I have loved beauty in all sorts, not least the beauty of women. But I have learned how an excess of love can waste the spirit and dull the senses. I believe that the flesh is lovely as a flower and withers like a flower. In Stratford I have come back to the flowers forever renewing themselves in the field and garden, and here, I believe, is my health and my fulfillment.

I believe in freedom, the freedom to own, and I am a lover of my lands as well as of my people. I believe in the beauty and the glory of words. This love of language has been the very stuff of all my being. I have believed in the splendor of laughter. Man may be born to sorrow, but he has his remedy, which is to laugh when he may. I can boast that I have done what few will do. I have laughed at myself, at my young follies and my old foibles.

So, though I have been through darkness and known the treachery of pomp and power and the frailty of human hearts, I can relish the rich and gusty humors of mankind. Out of pain does poetry spring. But it is mirth that ripens the fruit of it. I shall end with a smile.

Profile of William Shakespeare

◆§ WILLIAM SHAKESPEARE was born in 1564 into the competitive, litigious, acquisitive society of Elizabethan Warwickshire. His mother was more of an aristocrat than his father, a merchant in leather goods. He went to the Latin Grammar School at Stratford-upon-Avon. Later on he may have been a schoolmaster or apprenticed to a lawyer, or both. At eighteen he married a farmer's daughter, Anne Hathaway. Although he had a wife and three children to keep, he later abandoned security and took a chance with the players, whose calling was despised, on tour and in London.

He was quickly acclaimed as a "factotum," that is to say he both acted and wrote, first patching up other men's work and then developing his own. At the age of thirty he was one of the leading men of the Lord Chamberlain's Men; this very successful troupe was afterwards taken over by King James I as the King's Men. With this company he stayed through all his working life.

In 1596, when he was only thirty-two, he had become rich enough to buy the largest house in Stratford for his family. He also helped his father to recover the family's coat of arms and to style himself "Gentleman." He steadily invested in land in Stratford, and, though he must have been working in London most of the time, he remained at heart a countryman with a passion for possessing his own acres.

He had been a favorite of the wealthy Lord Southampton, to whom he made dedication of his poetry, and knew the life of the town from its social summit to the rough-and-tumble of the taverns. He had a black period, soon after 1600, when he wrote tragedies only.

About 1608 (aged forty-four), he seems to have recovered his calm and spent more of his time in Stratford with his wife and two daughters. (His only son died in 1596 at the age of eleven.) He matured in mental serenity, happy in his possessions and his friendships. He died in 1616 at the age of fifty-two.

◆§ IVOR JOHN CARNEGIE BROWN has for the past forty years done much to shape the dramatic tastes of England. He was born in Penang in 1891, was educated at Cheltenham and Balliol College, Oxford, and entered the Home Civil Service. He soon resigned to take up literary pursuits and, in 1919, he became the London drama critic for the *Manchester Guardian*. For the next twenty-three years, while continuing in this capacity, his writings also appeared in a variety of other British publications—*Saturday Review, Punch, Week End Review* and the *Observer*. In 1942 he was made editor of the *Observer*.

His sense of responsibility to the current world as well as his knowledge of the history of the theater is revealed in a score of works including *The Meaning of Democracy* (1919), *Heart of England* (1935) and *Shakespeare* (1949).

BENJAMIN FRANKLIN

by Henry Butler Allen

WHEN I WAS a boy, a book entitled *Essays to Do Good* had an influence on my conduct throughout life. It led me to set a greater value on the character of a doer of good than on any other kind of reputation.

My parents in Boston had early given me religious impressions and brought me through childhood piously in a dissenting way. I grew convinced that truth, sincerity and integrity in dealings between man and man were of the utmost importance to the felicity of life; and I formed resolutions to practice them while I lived.

My early thinking led directly into my matured convictions. I had never doubted the existence of the Deity; that He had made the world, and governed it by His providence; and the most acceptable service to God was the doing good to man; that our souls are immortal; and that all crime will be punished, and virtue rewarded, either here or hereafter. These I consider the essentials of every religion. And, being ground in all the religions we have in our country, I respect them all, though with different degrees of respect. For I find them more or less mixed with other articles which, without any tendency to inspire, promote, or confirm morality, served principally to divide us, and make us unfriendly to one another.

By the time I was twenty-two I had become firmly convinced that to carry out my conviction about a useful life, I must arrive at moral perfection. As I know, or thought I knew, what was right and wrong, I did not see why I might not always do one and avoid the other. I was then very young, for now I know that while perfection is not possible—striving for it is good and does good.

But as a boy I started a plan to make myself perfect. This plan I kept to all my life. I enumerated the moral virtues I wanted to acquire in a little book—one to a sheet.

I concentrated on one virtue for each week successively. I prayed every morning. And before going to bed I would mark by a spot every fault I committed respecting that virtue that day. I was surprised to find myself fuller of fault than I imagined.

Here are some examples of them. Can you improve on them?

Temperance—Eat not to dullness; drink not to elevation.

Silence—Speak not but what may benefit others or yourself; avoid trifling conversation.

Order—Let all your things have their places; let each part of your business have its time.

Resolution—Resolve to perform what you ought; perform without fail what you resolve.

Frugality—Make no expense but to do good to others or yourself; that is, waste nothing.

Industry—Lose no time; be always employed in something useful; cut off all unnecessary actions.

Sincerity—Use no hurtful deceit; think innocently and justly.

Moderation—Avoid extremes; forbear resenting injuries so much as you think they deserve.

Tranquillity—Be not disturbed at trifles.

Humility—Imitate Jesus and Socrates.

In reality there is perhaps nothing so hard to subdue as pride. Disguise it, struggle with it as much as one pleases, it is still alive. Even if I could conceive I had completely overcome it, I should probably be proud of my humility.

I have enemies—some in England who are enemies as an American—some in America who are enemies as Minister Plenipotentiary—some are enemies of my ideas. But there is not one enemy of Ben Franklin, the man. This, my friends, is, in old age, a comfortable reflection.

Profile of Benjamin Franklin

≈§ BENJAMIN FRANKLIN, one of the foremost statesmen, writers and scientists of his time, was born in Boston in 1706. As the youngest of seventeen children, he was slated for the ministry. But funds gave out, and he had to go to work after two years of formal education. He was apprenticed to an older brother as a printer. But he became dissatisfied and, at seventeen, moved to Philadelphia. Here he worked as printer for many years, set up his own shop and by the time he was forty felt that he could retire from active business and devote himself to science. By that time he had done remarkable research in the nature of electricity, which had won him international recognition.

But Franklin found the calls of civic duty too great for him to absorb himself in science. In Philadelphia he organized the first real fire-fighting company. He was appointed deputy postmaster for the colonies. He organized street-lighting and street-cleaning. He served on the Philadelphia Council. He organized military defense for Philadelphia during the trouble with the French and Indians and, as a colonel, led a regiment into the Lehigh Valley.

In 1757 he went to England as an agent for the Pennsylvania Assembly in a case of the citizens against the proprietaries of the province. Later, as the dispute of the colonies with the English Government broadened, he returned to England to represent Georgia, New Jersey and Massachusetts as well as Pennsylvania. He returned to Philadelphia in 1775, as secession drew near, and was immediately elected to the Second Continental Congress. He was made chairman of the Pennsylvania Committee for the Defense of the Province. The next year he served on the committee which drafted the Declaration of Independence.

As soon as hostilities began, he was back in Europe successfully soliciting financial and material help from France and Holland. At the end of the war, as plenipotentiary, he had a leading part in negotiating the treaty of peace with Great Britain. On his return to America, in 1785, he was immediately elected President of Pennsylvania, and two years later was delegate to the convention which wrote the Constitution of the United States.

In his originality, inventiveness, the breadth of his knowledge and extent of his patriotic services, Franklin was one of the most remarkable men of any era. He found the fullest scope for his genius with the band of illustrious men who created the American republic.

◆§ HENRY BUTLER ALLEN, executive vice president and director of the Franklin Institute of Philadelphia, is recognized as an outstanding authority on the life of Benjamin Franklin. He started out as a metallurgical engineer after graduating from the Columbia School of Mines in 1911. His first job was as United States examiner of iron and steel in the Port of New York. Later he held a number of important posts in private industry, coming to the Franklin Institute in 1935. He has occupied his present position and edited the Institute's *Journal* since 1947.

During World War I, Mr. Allen served as a captain in the A.E.F. World War II brought him the Presidential Medal for Merit. He has been given honorary degrees by Temple University, Drexel Institute of Technology and by Amherst College where he once was a student. The father of four married daughters, he lives in Chestnut Hill, Pennsylvania. His office is, appropriately enough, on Benjamin Franklin Parkway in Philadelphia.

THOMAS JEFFERSON

by Claude Bowers

I BELIEVE in the philosophy and ethics of Christ as expressed in his own words, that never from any source has come a purer or more sublime system of morality than is to be found in the four Evangelists; but believing that a man's religion is the reflection of his heart and soul, I cannot scorn or hate the religious creed and philosophy of others. Intolerance is the offspring of bigotry and ignorance, and I believe it has no place in the minds or hearts of rational men. The proscription or persecution of sects other than our own cannot be justified by the creed of Christ.

I believe it impossible for the human mind to contemplate the marvels of the universe without believing in the pre-existence of a Creator. And while I cannot visualize existence after this life on earth, I believe that when we leave our sorrows and suffering bodies we may ascend in essence to a happy meeting with those we have loved and lost. I believe in intellectual freedom, in the right to think, to write and speak as one feels without fear, to investigate without restraint, for only when the spirit is free and the mind unshackled can the race move onward to higher and better things.

I believe that the average man is moved by honest impulses, and that furnished with the facts he can be depended upon to reach rational conclusions, and on that belief I base my philosophy of democracy. I believe in the dignity of man and that he is no less worthy of respect if his skin in black, brown or yellow. Consequently, I believe that serfs and slaves are an abomination in the eyes of God.

I know that no nation can be both ignorant and free and that education can illuminate the darkness and make men free, and in consequence of this belief I believe that any society or state that ignores its duty to place education within the reach of the humblest is failing in a sacred obligation. I believe that to starve public education is to go far toward extinguishing the flame of freedom.

189

I believe in that peace among peoples that reason and justice can maintain when free of prejudice, bigotry and hate, since even successful wars bring destruction and demoralization and sow the seeds of future struggles and weaken the foundation of civilization. I have always hated war.

I believe that friendship is the most blessed possession man can have, and that in our friends we should cherish what is good in them and look with tolerance on what we think bad. The happiest moments of my life have been in the flow of affection among friends. I believe it better to live in a modest home with my books, family and a few friends than to move in the artificial atmosphere of Versailles. I believe that there is more lasting satisfaction in the woods, the wilds, the independence of the mountains than in the brilliant pleasures of Paris.

I truly believe that those who labor in the earth are closer to God than those who dwell amidst the distractions of crowded places with no time for meditation on elemental things, and that truth and sanity live close to the soil, and that soul-searching and creative thought comes easiest in the open spaces under the sky.

I believe in the civilizing influence of beauty, in houses that are not mere habitations to shut out the wind and rain, but structures of art and charm, and in surrounding them with refreshing lawns, with flowers and shrubbery, since these permeate the spirit and drive out hateful thoughts.

On these beliefs I base my relations with the Creator and my fellowmen. This is my personal philosophy.

Profile of Thomas Jefferson

◦§ THOMAS JEFFERSON, the greatest philosopher of American democracy, was born in Virginia in 1743. Before entering the Continental Congress, he had achieved national fame as a master of polemics in a pamphlet setting forth the grievances of the American colonies, and in Virginia's reply to the proposals of Lord North. Consequently, in his thirty-third year, he was unanimously designated to draft the Declaration of Independence. In the preamble of this immortal document he set forth in a few words the philosophy of democracy.

Returning to Virginia and its Legislature, he assumed the leadership of the democratic forces and fought through radical reforms that pulled down the sustaining pillars of feudalism by ending the Law of Primogeniture and Entail; by separating the Church and State; by humanizing the penal laws; by laying the foundation for the public school system of today; and by striking a deadly blow at religious intolerance with his immortal Ordinance of Religious Toleration.

He was our Minister in Paris when the Constitution, fresh from the Convention, reached his desk and he was shocked to find that, while it provided for a strong and stable government, it made no provision for the protection of the people against the abuse of power. He demanded the incorporation of a Bill of Rights and the first Congress wrote it into the Constitution in the first ten amendments.

Recalled by Washington to head his Cabinet, he laid the foundation of our foreign policy. He was Vice President when Congress enacted the Alien and Sedition laws, making a mockery of the Bill of Rights, and imposed them in a reign of terror, and he assumed the leadership in the bitter struggle to preserve the freedoms and our democratic institutions. The victory was his, and he was swept into the Presidency by the rising of the people.

The most spectacular achievement of his two Administrations was the purchase of Louisiana, and in his domestic policies he gave permanence to our republican and democratic institutions.

For many years he carried on a correspondence with statesmen, scientists, writers and philosophers throughout the world, and so universal was his interest, so profound his thinking, that this voluminous correspondence, now being published in fifty large volumes, is a deep well of wisdom.

The beautiful and imposing memorial recently built in Washington is the nation's tribute to one of the greatest thinkers the world has produced.

Statesman, philosopher, architect, scientist, inventor, he was a universal genius.

CLAUDE BOWERS has reached the top in three professions—journalism, history and diplomacy. It is as historian that he is most widely known, and his works on the Jefferson and Jackson eras and the decade after the Civil War have gone far to educate his contemporaries about the shaping of American democracy. Mr. Bowers was a Hoosier editor for years, before joining the editorial board of the New York *World* in its halcyon days. He had been up to his neck in Democratic politics, and had been chairman

of the Democratic National Convention in Houston in 1928 where Franklin D. Roosevelt placed Al Smith in nomination. President Roosevelt made him Ambassador to Spain in 1933, and he remained there till 1939. Then he moved to the embassy in Chile which he occupied until 1954.

His chief writings are *The Party Battles of the Jackson Period; Jefferson and Hamilton; The Tragic Era* and *My Mission to Spain,* the history of his services in Spain which did not appear till 1954.

SIMÓN BOLÍVAR

by Salvador de Madariaga

I BELIEVE that every man comes to this world stage to play his part in an endless drama and that he must play it to the full. The Playwright is wiser than any of us, and it avails nothing that we try to correct His script. We ourselves choose our parts—some of us by a slow process which gradually defines it through everyday retouches; others by a sudden flash of revelation that all but dazzles us. For my part, I know that when I witnessed the coronation of Napoleon that magnificent scene aroused my enthusiasm, but less owing to its pomp than because of the feeling of love which an immense people evinced for their hero. That general effusion of all hearts, that free and spontaneous movement of the people, excited by the glories, the heroic exploits of Napoleon, whom in that moment more than a million persons acclaimed, seemed to me, for the recipient of so many ovations, the highest degree of human aspirations, the supreme desire and the supreme ambition of man. The crown Napoleon laid on his head I looked upon as a miserable thing. What seemed great to me was the universal acclaim and the interest his person inspired. This, I own, made me think of my country's slavery, and of the glory which would be achieved by the man who would free her.

That scene was open to thousands of human beings. For each of them it would mean meat or poison, glory or misery, enthusiasm or indifference. For me, it meant revelation. When I saw the crown descend on that lofty brow, aglow with the light of thousands of eyes converging on it, I knew the part I was to play on the stage of world history. I knew that my life would not flow along some obscure channel of privacy to be lost in a pool of small endeavors. I knew that I should burn it in the open, on the wide stage of mankind's deeds. And the fact that I chose that part was in itself proof that I had the size for it and that it was the part for me.

I believe that greatness can only be achieved in grief and solitude; and that, as the peaks of the Andes have to pay for their height and majesty with the cold desolation of their eminence, so the men who choose the leading parts in history have to suffer for their choice. For I believe that great men, like those great peaks, live under high tensions, and that storms gather naturally round them.

I believe that there are men whose eyes were born to work closely on minute things, such as jewelers and watchmakers; and others whose eyes are made to see afar, such as sailors; and that the eyes that are born to see farthest are those of the men who shape nations. I was a "nationsmith." And I believe I know their ways and their weaknesses. I believe that nations should be free; by which I mean that their destinies should be in the hands of the men and women born of their earth, fed by their soil, lit by their skies. But I believe also that freedom is but a tender plant likely to wither unless it be rooted into the inner freedom of every man and woman of the people that would be free.

And I believe that the leaders of men must play the parts they have themselves chosen on the world stage without heed to the applause of the crowd that they lead. I freed my country. My country cast me out, and I died in exile—who knows, perhaps because I expected too much in return. Now, however, that the flesh has fallen away and that death has liberated me from myself, I believe that I am more than ever the Liberator.

❦

Profile of Simón Bolívar

Simón Bolívar was born in 1783 in the city of Caracas, then one of the intellectual centers of the Spanish Empire in America. His family was one of the wealthiest and most aristocratic of Venezuela, and his father took pride in the gold braid of his Spanish colonelcy. The time, however, called for a change in the regime which Spain had maintained in her American kingdoms for three centuries; and even Bolívar's father had advocated some form of home rule. Encouraged by the American and French Revolutions, the movement of emancipation came to a head when in 1808 Napoleon invaded Spain and eventually forced the King to abdicate. Spain rose against the invader and a Regency took charge. But every American "kingdom" of the Spanish Crown claimed then the right to take its destinies in its own hands; and on July 4, 1811, Venezuela declared its independence.

The moving spirit had been Bolívar. He had visited the British Foreign Secretary, Wellesley, in London and secured Britain's benevolence; he had sent his elder brother to the United States on the same errand. He became the natural leader of the "patriots" as soon as the struggle passed from the public square to the battlefield.

He improvised himself a general, was a born propagandist, and became a statesman. He wrote, fought, and made speeches. The ebb and flow of defeat and victory was spectacular. By August 1813 he had conquered Caracas and received that title of Liberator in which he was to take pride all his life. He lost Venezuela and won Colombia, and lost them both again until, in the battle of Carabobo (1821), he finally defeated the arms of Spain.

His task was then to organize on an independent basis the immense territories he had liberated. Venezuela, Colombia and Ecuador were unified under the name of Great Colombia. Guayaquil was wrenched from his rival San Martín, who withdrew from public life after a single interview with the Liberator. Peru was conquered; and its upper part, subjugated, took his name and became Bolivia.

But Bolívar's trials began with his victory. He was too ambitious, too high-minded and too astute to be popular; and at the early age of forty-seven, a victim of tuberculosis, he died in Santa Marta under a decree of expulsion by the very Venezuela he had liberated.

✥

᪣ SALVADOR DE MADARIAGA, writing in English and Spanish, is the author of many books on Spain and Spanish America. The son of a colonel in the Spanish army, he was educated in Madrid and Paris, and at twenty-five became an engineer with the Northern Spanish Railway. He turned to scholarship and diplomacy and from 1922 to 1928 was Director, Disarmament Section of the League of Nations. He was professor at Oxford, then at Mexico University, became a deputy of the Cortes Constituyentes and, in 1931, Ambassador to the United States. During the next five years he was Spanish delegate to the League of Nations, a member of the League's Council, a delegate to the Disarmament Conference, Ambassador to France, and Minister of Education and Justice. He is president of the Cultural Section, European Movement, and president of the Liberal International.

His many works include *Bolívar* (1952), one of several biographies of New World figures.

MICHAEL FARADAY

by Waldemar Kaempffert

I ONCE SHOWED Mr. Gladstone how an induced current of electricity could spin a little copper disk without touching anything. "What's the good of that?" he asked. He was a practical man of affairs, and I was not. So I gave him a practical answer. "Some day you will be able to tax it," I said.

I believe that the practical man is often very impractical. He wants an invention or discovery that will work—that is, make money. But the time comes when the invention fails to meet a new set of conditions, so that the theorist must step in and explain the failure and suggest a theory out of which some really practical good will come. No experiment is worth much unless it is explained by a good theory. Great inventions always spring out of good theories.

I never had a systematic education. As a pupil in a local day school, I learned no more than the rudiments of reading, writing and arithmetic. But I read much, especially when I was apprenticed to G. Riebau, a kindly bookseller. By chance I attended four lectures delivered by Sir Humphry Davy, made careful notes, transcribed them neatly, bound them and sent them to him with a letter in which I expressed the hope that with his aid I might forsake trade. To my astonishment he found a place for me in the Royal Institution. There I remained to the end of my days.

I belong to a small, despised Christian sect called Sandemanians. I believe with them that it is futile to bring religion and science into harmony. Religion is based on faith, science on reasoning. I ask myself: Why am I here? Science cannot answer. It is not concerned with purpose. But religion is concerned with purpose, and what that purpose is must be a matter of faith. I believe that without faith man would drift helplessly—that love, sacrifice, truth would have no meaning.

All told I have performed about 2,000 experiments. Without experimentation I am nothing. Not one of my many experiments was performed with a practical purpose in view, though many proved to be of industrial importance. I never patented anything. I foresaw the uses to which my discovery of electromagnetic induction might be put, but preferred to leave its application to others. In my earlier years at the Royal Institution I had to eke out my slender salary with outside work and in that way made a few hundred extra pounds a year. I soon gave this up. It is not too difficult to make money if there is self-denial and industry. To me money-making was an unpleasant distraction. It always took my mind off the work that I wanted to do.

But what was that work? As I look back at it I see that it was the quest of truth. I know that a scientist has no way of recognizing truth when he sees it. But the quest goes on and on. It must go on. Without it there would be no science.

Suppose that science had succeeded in creating a living man—something that could be accepted as a counterpart of the men we see about us. And suppose that this creature could think as we do. Unless it was concerned with the truth it would never be a real man, never a real scientist. That much I learned in my experimentation. I believe that there is something in the world of experience that is intent on truth. The responsibility of the scientist is a responsibility to seek and proclaim the truth as he sees it. We do not patent truths. We give them to others.

It is because giving is part of their creed that scientists constitute a world-wide intellectual fraternity. Religion may preach the brotherhood of man; science practices it. The lesson is not always heeded. I believe that mankind will prosper the more it widens and deepens the scientific habit of mind and that the greatest of all problems is that of making this scientific habit more effective. As that scientific habit of mind is acquired there will be more and more giving. I believe in giving. By giving I mean more than presenting a single precious discovery to the world. I mean that nothing may be withheld—not even a crumb of knowledge.

Profile of Michael Faraday

◄§ Morse would not have invented his telegraph, nor Bell his telephone, nor Edison his many electrical contrivances had it not been for MICHAEL FARADAY. He was probably the greatest experimenter that ever lived. Electrical engineering as we know it begins with him. When he did his work, which was largely in the first half of the last century, there was not even an electric doorbell. There were only two sources of electricity. One was the electric machine with glass plates that had to be rotated and rubbed with fur to produce electric sparks; the other was the battery.

Faraday was not only an experimenter but a theorist. As a theorist, he ranks with Newton and Einstein. He belonged to a very materialistic period; yet he was a spiritual force in the development of science. A devoutly religious man, his profound belief in the spirit played as much a part in his scientific success as his skill and his industry. As one of the most distinguished scientists of his time, he made scores of experiments and observations. His crowning achievement, the one that enabled society to pass from steam to electricity, was the generation of an electric current by moving magnets and coils of wire relatively to each other—the principle of the dynamo.

Faraday lived from 1791 to 1876. One could call him the most remarkable bookbinder who ever lived, for he was trained for this occupation and actually practiced it a little while. Then at twenty-two he unexpectedly was appointed a laboratory assistant of the Royal Institution of Great Britain through the influence of the eminent chemist Sir Humphry Davy. Soon he was to spend two years traveling through Europe with Sir Humphry, and he promptly began making his important discoveries. Right away he discovered two new chlorides of carbon and successfully liquefied several gases. By the time he was thirty he published a sketch of a history of electromagnetism and in that same year effected the revolution of a magnetic electric needle around an electrical current. He went on to discover the effect of one current on another in terms of their deflection and attraction, and the characteristics of the electrical current produced when a magnet is inserted in a coil of wire. It was this that led to the development of the magneto, the dynamo and the generator.

ᴇᴥᴦ WALDEMAR KAEMPFFERT is a lawyer and an editor, but his real vocation is writing about the discoveries of science in a way that non-scientific readers can understand. He was born in New York City, received his B.S. from City College and, while serving as assistant editor of *Scientific American*, was graduated from New York University's law school. He was admitted to the bar and registered as a patent attorney. From the position of managing editor of *Scientific Ameri*can he became editor of *Popular Science Monthly* and then director of the Museum of Science and Industry in Chicago. Since 1931, he has been science editor of the *New York Times*. He is the author of many articles in scientific and engineering periodicals, as well as popular books, including *Science Today and Tomorrow*. In 1954 he received the Kalinga Award from UNESCO, the first time it was given to a professional interpreter of science.

RALPH WALDO EMERSON

by Ralph L. Rusk

WHEN you ask what I believe, I am forced to admit that for me truth grows and changes and cannot be a settled thing. I do not wish any idea of mine to harden into the rock-like rigidity of a dogma. Being a lover of liberty, I shun a creed as I would a prison. Though I seem both inconsistent and insincere, I must be free to obey another mood tomorrow.

Yet certain fundamentals keep, in my eyes, a recognizable identity and seem, together, to make a unified scheme of things. I see one superior force or essence that gives laws to all else and offers each individual man beauty, truth, and duty. Between it and me stands nature, a physical presence which seems to be a sensuous symbol of mind and spirit, an interpreter. But, while I think I read the deeper meanings in nature, I sometimes feel that I receive directly into myself, by intuition, the strange yet intimate influence of the divine. And if I receive it at first hand, I do not much depend on any second-hand supply. And this explains what I mainly mean by self-reliance.

The self-reliance I persistently believe in is not separateness from the divine and the human, but a direct, free relationship with them, without any dependence on middlemen. In matters of spiritual truth I think I cannot afford to lose my immediate relationship with the source, and as for truth that comes by experience, which I also highly prize, I must value most what I get from my private plot of ground, however small. I study with excited interest the adventures of other seekers, but I must not be hampered in my own search by any person or institution that generously or officiously offers to be my guardian. I deny the right of church or state to encroach upon my personal dignity and my little area of freedom, just as I feel myself restrained from encroaching upon the dignity and freedom of others. Society has its part to perform and I have my share of responsibility for it, but I do not forget that the essential life is in individuals. Love? The one great force that has never been fairly tried in governing men. But lovers also must be individuals. Love must not be merely a mass hysteria.

Though I see clearly enough the existence of evil, of which I have perhaps suffered my share in the deaths of brothers, wife, and son, this self-reliance, which, at bottom, is God-reliance, gives me an affirmative feeling about life. Once I thought evil far outweighed good. It may be that a new scale of values and the sheer necessity of finding reasons for optimism account, as much as long observation does, for my firmly rooted conviction that there is such a thing as spiritual compensation and that good balances evil. At any rate I am an affirmer of life. If the human will looks frail when it is pitted against fate, and if experience seems empty and unreal, I still applaud Plato's act of pure faith and courage in making Socrates assert that whoever finds some truth is safe until another period.

I must end by confessing that I am too young by many centuries to make a system of thought. When I say, "This I believe," I am apt to rely, excessively you may think, on those sudden sallies of intelligence, the intuitions. I can only warn you not to lean too heavily on me. After all, I am an experimenter, and you have your own search for truth to carry on.

❧

Profile of Ralph Waldo Emerson

❧ RALPH WALDO EMERSON was born in 1803 at a time when the hopeful young republic was poised for the first great leap of expansion beyond the Mississippi and far toward the Pacific. His youth fell in a time when a new intellectual ferment, result of many liberal forces long at work in both the Old and New Worlds, was breaking the tight accustomed molds of thought and creed and giving men such freedom of mind and imagination as they had hardly had, except sporadically, in many centuries. He was the son of what was then perhaps the most liberal Christian church, and he actually prepared for and entered her ministry, but soon found even her broad, almost humanistic doctrines too confining.

Rapidly ending his initial phase as professional religious teacher, Emerson, at last a highly individualistic thinker, fully absorbing what he borrowed from the past into the blood stream of his own thought, emerged with an almost complete freedom as lecturer, essayist, and poet. Through his book called *Nature*, such piquantly original essays as "Self-reliance" and "Compensation" and "Love" and "Friendship" and "The Over-Soul" and "The Poet" and "Experience" and "Politics," such poems as "The Problem" and "Uriel" and "Brahma," such widely varied books as *Representative Men* and *English Traits* and *The Conduct of Life*, and such lectures as he read in many states of the Union year after year and, during some months, in England and Scotland, he spoke his liberal philosophy of life openly, while he generally escaped partisan narrowness and kept his temper and good manners, devoting himself, not to winning and organizing followers, but to making men conscious of themselves, their capabilities, and responsibilities.

His nearly seventy-nine years of life, from 1803 to 1882, witnessed the beginnings of a great change in Europe and America from the more adventurous romantic mood to a more pessimistic "realism." Today the core of his philosophy remains sanative for an age when there is a strong drift toward despair and when it is commonly taught that the life of man can be neither triumphant heroism nor immolation, but a thing to be regarded, at best, as tragedy without the element of nobility that the Greeks made a part of tragedy's meaning. In such an age, Emerson is an important admonisher that even-tempered courage, the will to live, and a sense of both duty and pleasure in living may still exist.

<hr/>

RALPH LESLIE RUSK is America's leading authority on the life and works of Ralph Waldo Emerson. He was born in Rantoul, Illinois, graduated from the University of Illinois, and took his Doctor's degree at Columbia. For two years he was an instructor of English at the University of the Philippines, then for ten years in the English Department at Indiana University. Since 1925, he has taught at Columbia where he has been a full professor for nineteen years. During that period he was co-editor of the quarterly, *American Literature*, and editor of many volumes of Emerson's letters. He is the author of *The Life of Ralph Waldo Emerson*, which won the National Book Award gold medal for non-fiction in 1950. He is also the author of a two-volume work on the literature of the Middle Western frontier, as well as various articles in the *Dictionary of American Biography*.

ABRAHAM LINCOLN

by Paul M. Angle

I CANNOT REMEMBER when I did not believe in God's omnipotence, although as a youth I used such terms as "fate" and the "doctrine of necessity" to express my conviction. On one occasion, when my old friend Joshua Speed was torn by indecision and I helped in my small way to give him resolution, I knew that the course I took was foreordained. When my father stood near death I urged him to trust in our merciful Maker, confident that He would not fail him. Even recently, I have been compelled to confess that with all the power at my command I was unable to control events, but that events, guided by Almighty God, controlled me.

The will of God prevails. Through His power over us and our adversaries He could have prevented this Civil War. He could, if He chose, have given victory to either side. I am forced to believe that He permitted the war to continue for some purpose which we were unable to comprehend. But that His purpose was beneficent I do not doubt.

Years ago I asked myself: "If man has no power over his own action, why should he trouble to choose one course over another?" But I came to see that God had placed an obligation on me to ascertain His will and to conduct myself as a humble instrument in His hands.

In this effort I could not achieve perfection. But when I have taken as my guide the precept: "Whatsoever ye would that men should do to you, do ye even so to them," I do not believe I have erred greatly. This is the teaching that has kept me from indulging in personal resentments against those who have opposed me. At the time of my contest against Douglas I was bespattered with every imaginable epithet, yet I held no grudges. I followed the same rule in 1860, and again in 1864. A man does not have time to spend half his life in quarrels. Still less can he afford to take all the consequences, such as the vitiating of his temper and his own chagrin at his loss of self-control. Rather than that I have tried to avoid doing anything in malice, and to forgive on the Christian terms of repentance.

This teaching, too, has led me to do what I could to elevate the condition of the Negro. As I would not be a slave, so I would not be a master. For years I saw no way to end human bondage except to put it in the course of ultimate extinction. Now I believe that the removal of this great wrong is assured. I see in this the realization of my long-standing wish that all men everywhere could be free. As I could not go calmly to my final reckoning, if I had to answer for robbing any man of his goods, how could I rob someone of this freedom? But even in this attitude I take no vainglorious satisfaction. For it is written: "Judge not, lest ye be judged."

To speak again of the will of God: Well-meaning men have urged one course or another on me on the ground that God so willed it. But I could not be sure. I believed it not irreverent to assume that if God would reveal my duty to others He would as soon reveal it to me. Lacking more specific guidance I have turned my thoughts from uncharitable passions, prejudices and jealousies. And for the final triumph of the right I strengthen my reliance on the Supreme Being.

Profile of Abraham Lincoln

◦§ ABRAHAM LINCOLN was born near Hodgenville, Kentucky, on February 12, 1809. His parents were poor and uneducated, but upright and God-fearing. When the boy was seven they moved to Indiana, where they lived for fourteen years. It was a primitive region and life was hard, yet young Lincoln managed enough schooling to aggregate, with what he had received in Kentucky, a year in all.

In 1830 the Lincoln family moved again, this time to Illinois. A year later, the son struck out for himself and soon settled in the village of New Salem, near Springfield. While there, he was elected to the Illinois legislature. Soon afterward he took up the study of law, supporting himself by surveying and by odd jobs. In 1837, after being admitted to the bar, he moved to Springfield and began practice. Before many years he became one of the leading lawyers of his state.

Lincoln served four terms in the legislature, and after an interval, a term in Congress. In these offices he was an honest, adroit politician, but in the slavery agitation of the 'fifties he took on new stature. His campaign for the U. S. Senate in 1858, marked by the famous series of debates with Stephen A. Douglas, made him a national figure. In 1860 he won the Republican nomination for the Presidency against better known rivals, and when the Democratic Party broke into fragments, carried the election as well.

When Lincoln took office, seven Southern states had passed ordinances of secession. He hoped for a peaceful solution, but the attack on Fort Sumter precipitated war. Thereafter, his was the responsibility of organizing for victory. Contending, originally, only for the restoration of the Union, Lincoln came to the conclusion that the war also called for the abolition of slavery, and issued the Proclamation of Emancipation (January 1, 1863). Although beset with difficulties, and often almost despairing of finding commanders who could make effective use of the superior resources of the North, he prosecuted the war to a successful conclusion, only to have his life cut short by a half-crazed assassin. He is venerated today for his achievements, but even more for the personal qualities he revealed in the years of national agony—gentleness, tolerance, honesty, resolution of purpose, mastery of language, staunch faith in democracy, and humility before God.

❦

PAUL M. ANGLE, historian and writer, has come to know Abraham Lincoln as well as any man in our time. He was born and brought up in the Middle West, about a half century after Lincoln's death, and studied at Oberlin College, Miami University and the University of Illinois. In 1924 he became executive secretary of the Abraham Lincoln Association. Since then, he has written a half dozen books on Lincoln and his times. The most recent of these is the well-known *Lincoln Reader*. In addition to the books in which he shared his knowledge of the great Civil War President with the general public, he has rendered much valuable service to other Lincoln scholars in his work with the Illinois Historical Library and later as director of the Chicago Historical Society.

The recipient of a number of honorary degrees, Mr. Angle is married and has two children. He lives in Chicago.

FLORENCE NIGHTINGALE

by Cecil Woodham-Smith

THE COURSE of my life has been decided by the single fact, the existence of suffering. When I was seventeen God spoke to me, and called me to His service. It was to be my work to lighten the burden of suffering in the world. I did not know how. I was not ready. I had to learn what was required of those who are to be the tools of God. For me it meant to give up almost all that made life pleasant. I had to renounce human relationships, my family, even the felicity of marriage. I had to learn to bear being misunderstood. I had to learn to be alone.

One of my greatest temptations was to be praised and admired and to be a general favorite. What I had to learn was to do God's work for the sake of the work, not for thanks. It took years to accomplish this. My actual work did not even begin before I had suffered enough to learn it.

I came back from the Crimean War knowing I had failed. I had left seventy-three per cent of eight regiments in their graves from disease alone. I had sat at the bedside of two thousand dying men. I could never forget. The blood of these dead men did not cry out for vengeance, it cried for mercy on the survivors. This was the work to which I had to give myself.

My family were wealthy and agreeable. But they had the conventional attitude of 1820. They planned my life. They stubbornly fought my going to the Crimea—and the career I chose. But every one must decide one's own life.

While my mind was made up, I knew my feelings were not enough. They had to be translated into action. I had to drive without surcease, drive myself first of all. I must allow no consideration of my own personal relations, or comfort or health to deflect me from putting forth the fullest effort of which I was capable. I faced a dual undertaking, to see that suffering was alleviated, that is by the development of nursing and sanitation, and to effect the reforms in government administration and habits and attitudes that would permit the condemned to live. I had to master the subject to the last detail, but to work always in the shadow of men to whom the decision was committed.

I believed in efficiency. Without it good intentions and enthusiasm are of little worth. I knew that efficiency could only come through training. I have insisted that those who elect to serve God by doing practical good be at least as competent as those who work for money. That view is unpopular. For many like the acclaim and credit for doing good but won't learn the job as a professional or work as hard as if paid. But competence in administration, accuracy in keeping accounts, foresight in arranging for supplies, can save lives as well as the tender and expert care in the sickroom. As I look back I believe the establishment of training has been almost the most important part of my work.

I believed in working wherever possible through existing regulations. I was not a rebel. I had to overcome great antagonism, but for my part, I always cooperated.

And I believed in the wisdom of modest beginnings. I went to the Crimea with forty nurses and would rather have had only twenty. The small beginning, the quiet work without publicity, the gradual struggle, these are the elements from which achievement can come.

I have been asked how, as a woman alone, I had the courage to set out to produce some of the greatest changes of our times. If there was courage, the glory is God's. God called me, sustained me, impelled me.

But though belief in God is my life, I do not attach importance to the doctrines of any particular sect. God may be reached by many roads. If I belong to any sect it is one that is small and has no churches and teaches no dogma. It is the sect of the Good Samaritan.

Profile of Florence Nightingale

◄§ FLORENCE NIGHTINGALE revolutionized the care of health throughout the world. Nursing was only part of her achievement; almost every aspect of everyday life has benefited from her work, while through her character and attainments she did more to raise the status of women than any other one woman in history. Yet when she was born, in 1820, everything seemed against her. Education and emancipation for women were undreamed of. When Florence grew up pretty enough to be called a beauty, her destiny became plain—she was to make a brilliant marriage.

But at seventeen she received a call from God. God spoke to her and called her to his service. A conflict followed with her own nature, for she loved the world, and with her parents. The service to which God called her was nursing. At that time the physical tending of the sick was thought to involve impropriety and, with the exception of religious sisterhoods, nurses were drunken and sexually promiscuous. Her parents refused to allow her to nurse. It was sixteen years before Florence left home for her first nursing post.

The years had not been wasted. She had secretly studied hospital administration and won powerful admirers. One was Sidney Herbert, Secretary at War in the British Cabinet. When in 1854 during the Crimean War, conditions in British military hospitals caused a scandal, he sent out Florence Nightingale with forty nurses to try to put things right. She put the hospitals into decent order, won the undying devotion of the troops and became a national heroine.

But she refused to exploit her fame. She knew that her work must be done through government departments, and publicity would be fatal. So she retired completely. In fact the great constructive period of her life began. For forty years she worked behind the scenes, accomplishing her great reforms in sanitation and health, first in England, then in India and throughout the world. Her health declined, but even as an invalid she worked sixteen and eighteen hours a day. Her influence was enormous, she was constantly consulted by kings, prime ministers and statesmen, treated with almost religious deference. When she died in 1910 at ninety, millions of her admirers were astonished. They thought she had died half a century before.

ᦒ Cecil woodham-smith belongs to an old Irish family—the FitzGeralds of Leinster. Her father served for many years in India and from stories he told her as a child, she derived her interest in military history and in Florence Nightingale. After reading English literature at Oxford, she worked in an advertising agency, did some journalism, married Mr. G. I. Woodham-Smith and had two children. She read steadily in the history of the nineteenth century. During the war, Mrs. Woodham-Smith began work on her biography, *Florence Nightingale*. Frequently interrupted by air attacks and overwhelmed by the wealth of available material, it took six years of persistent labor to complete the carefully documented work.

The research into the Crimean War and its origins, so basic to her study of the life of Florence Nightingale, led naturally to her newest book, *The Reason Why*, a brilliant history of the Charge of the Light Brigade.

QUEEN VICTORIA

by Hector Bolitho

How WELL I remember—being called from my bed by Mama—
sixty years ago—to receive the news of my accession. Last Sunday,
I was reading some of my journals from those early days. It is
frightening to see oneself coming to life from old pages on which
one wrote—oh, so long ago—with all one's follies and mistakes. I
suppose Lady Lyttelton was right when she spoke of the "vein of
iron" in me when I was young—it shows—so bitterly—in what I
wrote, on that first day as Queen. My dear mother had guarded me
through the sad and lonely years of my childhood—yet, from the
moment I got out of bed and went into the sitting-room, I thought
of the word, alone. I wrote in my journal—as if it were a sort of
challenge—I wrote—"I saw dear Lord Melbourne, quite alone."
And—"I took my dinner upstairs, alone." That night I slept in my
bedroom, alone—for the first time in my life.

Of course, I was very young. But the vein of iron was deeply
wrong. I know that. It showed—in a way I cannot forgive myself
for—when dear Albert came to England. I wrote of my fear of
marriage to him—of my great repugnance to change—those were
my very words. I was afraid he would thwart me—oppose me in
what I liked. I thought that would be a dreadful thing.

Then I beheld him—stepping from his coach, at Windsor—looking so beautiful. As the days passed—riding in the park—playing
duets—I knew that I loved him, and that he loved me. And this
I believe, with all my heart—that my character was changed by our
love. As he said—the way was "plentifully strewn with thorns." He
complained to a friend—soon after our very pretty wedding—that
he was only the husband—not the master, in the house.

But we walked clear of the thorns—because our love was blessed
by God. Albert and I always prayed together. Ours was a Christian
marriage.

During those early years, I prayed for humility. God listened to my prayer.

Our happiness endured for almost twenty-one years. Then—my husband died—in the terrible winter of 1861.

I have been blamed very much because I shut myself away during the years that followed. But I was lonely—walking through those big rooms—with nobody ever again to call me "Victoria," as he used to do. But I did not neglect my tasks—no one can ever say that. The endless papers—the problems of a growing family—and of a growing Empire. No—I did not neglect my tasks.

Slowly, my faith came back to me. I began to realize that, if one has loved—in the light of God—all that matters in one's love survives—even after death. My dear Albert seemed to emerge out of the darkness of my grief—to guide me.

I remember one day when Lord Tennyson came—he was very old and shaky on his feet then—and we sat together and had such a nice long talk. And he recited "In Memoriam" to me. It had always been such a comfort—in my dark times. Do you remember the words—

> "Strong Son of God, immortal Love,
> Whom we, that have not seen Thy face,
> By faith, and faith alone, embrace,
> Believing where we cannot prove."

Believing where we cannot prove. And then Lord Tennyson said to me, "You are so alone on that terrible height."

As I sit here in the garden, with all the millions of people waiting in the streets for me to drive by, I find myself thinking back—of what Lord Tennyson said—"Alone on a terrible height." But I am *not* alone.

My husband once said to me—"We don't know in what state we shall meet again—but that we shall recognize each other—and be together in eternity—I am perfectly certain."

These were my dear Albert's words—and I believe them with all my heart.

Profile of Queen Victoria

⋙ QUEEN VICTORIA was born on May 24, 1819, and she acceded to the throne on June 20, 1837. She was then eighteen. The monarchy in Britain was almost as unpopular as it had been during the reign of King Charles I. Through Queen Victoria's achievement, we trace the reason why, today, when few crowns matter, the British are devoted monarchists.

The story of Queen Victoria's influence really began with her marriage to Prince Albert, in 1840. Through the example of their scrupulous family life, they gave a standard of domestic behavior to the British people. Prince Albert was a remarkable, as well as a good man: he had a talent for government, also a gentle way of guiding his wife towards wisdom and inward greatness. When he died, in 1861, Queen Victoria succumbed to her grief, and the old republican cry was heard again. But, slowly, the Queen's influence inspired the life of her people. It was a simple influence, of character rather than power. She once said to a minister, "My Lord, I was brought up to know what was right and what was wrong. Never let me hear the word 'expedient' again." This was the force of her moral example, which endured for the sixty-three years of her reign—through fourteen wars, and the building of an empire that was not even a dream when she came to the throne.

She had been brought up to think in terms of life in Europe: the conflicts and intrigues of European courts provided the interests of her early years. But, from 1860, when her sons began their journeys to America, Canada, Australia and New Zealand, she came to think within a new, wider and more vital horizon. As her reign closed, the nation had learned that its destiny lay across the Atlantic and the Pacific.

Queen Victoria's greatness lay in her limitations. She was neither intellectual nor clever. She was obdurate as a monarch, believing in the divine right of her inheritance. But her humbleness as a woman was incredible. She sat on a river bank in Scotland, with the wives of the cottagers, sharing their grief when two children were drowned in the bourn. But when Bismarck visited her, he came away mopping his brow and saying, "What a woman." She knitted mittens for the poor soldiers when she was almost blind, but statesmen trembled before her simple and inviolate integrity.

⋙⋘

⋙ HECTOR BOLITHO's own statement of personal belief, and a short bio- graphical sketch of him, will be found in the first section of this volume.

LEO TOLSTOY

by Alexandra Tolstoy

I BELIEVE that the teachings of Christ are the substance of my life. If I doubted them, I could not go on living.

I believe that to remember God every day and every hour of the day, to fulfill His will by loving one's neighbor, raises us above mere animal existence. This is simple, so very simple that nothing can exceed its simplicity, and at the same time it is so important, and great, and such a blessing to all people, that nothing can be greater, because this is the Truth of God.

I believe that Christianity teaches us what every person must do to fulfill the will of the One who sent us into this life. Discussions about the possible results from these or other complicated theories, political parties, systems, have nothing in common with Christianity, these theories are very often false and can be destroyed only by Christianity. I believe that history is nothing else but a gradual evolution from the point of view of the personal animal interests to the understanding of social life, and from the understanding of social life to the understanding of God. All the history of ancient people which lasted for centuries and which ended with the fall of Rome is the history of the change from the narrow animal personal view of life to social, national and spiritual interests and the beginning of Christianity.

I believe that the Christian world with its prisons, forced labor, executions, with its factories, accumulation of capital, with its bars, corruptions, with its constantly growing armament and millions of misled people who, like chained dogs, attack others by the order of their masters, would be dreadful if it were the creation of public opinion, but all of this is the creation of evil forces and can be destroyed and is already being destroyed by public opinion, based on Christian principles.

I believe the main thing we must know is what we ourselves

must not be doing and what we must be doing, to create the Kingdom of Heaven on earth, and that we all know. And if every one of us will begin doing what we ought to do, and stop doing what we ought not to do, using the light of God we have in us, only then will we reach the Kingdom of Heaven. Every human being in the depths of his heart strives to reach this goal.

Christianity leads the way to self-improvement. I believe that moral laws are so simple that people cannot excuse themselves by saying that they do not know the law. They should not renounce their wisdom, which is what they are doing.

I believe that in subconscious atheism of people, and with the conscious denial of faith of the so-called educated people of the Christian world, lies the reason of the greatest misfortune of the people of our time.

I believe that life must and can be a constant joy. And a wise person is always joyful. The way to find joy in life is to understand that you are given life to enjoy it. If you don't, try and find out where you have made a mistake.

I believe that love, not exclusive love for some one person but one's inward readiness to love everyone around us, gives the feeling of the spirit of God within us.

It not only gives this spiritual inward joy to the one who feels it but in this world of ours love is the main source of joy.

⋅≼§≽⋅

Profile of Leo Tolstoy

≼§ Leo TOLSTOY at the age of five heard his brother Nicolas announce that he had the secret of happiness: everybody would love everybody else. And the rules whereby this Kingdom of Heaven could be attained, his brother said, were written on a green stick buried in the forest under oak trees near a deep, dark ravine. Symbolically one can say of Leo that he was to seek this green stick all his life. Today, he himself lies buried near such a dark ravine as Nicolas described, having gone far indeed in finding the rules of good living.

Leo Tolstoy, in the span of his years (1828–1910), was to have more readers and exert a wider influence than any writer of his day. He gained them with such masterpieces as *War and Peace*, finished when he was forty-one, and *Anna Karenina*, finished when he was fifty. But he was to sustain world interest by his unselfish search for truth in his later years. These decades saw him wrestling with creeds and doctrines, and finally inviting peace in a life of renunciation, in which he taught the virtue of non-resistance and the blessings of poverty. He gave up his own properties, turned over to his wife his copyrights up to 1881 and gave away all his writings save one after that date. That one, *Resurrection*, he wrote to raise funds for a Russian sect that refused military service.

As a young man, he had been a student at the University of Kazan but did not graduate. He put in five years of active military service and then devoted himself to writing. In his youth he did not always conquer his passions for women, his gambling or his laziness. But every time he fell he unmercifully punished himself, trying to learn from his mistakes. And this moral striving was to be the keynote of some of the finest characters in his fiction.

His religious writings occupied him after middle age, and he regarded them the most important products of his life. In the eighties he was disappointed in the Greek Orthodox religion, but felt he must find an answer to the questions that tormented him day and night. What is the aim of life? What do men live for? He was more helped by the Russian peasantry than anything else. He always had been close to simple people, and during his time of doubts came closer still. The peasants had patience, wisdom, humble obedience to the will of God, humility and faith. And all these helped Tolstoy find answers to his questions.

❦

ALEXANDRA TOLSTOY was born in Russia seventy years ago, the twelfth of Leo Tolstoy's thirteen children. From the age of seventeen, she acted as her father's secretary and, after his death in 1910, she edited the three volumes of his posthumous works. During World War I she was a nurse and relief organizer on the Turkish-Armenian and western German fronts, earning two St. George's medals. She was arrested five times after the Revolution and was condemned to prison, but after eight months she was released and later was appointed curator of Leo Tolstoy's museums. In 1929 she left Russia, going first to Japan, where she lectured and wrote *The Tragedy of Tolstoy*, and then to the United States. Since 1939, as the vigorous organizer and president of the Tolstoy Foundation, she has devoted herself to assisting Russian refugees. Author of *I Worked for the Soviets*, her most recent book is a biography, *Tolstoy, A Life of My Father*.

JANE ADDAMS

by Winifred E. Wise

I WANT to talk to you, as from a place that is very dear to me, the octagon, an eight-sided room for many years my working center at Hull-House in Chicago. I see a wall covered with the ever-changing population maps of the neighborhood, masses of color showing the location of the many different nationalities. Now, when I think how well on the whole this bright patchwork of races got on together because of the community of human needs, I wonder. Is there not perhaps a hope expressed here for the whole world?

It could be said later on that Hull-House lighted a candle in the middle of darkness. All of us who worked there hoped and prayed that this would be true. Those who continue to work there continue so to hope and pray.

I know, as I look back on my life, that I have had to live it from day to day, striving each day to do my best. Yet it was sometimes months later before I could tell whether that best had been adequate. I came to believe that the processes by which an end is achieved may be more important than the end itself. And also that the solution may be only "the best possible" under pressing immediate circumstances—not perfection. The learning and understanding developed by both parties to a problem may be the real gain.

My life taught me to believe deeply in people and in democracy. The whole thing has its roots in a simple acceptance of Christ's message. It is the joy of finding the Christ-spirit in our fellows, finding it unfold in the fellowship of common service and common aims under His will.

The founding of Hull-House with an old college friend was the outgrowth of a deep search for the inner meaning of life. My Quaker father had taught me early that I must be honest with myself inside—I must never pretend to understand. I had traveled extensively abroad seeking culture. But I found only dissatisfaction

213

with being an onlooker. I felt impelled in honesty to myself to step into the highway of life and at least realize the size of the burdens some of my fellows were carrying.

From the moment we moved into the old house on Halsted Street, any stuffy air of study swept away before the stir of life itself. Every room of this small beginning of a social settlement filled and refilled with folk of all ages. Calls came from every hand to perform the real human services—to wash the new babies . . . to nurse the sick . . . to mind the children. Yet from the first our neighbors and friends gave me so much more than I could possibly return, such spontaneity of emotion and gratitude . . . such rich experience of the inner goodness and understanding of people from many lands.

Sometimes it was necessary for me to restore myself and my perspective in rest . . . or in the countryside . . . or in travel. But I tried for the most part to stay close to my neighbors and my friends.

Now, as I look back, the belief is strong within me that there is ultimate hope for peace among the peoples of the world. Not through warfare or political pressures—not through dogma or decree. But through our understanding human needs and meeting them.

There is so much more to be said along these lines . . . some of it is now being said by others. And, happily, there are more and more who listen.

Profile of Jane Addams

☙ JANE ADDAMS' mother had ridden down country lanes with baskets for the needy in the simple charities of an earlier America. Later, Jane herself, in the complex Industrial Age, sought to assist her neighbors on Chicago's teeming Halsted Street and pioneer as an interpreter of the needs of the underprivileged and foreign-born to those in economic and political power.

Born in 1860 and early left motherless, she knew through her childhood the lovely country life of northwestern Illinois and the guidance of a Quaker father who was a prosperous miller and friend of Abraham Lincoln. She was a frail, thoughtful child who at seven first glimpsed the inequalities of fortune that were to haunt her all her life.

College days were passed at Rockford Seminary where many of her fellows later became missionaries, doctors, lawyers, teachers. Although shy and reserved, Jane Addams had even then a magnetism that drew others to her as a leader. Pictures of the time show a finely modeled sensitive face and eyes with great depth of expression and compassion.

When a recurrent spinal ailment blocked her plans for becoming a doctor among the poor, she traveled restlessly abroad. Slowly the plan of starting a social settlement crystallized in her mind. She was twenty-nine when in the fall of 1889 she opened the doors of a battered old mansion, "the Hull-House." Her own funds would not finance her far. She mounted the lecture platform and explained her purpose. Soon aid came in the form of both physical and spiritual support: money and many other dedicated men and women.

Hull-House and the distinguished residents who came to join Jane Addams exerted a strong influence on early factory legislation, cleaning up sweat-shops and protecting the child and woman worker. They achieved the world's first Juvenile Court and a league interpreting the immigrant to America, America to the immigrant. Hull-House became most famous of American social settlements, a mecca for visitors from all over the world.

She endured bitter years in a stand for pacifism during World War I. But when she died in 1935, she had been honored in her lifetime far beyond her own modest desires. She was co-recipient of the Nobel Peace Prize, and president of the Women's International League for Peace and Freedom. But until the end she was first of all a neighbor with the latchstring out.

◄§ WINIFRED E. WISE first met Jane Addams when, as a young writer from Wisconsin, she explored the thoroughfares and back streets of Chicago. In time, she came to regard the city as her own and to consider Jane Addams a close and valued friend. It was with her help that she wrote *Jane Addams of Hull-House.* She worked as a writer of biographies and as divisional advertising manager of Marshall Field & Company before leaving Chicago for the sunnier climate of the San Fernando Valley, California. Even the plenitude of trees and flowers in her new home has not overcome her loyalty to the Middle West.

Miss Wise in private life is Mrs. Stuart Palmer and the mother of three teen-age children. Her husband is national president of the Mystery Writers of America.

MARIE CURIE

by Eve Curie

LIFE IS not easy for any man or woman. We must have perseverance and, above all, confidence in ourselves. We must believe that we are gifted for something and that this thing, whatever the cost, MUST be attained. What ultimately matters is to be able to say, when the end comes, "I did what I could."

Once, in the spring, during weeks of forced idleness at home from a severe illness, I watched cocoons being made by silkworms that my daughters were raising. It interested me immensely. Looking at the caterpillars working with such obstinacy and such eagerness, I felt somehow that I resembled them very much; like them, I always drove patiently toward a single goal. I probably did so because something compelled me—just as the silkworm is compelled to spin its cocoon.

I have devoted almost half a century to scientific research which is fundamentally a quest for Truth. I have memories of marvelous happiness. They were in the solitary years of study as a young girl at the Sorbonne in Paris; they were in all the time when my husband and I, living with one single preoccupation, as if in a dream, toiled so hard in the miserable old shed where we were to make the discovery of radium.

What I always wanted from my existence was work, surrounded by silence, and a simple family life. I was given them, though the time came when I had to strive desperately to protect them from the invasion of publicity and the noise of fame.

I believe that in science we should be interested in things, not persons. When Pierre Curie and I had to decide whether to draw financial gains from our discovery, we both felt it would be contrary to our conception of pure research. So we did not take out a patent for the purification of radium, thereby throwing away a fortune. I am convinced we were right. True, humanity needs practical men who get the most out of their work. But it also needs the dreamers—those for whom the selfless development of an enterprise is so absorbing that they can have no devotion and no time left for material profit. My sole ambition was to work as a free scholar in a free country, and this particular privilege I never took for granted. Until I was twenty-four I had lived in a captive and oppressed Poland. I measured the price of French liberty.

I was not born with a peaceful soul. I understood very early that persons who felt things as sharply as I did, and could suffer absurdly even from one harsh word, had to try to conceal their sensitiveness as much as possible. I derived great help from my husband's gentle serenity. After the catastrophe of his sudden death I had to learn resignation. As I became older, I came to appreciate more and more such simple things as growing flowers, planting trees, building a house, recalling a piece of poetry, or looking at the stars and trying to identify them.

I have always been captivated by the beauty of the world, to which the science I love constantly adds new vistas. I also think science itself has great beauty. A scientist doing his research is not only a technician; he is also a child placed before natural phenomena that impress him like a fairy tale. This magic is perhaps the reason, above all others, which kept me at work in a laboratory all my life.

❦

Profile of Marie Curie

◄§ In 1897 a young woman scientist, MARIE SKLODOWSKA CURIE, while doing research on uranium rays, suspected the existence of one of the most closely guarded secrets of nature and resolved to bring it to light. Her husband, Pierre Curie, joined forces with her. Together, they discovered a new chemical element which emitted spontaneous radiations of an extraordinary kind. They named it "radium."

What the Curies had lit upon was not merely a new substance. The properties of radium flatly contradicted many established views as to the structure of matter. For all its seeming inertness, matter was the scene of what Madame Curie already called at the time "the cataclysms of atomic transformation." Amongst the far-reaching consequences of the Curies' discovery we find the creation of artificial radioactive bodies, the splitting of the atom by man. Radium was also to bring dramatic changes in the field of medicine: by destroying morbid cells it could cure certain types of cancer and relieve human suffering. Over a short period of fifty years the research on radioactivity has led on to our modern cancer clinics on the one hand—and to Hiroshima on the other. The use of atomic power in industry is the next great development before us.

Marie Curie was born in Poland in 1867, the daughter of a teacher of physics in a Warsaw high school. She had to work for six years as a children's governess before accumulating enough money to come and study in Paris. Her marriage to the scientist Pierre Curie made of her a French citizen. She lived and worked in France the rest of her life.

Monsieur and Madame Curie were awarded a Nobel Prize in physics in 1903. A second Nobel Prize (in chemistry) was given to Marie Curie alone in 1911—thus making of her the only individual, man or woman, who was ever awarded the Nobel Prize twice. Pierre Curie had been killed in a street accident in 1906 and his widow had to bear alone the responsibility of their joint work. For twenty-eight more years—until she died in 1934—Madame Curie, Professor at the University of Paris, Director of the Radium Institute, Member of the French Academy of Medicine and of a hundred and seven scientific societies and academies spread all over the world, remained one of the leaders of the new science of our century, Radioactivity.

◆◆◆

◆§ Eve curie, the daughter of Marie and Pierre Curie, is a French writer and journalist who has been welcomed on lecture tours in America ever since she was sixteen, when she accompanied her famous mother to this country. She was born in Paris, and attended Sévigné Collège. For several years she devoted herself to the piano. After her mother's death, she compiled the records and documents from which she wrote the biography, *Madame Curie*, which has been translated into twenty-seven languages.

During the war she was war correspondent in Libya, Russia, Burma and China before joining the Free French Army as a private in the Women's Auxiliary Forces. At this time, she published her second book, *Journey Among Warriors*. She returned to Paris after the war and became co-publisher of the evening newspaper, *Paris-presse*. She is now special assistant to the Secretary General of NATO.

WILL ROGERS

by Donald Day

A COMEDIAN is not supposed to be serious or to know much. As long as he is silly enough to get laughs, why, people let it go at that. But I claim you have to have a serious streak in you or you can't see the funny side of the other fellow. I use only one set of methods in my gags, and that is to try and keep to the truth. People used to ask me, "Will, where do you get all your jokes?" And I'd tell 'em I just watch Congress and report the facts. 'Course I may have sometimes exaggerated a little. But, whatever I've said I tried to base on truth.

I'd a whole lot rather have people nudge each other and say, "You know he is right about that," than get a big laugh.

Now, truth ain't always easy to come by. The only thing I've found that's absolutely necessary for a man to have is religion. Never mind what kind; but it's got to be something or you will fail in the end. Although I haven't been able to see where anyone has a monopoly on the right truth in religion, I do know that the Lord was pretty wise in making one thing common to all of them, and that is: the better life you live the better you finish. I have tried to live my life so that whenever I lose, I'm ahead.

Now, everybody got a scheme to set the United States back right again. Although, come to think of it, I can't remember when it ever was right. There been times when it has been right for you and you and you, but never all of you at the same time. I believe this country's pretty much the same as it always was, and always will be, because it is founded on right and even if everybody in public life tried to ruin it, they couldn't. Trying to stop this country now would be like trying to stop a train by spitting on a railroad track. No element, no party, not even Congress or the Senate, can really hurt this country now. And we're not where we are on account of any one man. We're here on account of the real common sense of the big normal majority. This country's bigger than any man or any party. They couldn't ruin it even if they tried.

But in believing this, I don't believe that you can just sit down and do nothing. There ain't no civilization where there ain't no satisfaction, and satisfaction don't come from just money and property and a bunch of bathtubs. I can be mighty rich, but if I ain't got friends, then I'm poorer than anybody.

And if I fell out with people because of a difference of opinion, I wouldn't have many friends. Difference of opinion is what makes horse racing and missionaries.

A white man gets lost and an Indian doesn't because an Indian always looks back after he has passed anything so he can see it both front and back. For that reason I never try to disagree with a man when I'm facing him. I like to go around behind him and look the same way he is looking, then I see things that I didn't see before. After looking over his shoulder and getting his viewpoint, then I can go back and face him.

Every man has an angle on living, or on life, or on something, and when you get it things are apt to look different. Every man's got something good or worth knowing in him.

Well, this is what I believe, and because I believe it, I can honestly say, I never met a man I didn't like.

Profile of Will Rogers

§ WILL ROGERS was born in Oolagah, Indian Territory, November 4, 1879, and died in a plane crash with Wiley Post, near Point Barrow, Alaska, in 1935. His homely philosophy, unfailing humor and keen observation had made him an American institution. His biography in a current encyclopedia calls him "by far the most popular American of his day." Rogers' parents both had Indian blood in their veins, but the assumption that Rogers was born in poverty and received no education is mistaken. His father was fairly well to do and Will was sent to William Halsell College, Vinton, Oklahoma, and later to Kemper Military Academy. He did work as a cowboy, and later joined a Wild West show. It was as a cowboy twirling a lariat that he had his start in vaudeville in New York in 1905. He added to this act a running monologue, and it was this formula that was to build his phenomenal success. The monologue developed into an easygoing and penetrating commentary on human nature and human affairs. Rogers' satire and humor were unpretentious but they were unabashed, and he feared no rank or person. He has been called "the greatest debunker of stuffed shirts and fanciful ideas."

As humorist, he became the star of many of the Ziegfeld productions. After 1918 he appeared in a series of moving pictures. Then he branched out to be radio commentator, syndicated newspaper columnist and public lecturer. His success was dazzling and he earned a huge income. But he never lost his spiritual balance. He kept himself sincere and always spoke for the "big honest majority" of his countrymen. He once said: "It is great to be great, but it is greater to be human." And for his part he never lost his sense of humor or his feeling that he belonged with his own kind of people back in Oklahoma. Insincerity, pomposity, selfishness and smugness melted beneath his words of satire, but he spoke without venom and the persons he quipped oftener than not ended by loving him.

His death in the crash of Wiley Post's private airplane came after a long devotion to flying. He had 500,000 miles of flying to his credit, and had visited all parts of the civilized world and many parts not civilized.

His writings include: *The Cowboy Philosopher on Prohibition* (1919); *The Cowboy Philosopher on the Peace Conference* (1919); *What We Laugh At* (1920); *Letters of a Self-made Diplomat to His President* (1927); *There's Not a Bathing Suit in Russia* (1927); and *Will Rogers' Political Follies* (1929).

❦

DONALD DAY's own statement of personal belief, and a short biographi- cal sketch of him, will be found in the first section of this volume.

FRANKLIN D. ROOSEVELT

by Robert E. Sherwood

SHAKESPEARE's Marc Antony said, "The evil that men do lives after them, the good is oft interred with their bones." I must say that I believe the opposite.

I believe that that which is evil in mankind is forever condemned to death.

I believe that that which is good in mankind is immortal.

It is written in the Book of Genesis:

"God created man in His own image."

This is the beginning of education. It is the foundation of faith.

Our faith may be challenged when we contemplate the evil of which men can be capable—and we have seen in our own age evil as terrible, as inhuman, as in the darkest ages of the past.

But the very fact that we use the word "inhuman" means that we know such evils to be against nature, against God—and therefore against the divine spirit that is in man.

This I believe.

I was born and brought up in the happy valley of the Hudson River. As a boy I traveled about Europe on a bicycle. You needed no passport to cross frontiers in those days—except in one country—and that one country was Russia, then under the tyranny of the Czars.

It was inconceivable to me that world war could be imposed upon countless millions of people who hated the very thought of war.

I was still a young man when I learned otherwise, and I continued to learn otherwise throughout my life.

And yet—all of the awful events that I have known and seen have only served to strengthen the faith in which I was born. For the more evil that has been generated on earth, the more good has emerged to combat and conquer that evil.

Twenty years of my life as a public servant were spent in Washington.

It is impossible to live for long in our national capital without developing a sense of the past, and of the future—a sense that the good that men do *will* live after them.

The story of our country did not begin on July 4th, 1776.

It did not begin with the Mayflower compact nor with Columbus and De Soto and Drake.

It began with the first men, in the earliest chapters of recorded history, who were ready to fight and die for the right to worship their own God in their own way—the right to love their neighbors as themselves, to trade honorably with their neighbors, to live with their neighbors at peace.

We are the inheritors of the greatness of all the centuries going back to the Magna Carta of old England, to the Athenians who built the first democracy, to the Israelites whom God delivered out of bondage because they had earned deliverance by their devotion to His word.

We of this Twentieth Century—in all free countries of the civilized world—we are the inheritors, and we are the perpetuators of freedom.

And "we" means each and all of us, not only the men in high places of responsibility.

On the morning of the day when I first went to the Capitol to take the oath of office as President, I prayed for help from all of the people.

I was given that help generously and unselfishly. And I am forever grateful and proud that this help was given voluntarily. It could not have been commanded.

For our freedom is a personal thing. It is the private property of every one of us:

Freedom of speech—freedom of religion—freedom from want—freedom from fear.

This I believe, in life and in death

Profile of Franklin D. Roosevelt

◄§ FRANKLIN DELANO ROOSEVELT, thirty-second President of the United States, was the first ever to be elected for more than two terms. He died five months after having been elected for the fourth time. As President during World War II, he was one of the leaders of the coalition that won the world's greatest war. So it is his secure place in history to rank among the most outstanding leaders of modern times. But he was a fighting President on the home front as well as in the war, and the controversy he engendered was so strong that it has not yet subsided. He still arouses political emotions in a measure that has postponed an agreed verdict of the nation on his qualities and achievements.

Having come into office in the gravest hour of the depression, in 1933, he and his advisers improvised a series of reforms, some of which have permanently changed the social structure of the country. The New Deal never was a homogeneous program and much of it was discarded. But the part that remained constituted a recognition of the Federal Government's responsibility for the social welfare of its citizens, and the system of social security Roosevelt inaugurated has been accepted as permanent by both parties.

Born of wealthy parents in 1882, he entered politics at twenty-eight, as a state senator. Within two years he was on the national political stage, backing Woodrow Wilson for the Presidency and serving as assistant secretary of the Navy in the Wilson Administration. In 1920 he was nominated for the Vice Presidency on the Democratic ticket.

But within a year he had contracted poliomyelitis and faced the greatest fight of his life. He emerged from it cheerfully victorious. He was always to be crippled, but he had been deepened and broadened for public service. By 1924 he could attend the Democratic National Convention and put Al Smith in nomination. In 1928 he did it again, and his candidate was accepted by the party. He himself reluctantly agreed to run for Governor of New York. Smith failed to carry the state but Roosevelt won and two years later was re-elected by the largest plurality ever to have been given a Governor. The next step to the White House was taken two years later. He stayed there for more than twelve years. He died when victory in the war had come clearly into view, and was mourned as no man in modern times.

◄§ ROBERT EMMET SHERWOOD, who has won three Pulitzer Prizes for drama, won his fourth Pulitzer Prize for a work of history, *Roosevelt and Hopkins.*

After graduating from Harvard he was, in succession, drama editor of *Vanity Fair*, editor of *Life*, motion picture editor of the New York *Herald.* His success as a playwright began in 1926 with *The Road to Rome.* Then came *Reunion in Vienna*, *The Petrified Forest, Idiot's Delight*, and *Abe Lincoln in Illinois.* After the production of the anti-Soviet *There Shall Be No Night* in 1940, he was invited to the White House. A warm friendship with President Roosevelt resulted and Sherwood served the President in various capacities.

His film script for *The Best Years of Our Lives* won the 1946 Academy Award. He has recently turned to the new medium of television.

GANDHI

by Louis Fischer

I BELIEVE that the core of all religions is the same—otherwise they would not be religions. I consider myself a Hindu, Christian, Moslem, Jew, Parsi, Buddhist, and Confucian. Rivalry among creeds degrades them. The idea of "My God is better than your God" repels me.

Nor do I believe in the superiority of nations or races. There is good and bad in all of them. I would not hurt England to help India. Peace at the expense of some nations is only an armistice. Peace between countries must rest on the solid foundation of love between individuals. Love gives men a partnership in the cares and needs of others. Hate and competition then yield to cooperation.

Love between individuals is the elixir of growth. I believe that I achieve my highest stature by merging my ego in other individuals. This is love, or tender identification.

My love of my fellowmen does not depend on their agreeing with me or following me. I smile on the dissenter. Disloyalty to my ideas is a gulf easily bridged by friendship and affection.

Civilization, I hold, is the acceptance, aye, the encouragement of differences. Civilization thus becomes a synonym of democracy. Force, violence, pressure, or compulsion with a view to conformity is therefore both uncivilized and undemocratic.

Force leads to fear and fear makes a small man. I have tried, throughout life, to banish fear, for if I fear I am not free.

Fear, I am convinced, resides in possessions. My heart is where my worldly goods are, and by worldly goods I mean not only treasure and property, I mean also power, popularity, even this body of mine. Were I to put a high value on these I would hesitate to give them up in payment for principles. An attack on my principles would then make me cringe and retreat.

I am not against wealth. I am against the wealth that enslaves.

No possession must have a veto power over my actions. I fast when the cause for which I fast is more important to me than life itself. I renounce because that which I renounce affords me less pleasure than the fruits of renunciation.

I am an ordinary person, subject to many frailties, and if I have any right to speak about myself it is only thanks to my successful experiments in living. My life is action. I believe that I must live what I believe. I have attempted to eliminate the conflict between what I believe, what I do, and what I say. This is truth. I preach what I practice. The result is an integration which brings inner harmony. In the face of a wrong I cannot remain supine and merely wring my hands, utter pious regrets, and thereby salve my conscience. I share responsibility for all the evils in the world unless I combat them.

The poor and the oppressed are my first and chief preoccupation, but I will not act for them, I act with them. They must not be passive or indifferent. I fear resignation more than failure. Action in a right cause ennobles, though the results be meager, for means are more important than ends. Actually there are no ends in life (there is even no end to life, for every end is a beginning and another incarnation), there are only means, every means is a means to another means. Means, accordingly, make the man and they must be clean and beautiful.

I believe that God is no dictator. He leaves us the freedom to master ourselves.

Profile of Gandhi

◄§ Born in 1869, MOHANDAS K. GANDHI was an ordinary youngster, a mediocre student, an average lawyer, indeed an average person until, confronted by experiences common to many human beings, he reacted as not a few might like to react but fail to. He remade himself, the better to serve his principles and humanity and the better to fashion his own weapon against which powerful governments were to find themselves powerless.

The weapon, called Satya-graha, variously translated Love-Force, Truth-Force, or Soul-Force, was the iron determination Gandhi instilled in thousands of simple, sometimes illiterate, Indian peddlers, miners and laborers in South Africa to renounce homes and jobs and invite imprisonment, beatings, even death, while defying racial discrimination embodied in legislation against Asiatics. They acted in obedience to a higher moral law. Events proved that this made them invincible, and after an eight-year struggle the government scrapped the legislation.

In 1914, accordingly, Gandhi went home to India. There, millions, responding to his selflessness, renunciation and love, as demonstrated on occasions by his fasts, sought to purge themselves of evil. At other times, more millions, united by his summons, "non-cooperated" with the British. In the end, the British realized they could not further postpone giving India independence and withdrew without resentment. It was the highest tribute to the Gandhian method.

Through the use of moral means, Gandhi grew to towering dimensions. A "Great Soul" (or Mahatma) inhabited his small yet sturdy body. He became a yogi, a saint, and a master politician dedicated more than anything else to the defense of the modern individual against the inroads of power and the assaults of materialism. He has been called the liberator of India, the father of his country. But his primary objective was not merely a free India; he wanted a new, innerly-free Indian in a free India.

Gandhi never remained above the battle. He fought in the thick of a thousand fights, but his hands remained clean, for his weapons were love, truth, trust, tolerance and moderation. People believed him, for his word, deed and creed were one; he was integrated.

When Gandhi was assassinated on January 30, 1948, George C. Marshall, then Secretary of State, said, "Mahatma Gandhi was the spokesman for the conscience of mankind." There could be no higher post.

◄§ LOUIS FISCHER started life as a schoolteacher in Philadelphia in 1917–18 after graduating from the Philadelphia School of Pedagogy. He entered journalism by contributing, from Berlin, to the New York *Evening Post* in 1921. A visit to Russia followed in 1922, and he was to devote much of his life to the study of that country and its place in world affairs. His two-volume *The Soviets in World Affairs* (1930) and *Machines and Men in Russia* (1932) were widely read. A profound change in his outlook was registered after a stay in India in the appearance of *Gandhi and Stalin* (1947). Later he edited *Thirteen Who Fled* (1949) and contributed to *The God That Failed* (1950). His *Life of Mahatma Gandhi* (1950) established him as an authority on the great Indian leader, and he has lectured widely about Gandhi and Indian affairs in this country.

The Editorial Board, who run "This I Believe" in its entirety, owe thanks to many for its development and dissemination.

Our greatest thanks go to the many hundreds who have accepted our invitation to write the hardest thing in the world—their beliefs in 600 words—with a special bow to the 100 co-authors of this book. Belated thanks are proffered also to the 20 Immortals chosen for the ideas they have left us, though the "authors" in every case are the world authority on each Immortal.

And then thanks . . . to the 193 U.S. Radio station owners who, as a public service, give free time daily to "This I Believe" . . . to the 85 newspapers which run "This I Believe" weekly . . . to the Armed Forces Radio Service which broadcasts it six days weekly on 140 overseas stations (in Korea three times a day) . . . to the Voice of America which broadcasts it in six languages weekly and plans for '55 an expansion to twenty-two languages including famous foreign guests speaking their native tongues . . . to the USIA, especially Theodore Streibert and Duncan Scott, for sending the second series of "This I Believe" to all foreign countries for major newspaper use, the first series two years ago having been the most successful feature they ever put out . . . to another section of USIA, Morton Glatzer and all our able Public Affairs Officers in every part of the world . . . to BBC, especially Basil Thornton, George Looker and Keith Kyle, for obtaining outstanding British guests and for the broadcasting of "This I Believe" on BBC . . . to the hundreds of educators who have used "This I Believe" in school work and those who urge and offer to

229

help develop it as a means of teaching moral and spiritual values in high schools . . . to Dr. Ruth Liepman and Dr. Ivar Lissner of Hamburg, Germany, who caused *Kristall*, the leading mid-European magazine, to contract to run "This I Believe" each issue for the next five years . . . to Hamish Hamilton for publishing the British book with 50 per cent British guests . . . to Datus C. Smith, Jr., of Franklin Publications, who ordered the Arabic book, and is publishing a *"This I Believe"* book next year in Iran and Pakistan . . . to Hassan Aroussy of Cairo who spent a year getting the Arabic beliefs written and translated and approved by our Editorial Board, with the result that the Arabic book sold 30,000 copies in three days, a record in Cairo (Mr. Aroussy is now collecting beliefs for another Arabic *"This I Believe"* book) . . . to the leading men and women of the world selected for their character and decency who have written or are writing their beliefs for international use in print and radio in 1955, including David Ben-Gurion, the King and Queen of Greece, General Naguib, Taha Hussein, Konrad Adenauer, the late Alcide de Gasperi, S. Radhakrishnan, Madame Pandit, Prince Wan Waithayakon of Thailand, Chiang Kai-shek, Chiang Monlin, Syngman Rhee, Ramon Magsaysay, the Begum Liaquat Ali Khan and Mohammed Ali of Pakistan . . . to all those working on the International edition for 1956, including the 16 foreign publishers who have expressed a desire to publish it . . . to Columbia Records, especially David J. Oppenheim, for the much-kudoed LP "This I Believe" Album of 10 outstanding Americans and 10 Immortals . . . to Simon & Schuster, especially M. Lincoln Schuster and Joseph Barnes, for their sympathetic interest and help in putting out this book as well as its predecessor, which sold more than 300,000 copies . . . to the Library of Congress who published *"This I Believe"* as a book in Braille for libraries and schools for the blind . . . to our small but hard-working, dedicated staff for their prodigious job, especially Ernest Chappell, Alice E. Colgan, Donald J. Merwin, Reny Hill, Gladys Chang, Ralph Richmond, Eugenia Marchello and Robert De Pue Brown . . . and then a very special thanks to the "This I Believe" representatives in 193 cities . . . but the list could well be interminable.

Lastly, thanks to the thousands who have written us what "This I Believe" has meant to them—how it has helped them. These letters are very heart-warming for us and for Help Inc., whose belief in the idea and financial support has made "This I Believe" possible.

Without this unselfish and untiring work of so many, "This I Believe" and this book would not be. It is greatly appreciated.

EVERY GUEST who appears on "This I Believe" is invited after careful consideration, through this invitation by the Editorial Board. Every belief is written according to the following rules which are inside the invitation. This will be continued.

But thousands of people have written their beliefs simply for their own benefit—many in classes in high school or college, many after a discussion of "This I Believe" with family or friends.

Why don't you write your beliefs, not to send to us, but for your own benefit? Why not put them in 600 words under the exact conditions confronting every guest?

The following quotation is taken from the inside of the invitation which goes to every guest invited for "This I Believe":

"THIS INVITES YOU to make a very great contribution: nothing less than a statement of your personal beliefs, of the values which rule your thought and action—all in 3½ minutes, as you yourself speak, about 600 words.

"We know this is a tough job. What we want is so intimate that no one can write it for you. You must write it yourself, in the language most natural to you. One faces an intensely personal moment when he draws up his will disposing of his belongings. Even more personal is the testament of his faith. It is this we ask you to write in your own words and then record in your own voice. You may even find that it takes a request like this for you to reveal some of your own beliefs to yourself. If you set them down they may become of untold meaning to others as well.

"We would like you to tell not only what you believe, but how you reached your beliefs, and if they have grown, what made them grow. This necessarily must be highly personal. That is what we anticipate and want.

"It may help you in formulating your credo if we tell you also what we do not want. We do not want a sermon, religious or lay; we do not want editorializing or sectarianism or 'uplift' or 'finger pointing' or the riding of hobbies. We do not even want your views on the American way of life, or democracy, or free enterprise. These are important but for another occasion. We want to know what you live by. And we want it in terms of 'I,' not the editorial 'We.'

"Although this program is designed to express beliefs, it is not a religious program and is not concerned with any religious form whatever. Most of our guests express belief in a Supreme Being, and set forth the importance to them of that belief. However, that is your decision, since it is your belief which we solicit.

"But we do ask you to confine yourself to affirmatives: This means refraining from saying what you do not believe. Your beliefs may well have grown in clarity to you by a process of elimination and rejection, but for our part, we must avoid negative statements lest we become a medium for the criticism of beliefs, which is the very opposite of our purpose.

"We are sure the statement we ask from you can have wide and lasting influence. Never has the need for personal philosophies of this kind been so urgent. Your belief, simply and sincerely spoken, is sure to stimulate and help those who hear it. We are confident it will enrich them. May we have your contribution?"